Aimar Arriola//Clare Barlow//Khairani Barokka//Dodie
Bellamy//Anne Boyer//Rizvana Bradley//Canaries//
Eli Clare//Patricia Domínguez//Taraneh Fazeli//John
Foot//Lauren Fournier//Dora García//Nancy Garín//
Tamar Guimarães//Sunil Gupta//Alice Hattrick//
Johanna Hedva//Martin Herbert//bell hooks//Sara
Jaspan//Alexandra Juhasz//Theodore (ted) Kerr//
Mahmoud Khaled//Eve Kosofsky Sedgwick//R.D.
Laing//Carolyn Lazard//Simone Leigh//Miguel A.
López//Catherine Lord//Audre Lorde//Catalina
Lozano//Portia Malatjie//Park McArthur//Margarida
Mendes//Mujeres Creando//Pedro Neves Marques//
Naomi Pearce//Peter Pál Pelbart//Paul B. Preciado//
Maria Puig de la Bellacasa//Filipa Ramos//Pedro
Reyes//Tabita Rezaire//Anne Charlotte Robertson//
Sur Rodney (Sur)//Lynx Sainte-Marie//Sarah Sharma//
Susan Sontag//Jo Spence//Patrick Staff//Mary Walling
Blackburn//Emily Watlington//Simon Watney

Health

Whitechapel Gallery
London
The MIT Press
Cambridge, Massachusetts

Edited by Bárbara Rodríguez Muñoz

HEALTH

Documents of Contemporary Art

Co-published by Whitechapel Gallery
and The MIT Press

First published 2020
© 2020 Whitechapel Gallery Ventures Limited
All texts © the authors or the estates of the authors,
unless otherwise stated

ISBN 978-0-85488-286-1 (Whitechapel Gallery)
ISBN 978-0-262-53946-3 (The MIT Press)

A catalogue record for this book is available from
the British Library

Library of Congress Cataloging-in-Publication Data
is available

Whitechapel Gallery   10 9 8 7 6 5 4 3 2 1
The MIT Press   10 9 8 7 6 5 4 3 2 1

Series Editor: Iwona Blazwick
Commissioning Editor: Anthony Iles
Project Editor: Francesca Vinter
Design by SMITH
Gemma Gerhard, Justine Hucker, Allon Kaye,
Claudia Paladini
Printed and bound in China

Cover, Patrick Staff, still from *Weed Killer* (2017).
Courtesy the artist and Commonwealth and Council

Whitechapel Gallery Ventures Limited
77–82 Whitechapel High Street
London, E1 7QX
whitechapelgallery.org

Distributed to the book trade (UK and Europe only)
by Thames & Hudson
181a High Holborn
London, WC1V 7QX
+44 (0) 20 7845 5000
sales@thameshudson.co.uk

The MIT Press
Cambridge, MA 02142
mitpress.mit.edu

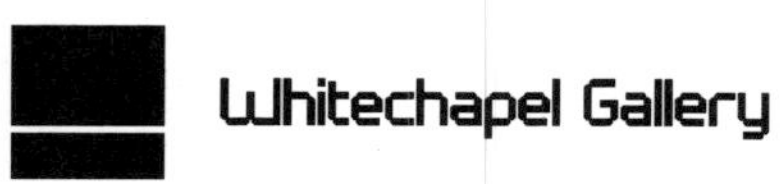
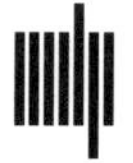

Documents of Contemporary Art

In recent decades artists have progressively expanded the boundaries of art as they have sought to engage with an increasingly pluralistic environment. Teaching, curating and understanding of art and visual culture are likewise no longer grounded in traditional aesthetics but centred on significant ideas, topics and themes ranging from the everyday to the uncanny, the psychoanalytical to the political.

The Documents of Contemporary Art series emerges from this context. Each volume focuses on a specific subject or body of writing that has been of key influence in contemporary art internationally. Edited and introduced by a scholar, artist, critic or curator, each of these source books provides access to a plurality of voices and perspectives defining a significant theme or tendency.

For over a century the Whitechapel Gallery has offered a public platform for art and ideas. In the same spirit, each guest editor represents a distinct yet diverse approach – rather than one institutional position or school of thought – and has conceived each volume to address not only a professional audience but all interested readers.

Series Editor: Iwona Blazwick; Commissioning Editor: Anthony Iles; Project Editor: Francesca Vinter; Editorial Advisory Board: Erika Balsom, Sean Cubitt, Neil Cummings, Sven Spieker, Sofia Victorino, Thomas Weaver

INTERDEPENDENCY IS NOT A CONTRACT, NOT A MORAL IDEA – IT IS A CONDITION

Maria Puig de la Bellacasa, 'Thinking with Care', 2017

WE ARE THE RELUCTANT VANGUARD REGISTERING MODERN IMBALANCE AND TOXICITY

Bárbara Rodríguez Muñoz
Introduction//The Wound is the Land of Healing

At the 2019 Whitney Biennale, Carolyn Lazard's installation *Extended Stay* featured a cream-coloured monitor placed an arm's length from a bench for viewers to sit at. Monitors like this are used in infusion centres, where patients receive intravenous treatments, and are held from the wall by a mechanical arm designed for a single user. The monitor at the Whitney was wired for cable (live) television, inviting the visitors to participate in a synchronised experience of passing time with hospital patients. Lazard has claimed that 'the hospital must be brought to the museum'.[1] This statement emphasises art institutions' inability to critically tackle illness and impairment in their programmes as well as their lack of inclusive and ethical frameworks with which to engage disabled artists, workers and visitors. In a parallel effort to establish illness as a serious subject for literature, in 1926 Virginia Woolf wrote the essay 'On Being Ill'. She notes how 'Considering how common illness is, how tremendous the spiritual change that it brings, how astonishing, when the lights of health go down, the undiscovered countries that are then disclosed [...] it becomes strange indeed that illness has not taken its place with love and battle and jealousy among the prime themes of literature.'[2] These lines convey the isolation, vulnerability and sense of alienation that disease can bring. Lazard's politicised approach to chronic illness as a significant matter in art is not centred in self-representation, nor in existential pursuits, but in changing ableist institutional dynamics. Lazard is also a co-founder of Canaries – a support group for people with autoimmune disorders and other chronic conditions whose manifesto poignantly claims 'We are sick. We are growing in number.'[3]

'Sickness'[4] is a constant in our lives, as it has been in artistic and literary production throughout history, yet this continuum is muted by the gloss of wellness that colours contemporary existence. Healing, self-care and therapeutic practices have become productive spaces for artistic exchange and intersectional resistance, yet these are also coerced by the marketplace and cultural initiatives that demand measurable health outcomes. When health is divorced from its politics, the entanglements between the individual and the social body are rendered invisible. More so, the language with which to articulate suffering becomes a grammar of heroic recovery and artworks depicting suffering are dismissed as self-absorbed. However, when health is reimagined as a space of agency, the intersections between body, sexuality, ethnicity, gender, species and coloniality are exposed, allowing ecosystems that sustain life to be reconceived. Since the 2008 financial crisis, health systems across the world have been systematically defunded and neoliberal-ableism discourses have taken centre stage in politics. As this book is being made, the COVID-19 pandemic is exposing the threats of, and to, our connectivity and interdependence – an aspect of the contemporary world which the global production and institutional system of art relies heavily on. Meanwhile, climate emergency menaces all life forms. As a response, or as a necessary consequence of this condition, there is a surge in the production, visibility and analysis of contemporary artistic and literary practices that articulate vulnerability. Their voices are amplified by nascent institutional programmes that push their missions of access and inclusion, creating spaces where the significance of health is both expanded and complicated.

This book focuses on the ethical, aesthetic and political significance of practices, positions and theories connected to health in contemporary art. It privileges and amplifies personal experiences that narrate how the vulnerability of our bodies and the maladies that seize them reveal structural aspects of our societies. The texts it features problematise the ideology of wellness that dictates our intimate and social acts, where a holistic 'care for the self' has become an elitist and coercive obligation to remain young and productive through the purchase of an endless chain of goods and practices. In this culture, only sanitised active bodies are allowed to fully participate in society and obtain visibility through its media. The included contributors, instead, reclaim existences beyond *a state of health as a norm* – beyond what is considered straight, healthy, neurotypical, or productive – ultimately questioning the myths, stigmas and cultural attitudes that shape widespread normative perceptions.

We can speak of a *turn in health* in contemporary art – a turn that is not happening in a void but informed by feminist and queer thinking as well as continuing the legacy of other 1970s–90s counterculture movements, ranging from artistic responses to the AIDS crisis, critical psychiatry, crip theory and decolonial practices. While some of the aforementioned grassroots movements experimented with DIY communication strategies, civil disobedience and institutional critique (e.g. AIDS activist collective Gran Fury's mass campaigns in New York public spaces, or Jo Spence's laminated panels addressing her responses to orthodox cancer treatment disseminated to community centres and hospitals[6]), contemporary artists are creating shared spaces on social media and reshaping art institutions by proposing new ethical paradigms for the production and display of their work (e.g. Oreet Ashery's absurdist film *Revisiting Genesis* (2017), which interrogates the rise of contemporary digital death industries that target individuals with chronic conditions[7]; or Lazard's access resource pack for small-scale arts non-for-profits[8]).

Within this genealogy of 'invisibility', there are major figures whose work tackling illness has been widely presented and studied. While their work is acknowledged, this collection also opens to other geographies, counter-narratives and contexts that remain obscured. What emerges in this book is the prevailing blind spot within diversity agendas in cultural programmes, where health intersectionality is still neither articulated nor nurtured. Over the last decade, there has been a visible growth in placing gender and sexuality at the core of institutional programming. Similarly, museum collections are increasingly (albeit slowly) being interrogated and activated in order to address the colonial violence they often display. The forms of devastation associated with forced migration and climate emergency has been the subject of various recent major exhibitions and biennales. However, institutions are still at the early stages of developing curatorial and educational practices tackling health marginalisation. Artists are leading these changes, not only making works that engage critically with health but also through the publication of access guidelines and involvement in public programmes where vulnerabilities can be made public and addressed practically. Curators are following closely but still struggling to reconcile static and rigid institutional dynamics with the ever evolving and fragile undertaking of embracing health diversity. In more mainstream areas of cultural production, self-narratives of sickness can be made to equate to positive thinking and restitution – as writer Anne Boyer puts it as she reflects on the representation of cancer, a disease she suffered from, 'the world is blood pink with respectability politics'.[9]

Biomedicine's ideological and epistemological framework began during the Enlightenment. During the eighteenth and nineteenth centuries new discoveries in biology and technological advancements in medical treatment materialised to produce the 'modern' medical model – one that implies a dualism between mind and body. However, prior to this, the practice of medicine evolved as civilisations improved, codified and disseminated their cures, with astrology and spirituality each having significant influence in conceptualising the individual as a physical and metaphysical entity. Colonial, patriarchal and corporate power has historically established a hierarchy of medicine's agendas and priorities, as well as dividing 'the healthy' from 'the sick'. We have inherited this complex landscape, which we are still struggling to navigate. On the one hand, public health is a shared space, an ecosystem we all should care for (this was once an abstract idea that is slowly becoming more tangible during the COVID-19 enforced lockdowns). On the other hand, subjectivity, cultural beliefs and the marketplace shape the understanding of health and healing as an individualised or localised pursuit. We have recently witnessed a threatening lack of trust in expertise and more widely in science – anti-vax movements, climate change deniers – often rooted in a combination of misinformation, sensationalism, nationalism, populism and the protection of what is misleadingly portrayed by certain leaders as individual liberties. The approach of this book is not anchored in a critique per se of modern medicine – an equitable and ethical application of scientific knowledge to our lives and ecosystems is vital to maintain human and non-human species. Thus, the conversation that is shaped through the different contributors in this book creates a more complex picture of the discussion and opens itself as much to answers as questions. How can we find a language to reconcile our individual experience of illness with the rigidity and totalising nature of biomedical analysis and treatment? How can we counterbalance established lineages of scientific knowledge with other systems disregarded as 'alternative'? How are artists and cultural institutions creating safer spaces to engage critically and ethically with illness and impairment?

Chapter 1, *Viral,* touches on the initial artistic and activist responses that arose during the early days of the AIDS crisis in the 1980s in the US and UK. It includes artists and activist groups: ACT UP, Gran Fury, David Wojnarowicz, Felix Gonzalez-Torres, who used strategies of queer humour, institutional confrontation and media interventions. The chapter then opens up to other geographies, periods and identities that have not been widely represented, exposing the continuity in artistic practices that strive to make epidemics visible – HIV, Zika, COVID-19 – demand political responsibility and challenge the stigmatisation and neglect of marginalised communities, from LGTBI to others labelled as 'risk groups'. Theodore (ted) Kerr speaks of an 'AIDS crisis revisitation' to reflect on the revisionist period that commences around 2008 with museum exhibitions such as 'Art AIDS America' (2015) and films like *Dallas Buyers Club* (2013).[10] This revisionist movement has been criticised by Kerr for missing the 'foundation of collectivism, intersectionality and feminism that the AIDS movement was built on'.[11] These absent voices arise in Kerr's conversation with Alexandra Juhasz, in which they discuss the re-emergence of AIDS activism through new intergenerational collectives such as What would an HIV Doula Do?, a community of people who respond to the ongoing AIDS crisis and reclaim the figure of the doula as 'somebody who holds space during a time of transition', reminding society that AIDS is not over. An appeal for universal kinship also emerges in Anne Boyer's immediate reaction to the COVID-19 pandemic, where she meditates on the ways the epidemic is making visible the invisible – the 'evils' that discriminate. In this short text, Boyer speaks of the rising deaths of what some consider 'the unproductive' and urges us to care for the vulnerable and come together spiritually, even when physically isolated.

Chapter 2, *The Institution Denied,* is devoted to questions of normativity and deviation. It borrows its title from psychiatrist Franco Basaglia's *L'istituzione negate* (1968).[12] This seminal book explores how radical practice within 'total institutions' could overturn power structures and expose society's contradictions. In recent years, the ideas and methodologies of Basaglia, alongside other thinkers associated with anti- and critical psychiatry such as R.D Laing and Félix Guattari, have been re-examined by contemporary artists – most notably Luke Fowler's film *All Divided Selves* which was nominated for the Turner Prize in the UK in 2012.[13] Informed by health reformers such as Basaglia, Laing and Guattari, as well as grassroots approaches to the therapeutic, artists, thinkers and curators are increasingly imagining alternative spaces for care and conviviality, both within and outside the art institution. In a local community setting, artist Simone Leigh's *Free People's Medical Clinic* (2014)[14] was inspired by the Black Panthers' community-based health care efforts in the 1960s–80s. In her essay, Leigh reflects on the involvement of local black diasporic communities and the importance of creating safe spaces and building self-resilience, while questioning the legacy and sustainability of social practices. This potential inadequacy of art practices to meaningfully reach diverse communities is exposed in Mary Walling Blackburn's essay, where the artist questions what is repressed and who is excluded from artists' *soft institutions*.

Chapter 3, *Narrating Illness*, explores how sickness and wellness are currently defined through diaristic and embodied approaches, weaving a dialogue between artistic and queer or feminist literary autopathographies (narration of one's own illness). Susan Sontag's seminal autobiographical essay 'Illness as Metaphor' (1978) continues to provide a framework – or an argument to push against – for the practices of many of the contributors to this book. Sontag's critique of the use of metaphoric language – particularly military terms used during cancer treatments such as invasion and battle – had a major impact on the work of artists such as Jo Spence. *The Picture of Health?* (1982–86) is Spence's large photographic project tracking her cancer diagnosis and treatment over four years, where she documents her lumpectomy and adoption of alternative health regime. In it, the artist articulated her feelings of being infantilised by male doctors, wittily questioning whether she is a hero or a victim. This productive artistic and literary exchange is further encapsulated in artist Patrick Staff's newly edited script for this book based on *Weed Killer* (2019). Staff's video was inspired by Catherine Lord's irreverent memoir *The Summer of Her Baldness*[15], a literary performance where Lord adopts the online persona of 'her baldness', exploring the queer affective land of breast cancer.

Chapter 4, *Self Caring*, engages with different approaches to the care of the self as a radical act, from the individual human body to those of non-human beings. The concept of 'self-care' was revived in 1988 by feminist writer Audre Lorde during her struggles with cancer and the political system. Nowadays, self-care has become ubiquitous in online cultures. But a perversion has occurred, more and more divorced from Lorde's statement – which asserts that, in precarity and as a minority, individuals and communities need to promote their own survival – self-care is disguised as an alternative to the medical-industrial complex, but still co-opted by the marketplace: glossy magazines and 'alternative' wellness brands. Sarah Sharma describes this perversion as 'selfie-care'.[16] The performances and writings of artist and author Johanna Hedva on the politics of intimacy, interdependence and mourning have been a catalyst for the development of this book. Hedva's autobiographical essay 'Sick Woman Theory' maps connections between disease and post-colonial/gender/class trauma stating that we need other forms of conviviality: '[a] radical kinship, an interdependent sociality, a politics of care'. Also drawing upon feminist ethics, academic Maria Puig de la Bellacasa suggests, in her essay 'Thinking with Care', that interdependency is a condition, not a contract or an obligation, it is vital to our entangled existences. This 'care' expands beyond us, it opens up to the multiple relations, human and non-human, that support life.

Chapter 5, *On Cripping*, interrogates the impact of 'crip theories' in artistic production and exhibition making. 'Crip theory' is a political concept that reclaims the often-derogatory term 'cripple' to describe disability as a viable identity. It celebrates non-normative embodiments, often intersecting with sexuality, race and gender. This chapter contextualises current and nascent shifts in the institutional treatment of disability to one driven by disabled artists, academics and activists who are changing the ethics of engagement and representation. Writer and activist Eli Clare's autobiographical account focuses on listening to his body, reclaim his non-binary identity and denouncing ableist constructions of gender. Paul B. Preciado's essay covers the life and work of Lorenza Böttner on the occasion of the artist first international retrospective 'Requiem for the Norm' (2019). Böttner's paintings and photographic sequences interrogate the technologies of normalisation, eroticising the disabled body and as Preciado suggests 'endowing it with sexual and political potency'. The representation of non-normative bodies in large museums are further scrutinised by Clare Barlow's newly commissioned text for this book, as she reflects on the curatorial strategies for 'Being Human'. This new permanent display at Wellcome Collection embraces the social model of disability as a curatorial framework and a move towards pluralising the 'fictive body' that museums often affirm.

Chapter 6, *Decolonial Healing*, tackles critical responses to biopower and the consequent renewed interest in shamanic, ritualist and transcendental experiences in contemporary art. It takes as its starting point philosopher Peter Pál Pelbart's approach to biopower, a form of power which has penetrated all levels of existence: 'from the genes, the body, affectivity and psyche, to intelligence, imagination and creativity', reducing the body to its health or aesthetics. Margarida Mendes' essay 'Molecular Colonialism', on the merger between the multinationals Monsanto and Bayer, defines the contemporary body as corporate territory, biologically shaped and partially owned by big corporations. The question of the rationality of medicine is always subject to polemics, with the figure of 'the healer' set against the validated expertise of the modern doctor. Portia Malatjie's newly commissioned text on artist Dineo Seshee Bopape reflects on ancestral healing practices that are at the core of black culture, contextualising how Bopape's enactments of ritual, song and healing herbs convey a healing space against the ills of colonialism, from the body to the land. A more profound scrutiny of this clash between indigenous and 'modern' medicine reveals how most systems have been both politicised and pitted against each other in the global market. In artist Patricia Domínguez's contribution to this book she observes the mushrooming of alternative healing centres hidden in basements across Canary Wharf, the second financial district in London – a trend that speaks to our desire to undergo a holistic process of re-enchantment with our bodies as well as the market exploitation of so-called 'traditional' practices.

Since the last revisions to this book in March 2020, museums are closing their doors, artists losing their livelihoods and rethinking what their practice means in isolation, while institutions continue to overproduce developing online programmes and stay-at-home artists' residencies. Meanwhile we are being inundated by reflective writings trying to reimagine the paradigmatic shifts necessary to inhabit and exist beyond the COVID-19 pandemic. The object of critique here is governmentality: the ethical frameworks used to implement, communicate or deny science and data, following moral or economical imperatives, which is further othering minoritised individuals and communities. Amongst these voices, philosopher Judith Butler warns us against the prevalent rhetoric that reinforces the hierarchy between 'grievable and non grievable bodies' in a passionate appeal to treat all lives equally.[17] Moving forward, we lack the language and frameworks to define how months of physical distancing will shape our lives and our practices. Writer Josh Gabert-Doyon returns to Eve Sedgwick's 'reparative reading'[18], articulated in 'Touching Feeling: Affect, Pedagogy, Performativity' (2003), an essay where she relates to the legacy of AIDS activism. 'Reparative reading' involves a certain degree of paranoia – 'a suspicious eye' – on the powers at play, while offering a way forward through new forms of conviviality and affect. Philosopher Amador Fernández-Savater movingly tempts us to transform ourselves, create new logics, populating this 'exception' with our thoughts, affects and desires so we don't merely become spectators or victims of this crisis: to 'inhabit the exception so we don't simply return to a 'normality'.[19]

In this spirit, the title of this introduction is taken from Tabita's Rezaire's essay 'Decolonial Healing: In Defence of Spiritual Technologies', an embodied critique of conventional lineages of scientific knowledge (medical, technological, epistemic) and a raw appeal against modern colonialism (of the land, mind and body).[20] For this book the phrase 'the wound is the land of healing' can be used as a navigational tool to engage with the texts selected: an ongoing search for language to convey the sense of alienation that may come with illness – *the wound* – and a space for nurturing care, shifting identities and conviviality – *the land of healing*.

1   Giulia Smith, 'Carolyn Lazard', *Art Monthly*, no. 429 (September 2019).

2   Virginia Wolf, 'On Being Ill' (London: The Hogarth Press, 1930) 3.

3   See Canaries and Taraneh Fazeli, 'Canaries Manifesto' (2017); reprinted in this volume, 163. For more information about the group see: www.canaries-collective.com

4   The terms used in this text are based on the guidelines 'Languages of Respect' in Equality Training (www.equalitytraining.co.uk/images/news/language_of_respect.pdf"www.equalitytraining.co.uk/images/news/language_of_respect.pdf'.

6   See Jo Spence, 'The Picture of health?'(1988); reprinted in this volume, 98–103.

7   See Rizvana Bradley, 'Incalculable Lives: Oreet Ashery's *Revisiting Genesis*' (2019); reprinted in this volume, 213–16.

8   See Carolyn Lazard, *Accessibility in the Arts: A Promise and a Practice* (2019), reprinted in this volume, 159–62.

10   Some examples include museum exhibitions such as 'Art AIDS America' (2015); retrospectives of General Idea (2011, Musée d'Art Moderne) and Gran Fury (2012, 80WSE, New York University; 2017, Auto Italia East, London).

11   Theodore (ted) Kerr, 'Time is not a line' (2014) (https://visualaids.org/blog/time-is-not-a-line-introduction-by-ted-kerr).

12   Franco Basaglia (ed.), *L'istituzione negata* (Turin: Einaudi, 1968).

13   See Martin Herbert, 'Undivided Attention: on the art of Luke Fowler (2012); reprinted in this volume, 79–81.

14   Commissioned in 2014 by Creative Time for their programme 'Funk, God, Jazz, and Medicine: Black Radical Brooklyn'.

15   Catherine Lord, *The Summer of Her Baldness: A Cancer Improvisation* (Austin: University of Texas Press, 2004).

16   See Sarah Sharma, 'Antinomies of Self-Care' (2017); reprinted in this volume, 147–8.

17   Judith Butler, 'Capitalism Has its Limits' (March 2020) (www.versobooks.com/blogs/4603-capitalism-has-its-limits).

18   Josh Gabert-Doyon, 'Paranoia and the Coronavirus: how Eve Sedgwick's Affect Theory Persists Through Quarantine and Self-isolation' (March 2020) (www.versobooks.com/blogs/4597-paranoia-and-the-coronavirus-how-eve-sedgwick-s-affect-theory-persists-through-quarantine-and-self-isolation).

19   Amador Fernández-Savater, 'Habitar la excepción: pensamientos sin cuarentena I', *Filosofía Pirata* (March 2020) (www.filosofiapirata.net/habitar-la-excepcion-pensamientos-sin-cuarentena-i/).

20   See Tabita Rezaire,'Decolonial Healing: In Defence of Spiritual Technologies' (2019); reprinted in this volume, 225–31.

What can ART do in an ongoing EPIDEMIC?

Sur Rodney (Sur), 'Activism, AIDS, Art, and the Institution', 2016

VIRAL

Simon Watney and Sunil Gupta
The Rhetoric of AIDS//1986

The following quotes on homosexuality, AIDS and its representation were selected and arranged by Sunil Gupta and Simon Watney for 'The Rhetoric of AIDS', Screen, vol. 27 (1986). They were originally accompanied by visual material including sensationalistic articles on the AIDS crisis at Time Magazine, The Sun, The Daily Mirror, Der Spiegel, amongst others, as well as microscopic images of the HIV virus and articles in gay magazines featuring HIV positive individuals. This version presents a more tightly focused selection of quotes without the original visual material.

'The central issue then... is not to determine whether one says yes or no to sex, whether one formulates prohibitions or permissions, whether one asserts its importance or denies its effects, or whether one refines the words one uses to designate it; but to account for the fact that it is spoken about, to discover who does the speaking, the positions and viewpoints from which they speak, the institutions which prompt people to speak about it and which store and distribute the things that are said. What is at issue, briefly, is the overall "discursive fact", the way in which sex is "put into discourse".'
– Michel Foucault, *The History of Sexuality: An Introduction* (New York: Vintage Books, 1980).

'[I]n order for the reweaving of ideology to be truly invisible, the narrative is necessarily chiasmic in structure: that is, that the subject of the beginning of the narrative is different from the subject at the end, and that the two subjects cross each other in a rhetorical figure that conceals their discontinuity.'
– Eve Kosofsky Sedgwick, *Between Men: English Literature and Male Homosocial Desire* (New York: Columbia University Press, 1985).

'The gay identity is no more a product of nature than any other sexual identity. It has developed through a complex history of definition and self-definition, and what recent histories of homosexuality have revealed clearly is that there is no necessary connection between sexual practices and sexual identity. But since the late 1960s, with the emergence of a gay movement and the huge expansion of the gay subcultures, coming out as a homosexual, that is openly assuming a gay identity, has been crucial to the public affirmation of homosexuality. Homosexual desire was no longer an unfortunate contingency of nature or fate; it was the positive basis of a sexual and, increasingly, social identity. AIDS implicitly threatened that, firstly by offering fearful consequences for being

actively gay, but secondly, more subtly, by undermining the assumption that homosexuality is itself valid. AIDS, like nineteenth-century cancer, is seen as the disease of the sexually excessive just as "the homosexual" is seen as the embodiment of a particular sexual constitution.'
– Jeffrey Weeks, *Sexuality and Its Discontents* (London: Routledge & Kegan Paul, 1985).

'Any male person who, in public or private, commits, or is a party to the commission of, or procures or attempts to procure the commission by any male person of any act of gross indecency with another male person, shall be guilty of a misdemeanour, and being convicted thereof shall be liable at the discretion of the court to be imprisoned for any term not exceeding two years, with or without hard labour.'
– Criminal Law Amendment Act, 1885, section 11 (the 'Labouchere Amendment').
[…]

'Histories are not backdrops to set off the performance of images. They are scored into the paltry paper signs, in what they do and do not do, in what they encompass and exclude, in the ways they open onto or resist a repertoire of uses in which they can be meaningful and productive. Photographs are never "evidence" of history: they are themselves the historical.'
– John Tagg, 'The Burden of Representation', *Ten.8*, no. 14 (1984). […]

'Certain forms of sexuality, socially deviant forms – homosexuality especially – have long been promiscuously classified as "sins" and "diseases", so that you can be born with them, seduced into them and catch them, all at the same time. But today you are less likely to be condemned as immoral and more likely to be labelled sick. Disease sanctions govern and encode many of our responses to sex. It is this that makes the moral panic around AIDS […] so important. It condenses a number of social stresses and throws unprecedented light on them. What is so very striking about the moral panic around AIDS is that its victims are often being blamed for the illness.'
– Jeffrey Weeks, *Sexuality and Its Discontents* (London: Routledge & Kegan Paul, 1985).

'Another crisis coexists with the medical one. It has gone largely unexamined, even by the gay press. Like helpless mice we have peremptorily, almost inexplicably, relinquished the one power we so long fought for in constructing our modern gay community: the power to determine our own identity. And to whom have we relinquished it? The very authority we wrested it from in a

struggle that occupied us for more than a hundred years: the medical profession.'
– Michael Lynch, 'Living with Kaposi's', *Body Politic*, no. 88 (November 1982).

'The relation between the subjugation of the voice in favour of the visible has important consequences for understanding the zeal with which the medical profession took up photography.'
– Roberta McGrath, 'Medical Police', *Ten.8*, no. 14 (1984).

'The Moral Majority view that it is a reward for two decades of increasing sexual licence, a plague on gays, has disturbed deep-rooted fears. The AIDS scare has reinvested a fashionable, almost mundane homosexuality with taboo, rendered it marginal again. Despite the frank admissions and frantic gender-bending of pop stars in the not-so-gay Eighties, acceptance of homosexuality has now joined the other liberal causes in retreat... . The spectre of the decade: Transmission Electron Micrograph of stages in the growth of Human T-Cell Leukemia Virus 111, identified as the cause of AIDS.'
– 'Panic', *The Face*, no. 61 (May 1985).

'DISAVOWAL (DENIAL): Term used by Freud in the specific sense of a mode of defence which consists in the subject's refusing to recognise the reality of a traumatic perception... . Inasmuch as disavowal affects external reality Freud sees it as the first stage of psychosis, and he opposes it to repression: whereas the neurotic starts by repressing the demands of the id, the psychotic's first step is to disavow reality.'
– J. Laplanche and J-B. Pontalis, *The Language of Psycho-Analysis* (London: Hogarth Press, 1973). [...]

'Ultimately, the question posed by venereal diseases that remain dormant for long periods of time is, whom can I trust? The answer clearly involves the establishment of intimacy and a bond of mutual concern between sexual partners. But that is hardly the same as suggesting that sexual activity, or sexuality per se, leads to illness. Yet, that is the animus underlying AIDS hysteria, the infectious agent that has suppressed our immunity from guilt [...].'
– Richard Goldstein, 'Heartsick: Fear and Loving in the Gay Community', *The Village Voice* (28 June 1983).

'HYSTERIA: Class of neuroses presenting a great diversity of clinical pictures. The two best isolated forms, from the point of view of symptoms, are conversion hysteria, in which the psychical conflict is expressed symbolically in somatic symptoms of the most varied kinds: they may be paroxystic (e.g. emotional

crises accompanied by theatricality) or more long-lasting (anaesthesias, hysterical paralyses, "lumps in the throat" etc.); and anxiety hysteria, where the anxiety is attached in more or less stable fashion to a specific external object (phobia).'
– J. Laplanche and J-B. Pontalis, *The Language of 'Psycho-Analysis* (London: Hogarth Press, 1973).

'There are many causes, none of which alone is sufficient to cause the disease. But if you add them all up, they interact in such a way to cumulatively, over a period of time, produce this disease [...]. The problem is that the doctors who've written about this disease are in medical centres. The people researching this disease, the physicians who write in the journals, just see men who have been referred to them. They know nothing about the setting, the overall environment, of the patient. They don't look at the disease in totality. In the 1950s, we had certain ideals or objectives in terms of the practice of medicine which I think we've lost. One of them was that we should understand our patients as a whole – we should understand their environment, all the settings, and all the contributions to illness, not simply look at an isolated bit of a body. To the extent that we've lost this, we've become confused. We're not really equipped to deal with the disease in its totality.'
– Dr. Joseph Sonnabend, 'Looking at AIDS in Totality: A Conversation', *New York Native*, no. 129 (7/13 October 1985). [...]

'They appeal to the sadistic. Unlike most photographs which provide us with the familiar and known, they impinge on and break the fragile base upon which our lives are built – the disavowal of mortality, of disfigurement; a breakdown of barriers between the internal/external. We are shown the body cut open, flesh minus skin.... These are subjects which are marked, a split not only within the subject itself but one which divides one subject from another. This split is either healed and the subject allowed to return to the normal productive world in which her/his right to speak is returned or she/he dies within this space literally or in terms of a continued silence in the forms of confinement.'
– Roberta McGrath, 'Medical Police', *Ten.8*, no. 14 (1984). [...]

'[T]o call homosexuals liars is equivalent to calling the resistors under a military occupation liars. It's like calling Jews "money lenders" when it was the only profession they were allowed to practice.'
– Michel Foucault, 'Sexual Choice, Sexual Act: An Interview', *Salmagundi*, no. 58/59 (Fall/Winter 1982/83). [...]

'Subject to the gaze of the camera the body became the object of closest scrutiny, its surface continually examined for the signs of innate physical, mental and moral inferiority. From this science of corporeal semiotics there emerged new forms of knowledge about the individual and new ways of mapping depravity.'
– David Green, 'On Foucault: Disciplinary Power and Photography', *Camerawork*, no. 32 (Summer 1985). [...]

'"The most truthful way of regarding illness – and the healthiest way of being ill – is the most purified of, most resistant to, metaphoric thinking", Susan Sontag writes. I wish I could agree. I also wish sex could be stripped of its metaphors and reconstituted along the lines of pure pleasure. But I'm not convinced arousal can be sustained without fantasy, or fantasy composed with morality and myth. Since we are so vulnerable to the erotic potential of metaphor, how can we hope to be less susceptible when illness intersects with sex and death?'
– Richard Goldstein, 'Heartsick: Fear and Loving in the Gay Community', *The Village Voice* (28 June 1983). [...]

'Suddenly women and homosexuals find that they are being threatened, as a community of interests, by cervical cancer, Hepatitis B and AIDS, and resources are not being made available to these problems with sufficient speed or diligence. This is partly because these diseases have a marginal effect on the economic life of nations – neither women nor homosexuals are seen as primary, wealth-producing agents – and because these groups can be seen as destabilising agents. A Conservative MP has identified the women who are demanding smear tests as young, middle-class scroungers and by implication educated, politically aware and liberated. Health issues are usually politically important in the sense that they concern the relative quality of facilities such as childcare, hospitals – in other words they are to do with resources and are economic. These three diseases are politically important however because they represent a direct conflict of interest between the government and groups they find threatening to the moral orthodoxy of the family and the attendant political philosophy invested therein.'
– 'Pathological Language', *Square Peg*, no. 10 (1985). [...]

Simon Watney and Sunil Gupta, extracts from 'The Rhetoric of AIDS', *Screen*, vol. 27, no. 1 (1 January 1986) 72–85.

Sur Rodney (Sur)
Activism, AIDS, Art, and the Institution//2016

What You Don't Know Could Fill a Museum

I've recounted too many times that the most celebrated of my queer friends are dead. They all died from AIDS. Fewer of those who were diagnosed with AIDS in the 1980s survived. In 1982 what we refer to today as AIDS (acquired immune deficiency syndrome) was then called GRID (gay-related immune deficiency) after public health scientists noticed clusters of Kaposi's sarcoma and *Pneumocystis pneumonia* among gay males. At a moment in history when homosexuals were held in the highest esteem in the literary, film, performing and visual arts, the perception of us as engaging in an oversexed, drug-infested lifestyle was used by policymakers and gatekeepers of religious and familial order to have many believe we were expendable in the pandemic because of our behaviour: in other words, we had brought the disease upon ourselves. This heightened social stigma played into social mobility and identity politics, affecting the geography of the art world and the way in which art history was loaded into the canon and recorded. This was particularly relevant to the New York art scene, especially regarding gay men and the women who loved them. When we examine that scene over the last quarter century, we find that both groups were in outstanding evidence and that too many lives were lost to revisionist histories.

More deaths from AIDS occurred during the early years of the 1990s – before 1996, when the 'AIDS is over' campaign announced a new cocktail drug therapy known as HAART (highly active antiretroviral therapy). For those who had access to the treatment, were trusting enough to try it, and were able to tolerate the medications, HAART extended lives. Throughout this time, the gay community lived in a perpetual state of panic, protests, government neglect, medical and legal interventions, and memorials – memorials that reinforced the dimensions of our loss in a larger world that believed we were responsible for our own misfortune. Authorities wanted to quarantine us! This blaming had a huge impact on the production of visual imagery and on the anger and fear that stood behind so much of the art, especially in the works of many artists living with AIDS. Imagery and presentation were fought for as a means to encourage social action, freedom of expression, education and respect for human rights that were (and still are) continuously under siege in the gay community – our legacy.

Embracing our queerness, we went into battle, a battle that is still ongoing, So much of our time was spent organising collectively in order to educate ourselves against the disease and save ourselves – because no one was going to do it for us, or even really listen to what we had to say. We were expendable. We're still organising now, but it manifests differently than it did in the 1980s. Many issues remain the same, as do the denial and the stigma.

Some of us remain to bear witness of that time. Many of us have been targeted as carriers of AIDS and for our queerness, our bodies under attack. We're left wondering: what effect does a health crisis have on art and on its relation to the art world? How did all of this play out in art and how it has been represented in exhibitions until now? We were angry then; what does our anger look like today? Over the past few decades, how have the generations, the media, institutions, practitioners and social relations in the art world changed, especially with the advent of technology, and why? In an effort to find the answers to these questions, I reviewed roughly 25 years' worth of New York City exhibitions focusing on AIDS. The results of my research reveal much to satisfy the grand question: what can art do in an ongoing epidemic?

In 1984 Gracie Mansion moved her East Village gallery, of which I was co-director, to a storefront on Avenue A. That same year, artist and art critic Nicholas Moufarrege, who championed the gallery and its artists as well as the East Village scene, was hospitalised with AIDS. It was also the year David Wojnarowicz stormed into the gallery's office after removing his consignment of art works from Civilian Warfare, the gallery which had been representing him, and deposited them with Gracie and me to manage. Wojnarowicz had not yet been identified as living with the virus but would test positive later. He eventually became a poster child in the ongoing AIDS warfare and continued to be – even more so – after his death in 1992. His critiques on organised religion, class struggle, nature and the environment, homophobia, dreams and fears would all be collapsed into metaphors for AIDS, to better serve his hugely marketable writing on the subject.

In March 1987 the AIDS Coalition to Unleash Power (ACT UP), an advocacy group for people with AIDS, was formed. A call to arms had already been implored by the Silence=Death Project, initiated the year before by a group of gay activists who designed the now iconic poster and wheatpasted them around New York. A relationship to ACT UP was characteristic of most who organised the first AIDS exhibitions; indeed, many prominent art world figures counted among its ranks. For example, in 1987, ACT UP member William Olander, senior curator at the New Museum, invited Gran Fury and ACT UP to install *Let the Record Show…* in the front window of the museum, located on a heavily trafficked strip of lower Broadway. According to the group's statement in the accompanying brochure, the installation 'provides current information regarding the AIDS epidemic, as well as depicting the crisis in historical perspective. The intention is to make the viewer realise the depth of the problem and understand that history will judge our society by how we responded to this calamity, potentially the worst medical disaster of the century'. It goes on to say, 'the installation is more pointedly directed to those national figures who have used the AIDS epidemic to promote their own political or religious agendas. It is intended to serve as a reminder that their actions or inactions will soon be a matter of historical record'.[1] Evidence of which we would continue to see propagated throughout the culture wars in the following decade.[2]

That same year, in response to experimental film venues' marginalisation of queer film work, ACT UP members Sarah Schulman, a writer, and Jim Hubbard, a filmmaker, joined forces with other ACT UP members: curators Jack Waters and Peter Cramer from Naked Eye Cinema and filmmaker Ela Troyano, who programmed the New York Film Festival Downtown. In concert with the emerging AIDS activist and queer activist movement, they formed the New York Lesbian and Gay Experimental Film Festival (now called MIX), which became a mass cultural event in the LBGT underground. Film played an important role in presenting AIDS through artistic vision at film festivals, museums and galleries worldwide and continues to do so today. The importance of film in the struggle against AIDS cannot be overestimated, as so many of the cultural producers have used this medium. In his essay 'AIDS: Cultural Analysis/Cultural Activism', Douglas Crimp writes, 'Much of the dominant discourse on AIDS has been conveyed through television, and this discourse has generated a critical counterpractice in the same medium; video can sustain a fairly complex array of information; and cable access and the widespread use of VCRS provide the potential of a large audience for this work.'[3] Crimp cites a group of examples in his text and goes on to mention what he discovered in preparing the text for publication: 'Amber Hollibaugh of the New York Commission on Human Rights, was at work on *The Second Epidemic*, a documentary about AIDS-related descrimination…. . There was a critical, theoretical, activist alternative to the personal, elegiac expressions that appeared to dominate the art-world response to AIDS. What seemed to me essential was a vastly expanded view of culture in relation to crisis […] AIDS intersects with and requires a critical rethinking of all of culture: of language and representation, of science and medicine, of health and illness, of sex and death, of the public and private realms.'[4]

In 1988 a small group of curators and critics, all gay white men – some members of ACT UP and prominent in art institutions – who were committed to tracking a growing body of artwork about AIDS and trying to give it visibility, formed an advocacy group for artists living with AIDS and called it Visual AIDS. Curatorial practices engaged through the organisation's efforts provided an invaluable resource to organisations and institutions nationwide. Without Visual AIDS, many initiatives and the visibility of art and AIDS would not have been considered or presented, and even more lives would have been lost. What do artworks inspired by the experience of living with AIDS or in response to AIDS create? Or, as Jonathan Leiter, an artist with the Visual AIDS Archive, put it: 'How do you create something beautiful when all you feel is anger and decay?'[5] The answer may be that anger gives rise to action; decay brings about germination.

[…] The following year several landmark exhibitions appeared in response to AIDS and art. *Until That Last Breath: Women with AIDS* showed at the New Museum, organised by the museum's director, Marcia Tucker, along with Ann Meredith and Janet Goldner. On the second annual World AIDS Day, 1 December 1989, Visual AIDS organised the first Day Without Art as a national day of action and mourning, using art and art institutions to make the public aware that art can touch everyone and to inspire activism.[6] More than eight hundred arts institutions and AIDS organisations across the country participated by covering up artworks, presenting exhibitions about HIV/AIDS, or closing museum doors and sending staff to volunteer at AIDS service organisations.

Later that year, *Witnesses: Against Our Vanishing* appeared at Artists Space, curated by photographer Nan Goldin. Wojnarowicz's controversial essay in the exhibition catalogue set off a funding firestorm[7] and forever aligned Wojnarowicz with AIDS in the art world. In Steven Dubin's 1990 interview with Wojnarowicz published years later in the College Art Association's *Art Journal,* Wojnarowicz recounts what Nan Goldin had discussed with him about organising the exhibition: 'We talked about looking at how the disease was dealt with by a group of people who had died from it, and other people who had watched them die.'[8] […]

What Can Art Do in an Ongoing Epidemic

My research on art exhibitions dealing with AIDS reveals a grouping of exhibitions at the turn of the decade that started to wane leading up to the mid-1990s. We had lost many more celebrated artists and in 1989 exhibitions and actions called attention to the epidemic and its consequences. Several noteworthy examples: Gran Fury published *New York Crimes* on 28 March 1989, a four-page newspaper that appeared in addition to other poster campaigns the group had been creating since its formation a year earlier, when it produced *Wall Street Money.* For this 1988 action, reproductions of $100 bills were thrown from garbage bags onto the trading floor of the New York Stock Exchange. The overside of the bills was printed with slogans such as '*WHY ARE WE HERE? Because your malignant neglect KILLS. Fight Back. Fight AIDS*' and '*White Heterosexual Men Can't Get AIDS… DON'T BANK ON IT. Fight Back. Fight AIDS.*' 'We have to get out of SoHo, get out of the art world', the group declared.[9] In 1988 I left my position at Gracie Mansion Gallery in order to make myself available as a full-time caregiver to artist friends struggling with their day-to-day survival. But how would art institutions address any of these concerns regarding AIDS and the artwork produced around it? With fundraising as their comfort zone, they organised auctions for amfAR (The Foundation for AIDS Research) and other organisations.

Projects and exhibitions continued to be plentiful around the turn of the decade. The still popular Keith Haring poster *IGNORANCE=FEAR · SILENCE=DEATH · FIGHT AIDS, ACT UP* was created in 1989 and was printed on T-shirts; General Idea produced *Imagevirus* (1987–94), a poster project on streets and public spaces. Marlon Riggs directed the 1989 semi-documentary *Tongues Untied*, which introduced a group of gay black poets celebrating their sexuality; it stirred controversy over public funding and censorship.[10] The Guggenheim Museum shrouded its façade for World AIDS Day, 1 December 1990; P.S.1 Clocktower and the Longwood Arts Project in the Bronx began a public competition for temporary public artwork about AIDS in recognition of a Day Without Art. [...]

Public vigils began occurring in cities across the nation as early as 1982. When invited to speak at a vigil in Central Park on 17 June 1987, Rodger McFarlane expressed his feeling that AIDS survivors had raised mourning to an art form years ago. Douglas Crimp echoed that sentiment when he wrote, 'Art is what survives, endures, transcends; art constitutes our legacy.'[11] How much of that 'art form' has survived? I call for representing memorials in institutions and for the generation that lost family and devoted relationships to speak out [...].

In 1996, for *Arts' Communities/AIDS' Communities: Realizing the Archive Project*, the work of more than 120 artists who had died of AIDS or were living with AIDS was collected for the Visual AIDS Archive Project. The largesse of the exhibition encouraged a more selective presentation of under-recognised and living artists. From the Visual AIDS Archive Project, curators Geoffrey Hendricks, Frank Moore and myself chose twelve artists to participate in *A Living Testament of the Blood Fairies* and another fourteen for *A Living Testament of the Blood Fairies: Part II*.[12]

For the next decade and until recently, the majority of AIDS-related programmes has consisted of events, exhibitions and panels by or in partnership with Visual AIDS. By the time the 'cocktail party' arrived in 1996, too many artists and arts programmers had died, were burned out, or were in need of escaping the horrors they had been through. AIDS created an intergenerational divide – a split in the socialisation of the AIDS art world, where the generation that grew up during the crisis was abandoned to live in a different dimension. The year 1995 was not a moment when museums and institutions were considering AIDS as a subject to present, yet the horrors of AIDS were not over. Today, many more are living invisibly with HIV/AIDS and negotiating stigma, a barrier to their visibility.

The global AIDS pandemic necessitated the purview of human rights and medical conferences, and activity within departments of academic institutions. Each entity stimulated symposiums, generating a wealth of material published in books and periodicals, followed by archiving. Uploads to the web served as cocktail chatter that shifted, depending on your relationship to the global map in actual or virtual space. Visual AIDS took 'Bodies of Resistance', curated by Barbara Hunt, to the XIII International AIDS Conference in Durban, South Africa, in July 2000. The 'East Village: USA' exhibition in 2004–5, curated by Dan Cameron at the New Museum, presented a memorial room to artists lost to AIDS. Discourse about art and AIDS remained frozen in the pre-cocktail era of the AIDS crisis, not to be resuscitated until a decade later, this time initiated and revisited by curators inside New York art museums after years of neglect.

Is Our Nostalgia Killing Us?

> AIDS ART. THIS ART IS
> ABOUT AIDS. THIS ART
> RAISES AWARENESS ABOUT
> AIDS. I AM TALKING
> ABOUT AIDS. THIS ART
> MAKES YOU AWARE OF
> AIDS. YOU ARE THINKING
> ABOUT AIDS. I HAVE AIDS.
> I HAVE RAISED AWARENESS
> ABOUT AIDS. THIS ART
> HAS RAISED AWARENESS
> ABOUT AIDS. YOU ARE
> AWARE OF AIDS ART.
> I AM AN AIDS ARTIST.
> – Vincent Chevalier, text from a draft version of *AIDS ART* (2013), posted on his blog Hyperflesh Markup Language (HFML)[13]

Many of the concerns introduced here stretched into the twenty-first century and involved many adults who were born during the early stages of the AIDS pandemic. What have they lost during this troubled time, and what remains for them to grow into? All of the issues discussed here inform their work today. We need to hear more of their voices in the landscape of visual arts, and we need to see them recognised in exhibitions on the subject of how AIDS informed their art perception. We must not dwell on our nostalgia; to do so would be to drown out the voices of a generation that grew up in silence and stigma. These artists were rarely included in the conversation, but they are so necessary now, and we can learn from what they have to say.

Beginning in 2011 a number of exhibitions organised through Visual AIDS brought into focus what a show addressing art and AIDS could look like. [...] Other exhibitions that ran concurrently with many of these shows – although some not directly promoted as exhibitions about AIDS – were presented in museums and included elements that addressed artists and AIDS by looking back nostalgically at work produced by an earlier generation of artists, with no recognition of the current generation. Two exhibitions of note were mounted in the Smithsonian institutions. The first, at the National Portrait Gallery, was 'Hide/Seek: Difference and Desire in American Portraiture' (2010–11), curated by Jonathan Katz and David C. Ward. The curators' 2010 edited version of Wojnarowicz's 1986–87 silent video *A Fire in My Belly*[14] was censored from the exhibition, creating a firestorm of controversy. The second exhibition at the Archives of American Art, was 'Lost and Found: The Lesbian and Gay Presence at the Archives of American Art' Presented through letters, photographs, unpublished writings and rare printed material, it provided glimpses into the sometimes private, sometimes 'out' lives, careers and communities of gay American artists. Both shows marked the 30th anniversary of the first official reports on AIDS.

We were also introduced to 'AIDS in New York: the First Five Years' (2013), at the National Library of Medicine; 'I, You, We' (2013), curated by David Kiehl, at the Whitney Museum of American Art; 'Blues for Smoke' (2013), curated by Bennett Simpson, at the Museum of Contemporary Art, Los Angeles, and also shown at the Whitney.[15] Part of the programming for 'Blues for Smoke' at the Whitney reintroduced the poetic voices of gay black men. In a programme organised by Gregg Bordowitz, many in the audience heard these voices from the 1980s for the first time.

[…] When I was asked to co-curate, with Kris Nuzzi, an exhibition for Visual AIDS' 25th anniversary to be titled 'Not Over: 25 Years of Visual AIDS' (2013), we knew it would be imperative to undertake a different, if obvious approach. We first looked at the generation of artists working today who were at the same age as many of the celebrated artists working in the 1980s. We wanted to know what these younger artists were thinking about in relation to AIDS. What and who inspired them? What did they remember and what was their experience of the AIDS/art scene?

[…] Two important questions for me arose from this show. One was posed by Nancer LeMoins in her remarkable linocut *Will Art Save My Life?* (1996). It pictures a black and white classicised motif with the title of the work in a banner across the top and a response to the question along the bottom: 'will it bring my fucking friends back?' Maybe not, but it does invoke their presence in our memory. The other important question was introduced with our announcement card for 'Not Over: 25 Years of Visual AIDS', which showed a twelve-year-old boy wearing a blonde wig on a video screen. At the bottom of the screen, a subtitle reads: 'when did you figure out you had AIDS?' The card was meant to call attention to our youth and prompt us to think about where they are today in an age in which AIDS is *not over.*

1   William Olander, 'The Window on Broadway by ACT UP' (http://archive.newmuseum.org/index.php/Detail/Object/Show/object_id/7910).

2   The expression 'culture wars' was reintroduced by the 1991 publication by James Davison Hunter, *Culture Wars: The Struggle to Define America* (New York: Basic Books, 1991). A sociologist at the University of Virginia, Hunter described what he saw as a dramatic realignment and polarisation that had transformed American politics and culture.

3   Douglas Crimp 'AIDS: Cultural Analysis/Cultural Activism', *October*, no. 43 (Winter 1987) 14.

4   Ibid., 15.

5   www.visualaids.org/history/year/2014; see entry for 1997.

6   Visual AIDS organised the first 'Day Without Art' in 1989, held on 1 December to coincide with the World Health Organisation's World AIDS Day. For more information, see www.visualaids.org/projects/

7   'The showdown between the National Endowment for the Arts and the non-profit Tribeca gallery Artists Space over the exhibition "Witnesses: Against Our Vanishing" ended last Thursday. The suspended NEA grant of $10,000 was restored; funding for the show's catalogue was categorically denied. It was not a victory for the arts community, or for the new NEA chairman John Frohnmayer, or for Senator Jesse Helms, and especially not for David Wojnarowicz, the artist in the eye of the storm.' Robert Atkins, 'Black Thursday: Frohnmayer Fiddles, Artists Burn', *Village Voice* (28 November 1989) 31–4. Available at http://robertatkins.net/beta/witness/culture/nea/critics.html

8   Steven Dubin, 'David Wojnarowicz: Against His Vanishing', *Art Journal* (25 March 2011). Available at www.artjournal.collegeart.org/david-wojnarowicz-against-his-vanishing. Though the interview took place in 1990, it was previously unpublished; see www.collegeart.org/news/2011/03/30/previously-unpublished-interview-with-david-wojnarowicz-on-the-new-art-journal-website/

9   'AIDS: Cultural Analysis/Cultural Activism', op. cit., 12.

10   Marlon Riggs, producer and director, *Tongues Untied* (distributed by Frameline & California Newsreel, 1989), 55 minutes. An excerpt is available online at https://youtube.com/watch?v=tWuPLxMBjM8

11   [15] 'AIDS: Cultural Analysis/Cultural Activism', op. cit.

12   [16] 'A Living Testament of the Blood Fairies' showed at Artists Space, in New York, 9 November 1996–4 January 1997. 'A Living Testament of the Blood Fairies Part II' showed at Printed Matter, in New York, 15 January–1 March 1997.

13   [17] See http://heterogeneoushomosexual.tumblr.com/post/42602187307/vincent-chevalier-aids-art-2012-hfml-aids.

14   [18] The full version is available online at www.youtube.com/watch?v=gHRCwQeKCuo

15   [19] 'Blues for Smoke' was curated by Bennett Simpson for the Museum of Contemporary Art, Los Angeles, where it appeared 21 October 2012–7 January 2013. It then travelled to the Whitney Museum of American Art, where it appeared 6 February–28 April 2013.

Sur Rodney (Sur), extracts from 'Activism, AIDS, Art, and the Institution', in *Art, AIDS, America,* ed. Katz Hushka (Tacoma: Tacoma Art Museum and Washington: University of Washington Press, 2016) 74–81.

bell hooks
Subversive Beauty: New Modes of Contestation//1995

When Keats wrote the lines 'a thing of beauty is a joy forever, its loveliness increases, it will never pass into nothingness', he attributed to beauty the subversive function of sustaining life in the face of deprivation, unrelenting pain, and suffering. In the work of Felix Gonzalez-Torres beauty is also a life force, affirming the presence of intense intimacy, closeness, our capacity to know love, face death, and live with ongoing yet reconciled grief. Unlike Keats, Gonzalez-Torres insists in his work that beauty is not best expressed or contained in the enduring art object but, rather, in the moment of experience, of human interaction, the passion of remembrance that serves as a catalyst urging on the will to create. The art object is merely a mirror, giving a glimpse that is also a shadow of what was once real, present, concrete. It is this invitation to enter a world of shadows that Gonzalez-Torres' work extends.

Shadows become the location of our destiny, outlining the shape of past, present, and future possibility. There is always in Gonzalez-Torres' a work – whether expressed in the enfolding blackness that serves as background for signs of decontextualised history (seemingly random but connected events); in the photographic image of a once inhabited but now vacant bed; or in a pattern of birds' flight among grey clouds – the insistence that elegance and ecstasy are to be found in daily life, in our habits of being, in the ways we regard one another and the world around us. It is sacrilege to reserve this beauty solely for art.

Taking the familiar, the everyday, the mundane, and removing them from the veiled and hidden realm of domesticity, Gonzalez-Torres' work disrupts boundaries, challenges us to see and acknowledge in public space all that we have been encouraged to reveal only in private. Bringing us face to face with our emotional vulnerability, our lack of control over our bodies, our intense longing for nurturance (for example, the bits of candy in an installation we are allowed to take and suck remind us of our engagement with the world of the senses), this art restores the primacy of our bond with flesh. It is about exposure and revelation. It indicts the audience. We are witnesses unable to escape the truth of what we have seen.

Jet-black backgrounds provide the perfect blank screens for the projection of our individual understanding of realities named yet undefined by the printed text. When we see photographs of a billboard that reads '*People With AIDS Coalition 1985 Police Harassment 1969 Oscar Wilde 1895 Supreme/Court 1986 Harvey Milk 1977 March on Washington 1987 Stonewall Rebellion 1969*', we are not innocent onlookers asked to escape into a world of the artistic imaginary.

Here, in this moment of testimony, art returns the gaze of the onlooker, demanding an interrogation of our individual subjectivity – our locations. Who were we, where were we, how did we experience these events?

All the pieces by Gonzalez-Torres that make use of 'datelines' resist consumption as mere artefact by the inherent demand that audiences participate, that we make 'sense' of the world mirrored here. As counter-hegemonic art, Gonzalez-Torres's work requires not that we identify with the artist as iconic figure or with the beautiful art object but, rather, that we identify ourselves as subjects in history through our interaction with the work. This is not art that subliminally subjugates, coercively enthrals or enraptures. It welcomes our presence, our participation.

That presence is made more manifest by the spaces left vacant in the work that leave room for us. This was most evident in the photograph of the unmade bed, rumpled, marked by the imprint of missing bodies, [*Untitled*, 1991] that loomed large on billboards throughout New York City. This image taunted us with remembered connection. Where the body of love could be, where the intimacy of lying close could be seen, there was only absence. Each individual looking into that vacant space must come to terms with what is not there. Once again Gonzalez-Torres gives us art that is not meant to usurp, stand in for, or replace experience.

This art returns us to experience, to memory. What we feel and know with our senses determines what this absence means. There are many ways to 'read' the image of the empty bed. Those who come to it with autobiographical details from Felix Gonzalez-Torres' life can see projected here the loss of his lover, the impact of AIDS, the power and pleasure of homosexual/homoerotic love and loss, the anguish of grief. Yet for the masses of viewers who saw this work without knowing the intimate details, this black and white image of an empty bed is a shadowy place to be entered, not simply through empathy with the artist but by way of our own relationship to loss, to absence, to leave-taking, to remembered grief.

Inviting audiences to remember moments of closeness and separation, this image is a passage linking the particular losses we experience with a culture of collective grief. All our diverse losses, unnamed sorrows, undocumented deaths can find expression as we gaze upon this bed where living bodies might lie together, leave their mark. We confront an absence that is also a trace leading back so that we can we bear witness to the intimacy that was present. Although the bodies are gone, memories sustain the experience, allow the feelings these bodies generated – the warmth and passion – to be revealed, recalled, recorded.

In the stillness of this image can be heard the sounds of lives content, fulfilled. It is that aura of satisfaction which this image embraces, resurrects, bringing to life a vision of hope and possibility. The absence in this image is not meaningless death. What we see is a pedagogy of mourning that teaches us to understand that life well-lived shapes the nature of our journey, our passage from the moment we are born to the day we die. There are intimations of immortality in this and in Gonzalez-Torres' newer work, a sense of eternity that extends from this image into the artist's recent images of dark clouds where solitary birds fly. Gonzalez-Torres gives us a 'passport'. This passport has no places for 'irrelevant' details: where we were born, in what country, dates or numbers. A passport of dark clouds, of birds in flight, moves us into a space beyond history, a space of mystery where there is no record, no documentation, nothing to recall. What is captured here is a moment of utter oneness where the experience of union, of perfect love transcends the realm of the senses. No boundaries exist. There are no limits.

In the work of Felix Gonzalez-Torres this call for reunion is a political moment, an act of resistance. Once we embrace his vision of the collapse of public and private, the convergence of the individual and the collective, we open ourselves to the possibility of communion and community. The beauty of that union is celebrated in Gonzalez-Torres' work. Yet as the signs, symbols, and datelines tell us, that union will not come without struggle and sacrifice, without active resistance against those forces of domination that seek to shut down our agency, our will to be self-actualised. Gonzalez-Torres' art declares that to be political is to be alive – that beauty resides in moments of revolution and transformation – even as his work articulates 'new modes of contestation'. In his grappling with subversive beauty, with an aesthetics of loss, Gonzalez-Torres insists that our lives be that space where beauty is made manifest, where the power of human connection and interaction creates that loveliness that 'will never pass into nothingness'. […]

bell hooks, extract from 'Subversive Beauty: New Modes of Contestation', in *Art on My Mind: Visual Politics* (New York: The New Press, 1995) 49–53.

Alexandra Juhasz and Theodore (ted) Kerr
On Care, Activism, and HIV//2017

Since 2014, academic and filmmaker Alexandra Juhasz and writer and organiser Theodore Kerr have been engaging in conversation about the confluence of the ongoing AIDS crisis, history and representation. They began their first published conversation[1] by reflecting on films from across the ecology of AIDS media, looking at trends, absences, and meanings. Crucial to that conversation and ones that followed was thinking around the Second Silence and the AIDS Crisis Revisitation. For Kerr, the Second Silence is the period that comes after the release of life-saving drugs in 1996 and continues until around 2008. In this period, the production of AIDS-related culture slowed down, as did related dissemination and discussion. It was an echo of the first silence in which the Reagan administration and the media at the time were largely quiet around the, then emerging, crisis, which allowed a virus to become an epidemic; during the Second Silence stigma and discrimination became more insidious. The Second Silence broke with the dawning of the AIDS Crisis Revisitation, a new wave of cultural production starting late in the first decade of the twenty-first century, one rooted in looking back at early responses to HIV/AIDS primarily through the lens of white middle-class gay men and their communities. Within this lens, Juhasz and Kerr posit, the crisis is often represented as something that can be and was overcome with medication and personal ingenuity. Seldom included within the Revisitation is work that wrestles with the intersectional foundation of the AIDS crisis and the examples of activism and other forms of critical response that addressed AIDS in its full cultural, community and political complexity. [...]

Juhasz was an active member of the AIDS response in NYC in the 1980s and 90s. She lost friends, participated in demonstrations, created work with collectives, and made videos. The work she did then and now honours the people, time and work of the past while also bearing witness to and activating connections and divergences in the present. Kerr came of age in a different time and place. For him, as a gay man, AIDS was an ever-present cultural inheritance, hanging over his head, throwing shadow on every path ahead. But by the time he became involved in AIDS work at HIV Edmonton, the AIDS service organisation in the Canadian city where he grew up, there was little-to-no gay community to be found (at least in the AIDS service world). Instead, there was a multicultural, multiracial, mostly female-run response that focused on first nation and immigrant communities and people who were active users of illegal drugs, who were living in poverty, as well as dealing with mental health issues and unstable housing. For Kerr, this was a vastly different AIDS world than he had seen represented, but as he would come to find, it was directly in line with less-known aspects of AIDS history and the stories that were rarely preserved and passed on. [...]

Alexandra Juhasz Let's start by talking about how our encounters can be seen as a form of care. In reaching out to each other, we have found a conversation partner with whom we can listen, bounce ideas off of, and continue to think, consider and propose along side with. Over these many interactions, we have built not just ideas about AIDS but a collaborative thinking and writing process that allows for our differences. We come together to ask and learn how media about AIDS can best hold stories that centre the lives of those most under-seen: people of colour, women, trans people. And once it is made, overcoming many obstacles to get there, why from one generation to the next there is inevitably, perennially, a quick and ready loss of the ideas and experiences produced about these least-seen people.

We are not alone in trying to make sense of these questions and gaps. There are many projects right now, done with care and exploration, in video, dance, theatre and other artistic and social registers that seem to be engaging in an inter-generational structure of remembering, revitalising, sharing and seeing anew much like our ongoing work together.[2]

[…] And I can tell you from my side of things, this model of dialogical care in which we and many others are working is rewarding, exhausting, productive, frustrating, sad and energising. As this cycle of discovery between us transitions into a long-term project, it seems that along the way we have created a foundation of mutual understanding, while also unearthing and participating in projects that are at once about video, remembrance and HIV/AIDS, as they are about means and modes of caring, me with WAVE (The Women's AIDS Video Enterprise) and you with the What Would an HIV Doula Do? collective.

Theodore (ted) Kerr   It is no accident [how], in the years we have been speaking about, HIV/AIDS gets understood and represented. We have both dug deeper into AIDS-related projects where care is central. To make sense of HIV/AIDS it is crucial to wrestle with what we mean by care and to consider how care is done, represented and passed down. Many of us have been quick to think of AIDS activism as the model instantiation of the history of AIDS, but more complicated and less considered is the idea of AIDS caring, which sets the stage for this fourth conversation.

A few years ago I was hearing a lot about doulas. I was meeting people who did it for work, and reading about how not only were there birth and end-of-life doulas, but also abortion and gender doulas. Being entrenched in the AIDS response I wondered if there could be a doula focused on HIV? I set out to think about this question with others. In 2015 I organised a one-day think tank where I invited folks involved in social justice activism and work to discuss many AIDS-related topics, including a session asking: 'What Would an HIV Doula Do?' It was lively and meaningful, and those of us involved ultimately ended up creating a collective that took the question as its name.[3]

Two years later the What Would an HIV Doula Do? (WWHIVDD?) collective has as a working definition of doula: a person in community who holds space during times of transition. We see living with HIV as a series of transitions that do not necessarily begin with testing positive and do not end once you get on medication. This idea of holding space can mean many things to different people. At that first think tank, which is documented in a transcript online, writer and chaplain Michael Crumpler talked about how when you are living through trauma you can lose track of the assets and capacities you have worked hard to cultivate. In these cases, someone holding space for you can mean a person reminding you who you are, what you can do and where to go.

[...] We are doulaing the system and ourselves – a term that comes to us from activist, doula and powerhouse, Jessica Danforth. As a group of people our awareness of HIV is all over the place. Some people are still working with a 1996 level of information about HIV, others are up to date because AIDS is our life or our job. Together we are working past the wrong information that circulates and are pushing past prevailing silences that still surround HIV. We are addressing issues such as HIV criminalisation, HIV testing, and ways HIV is being remembered and disremembered within mainstream culture. Along the way we are also bringing together people who have not seen each other in generations, mourning people who have been largely forgotten, and introducing people across generational divides. Through our meetings, public programmes and online presence we are working to make AIDS-aware communities in the twenty-first century.

Juhasz   WAVE is one of those groups from the past that WWHIVDD? have been engaging with. We've now had two immensely productive public encounters where WAVE shows and talks about our work from the early 1990s and then we connect this to needs and activism for today. [...] I built WAVE in conversation with the community-based AIDS organisation Brooklyn AIDS Task Force (BATF). I had reached out to them, after acquiring a grant that would support the project from the NY State Council for the Humanities (thinking today about the ongoing threats to the NEH, and also that community-based AIDS educational media-making by and for urban women of colour doesn't seem to be the kind or project our stifled and current humanities granting can support – the person who shepherded my grant application was Coco Fusco! – we see how climates of cultural support, and related ideologies of media practice, really affect what can be and is made). After making three very early tapes about issues affecting women in relation to HIV/AIDS for the Gay Men's Health Crisis 'Living with AIDS Show', I knew that I wanted to create an AIDS media production model that would facilitate media by and for (not just about) the communities of women most impacted, and least represented, that is urban women of colour. The model for WAVE (which I discuss in great detail in AIDS TV) put media literacy within an AIDS support group, so that as we think and learn about theories and practices of representation together this is occurring in a safe or even therapeutic space where the social and personal needs of often disempowered and new media makers is part of the process. [...]

Kerr   I love how WAVE makes visible the multiple ways that community was the response within the early AIDS crisis, and the people involved and their needs needed to be attended to. One of the goals of WWHIVDD? is to both draw attention to the role that community has always played in AIDS work, but also push forward the role of community in the face of a much needed but deeply problematic professionalised response. As you well know, long before Highly Active Anti-Retroviral Treatment (HAART) was released in the mid to late 1990s, something like an AIDS industrial complex began. AIDS Service organisations grew in size, lesbian and gay non-profits took on AIDS in a serious way, and a once cottage industry of responding to AIDS ballooned into multiple marketplaces and responses. [...]

Juhasz   Now that AIDS 'is over' (for some!) it is safe to look back at what it was.

Kerr   But as we know, for others, for whom medication was only one pillar of support they needed in the face of being HIV positive in America, the crisis was not over, it was very much the same or made worse because complex realities of HIV were no longer being broadcast or privately attended to. This is the start of the Second Silence. At the very same time that intricate stories of AIDS most needed to be driven home for maximum impact, it was erroneously suggested that AIDS was over.

Juhasz   The Second Silence buried for many of us our passion, community, and our previous work and analysis because the social, political, infrastructural and, as we've been arguing, technological conditions that supported it went away. Everyone went home and mourned, or raged, or learned alone.

Kerr   Right! And it's in the face of that last turn that we now found ourselves immersed in an interesting tension. In the face of inaction, care can seem like activism. [...]

Juhasz   The function of supporting a movement by cooking, planning, taking care has always been taken up disproportionately by women and those who take pleasure or power in these 'female' roles.

Kerr   What strikes me now is that in all the planning of the event, none of us stopped to think about how we could make more visible contributions to the AIDS response that were not only activist in nature. While we were trying to make everyone feel seen and valuable, we actually ended up participating in a narrative that suggests activism is the only action that matters within a movement, thereby erasing the other kinds of labour that make social change possible, labour that gets lost within much of the Revisitation. […]

Juhasz This is a beautiful way to think of this labour, and the role of caring within the ongoing epidemic: as the intentional making of support systems by frame shapers, those devoted to holding space for comfort, memory and love that enables more; the doulas and the media makers.

1   See 'Home Video Returns', *Cineaste* (April 2014). Available at http://cineaste.com/articles/aids-article
2   We are thinking here of the many feature documentary films, exhibitions, books and theatre productions. And we are also thinking about undertakings such as 'Lost & Found: Dance, New York, HIV/AIDS, Then and Now', a multi-pronged series of events curated by Dancespace Projects in the winter of 2017.
3   See: 'What Would an HIV Doula Do?', *HIVDoula* (Spring 2015) (http://hivdoula.tumblr.com/post/138557273724/what-would-an-hiv-doula-do).

Alexandra Juhasz and Theodore (ted) Kerr, extracts from 'On Care, Activism, and HIV', *Hema*, no. 2 (July 2017).

Aimar Arriola and Nancy Garín
Global Fictions, Local Struggles//2014

The original title of this essay is 'Global Fictions, Local Struggles (or the distribution of three documents from an AIDS counter-archive in progress)'. The three 'documents' mentioned are: 'Document 1: AIDS And Dictatorship, Embodied In The Public Sphere' on Chilean artist and activist Guillermo Moscoso; 'Document 2: Other Forms Of The Political' on activist, cultural producer and member of performance group Las Pekinesas Miguel Benlloch; and 'Document 3: AIDS Interrogates The Museum' on Spanish artist Pepe Espaliú. This edited version focuses on 'Document 2'.

This text looks at some of the aesthetic practices, representations, collective experiences and performative tactics that emerged in response to the HIV/AIDS crisis in various contexts in the so-called 'South', in order to critically revise the widely accepted notion that the 1980s introduced a new global order, one that was stripped of borders and accessible to all. As Chilean writer Lina Meruane wrote in her recent survey of AIDS-related literature in Latin America – the 2012 book *Viral Voyages* – this fiction of increasing freedom 'gradually proved to be an affliction.'

In *Viral Voyages*, Meruane connects two previously unrelated spheres: Latin American literature and the disciplinary discourse of illness. Based on literary narratives of AIDS, the book traces the representations and the demand for signification that the pandemic unleashed from the 1980s onwards. Drawing on the work of early cultural critics of AIDS such as Susan Sontag, John O'Neill, Cindy Patton and Paula Treichler, as well as theorists like Richard Sennett who analyse financial or globalised capitalism, Meruane devotes the first part of the book to examining the cultural, social and political context that is inseparable from the discursive production around the pandemic. The second part of the book uses literary texts as evidence, based on works of fiction by authors such as Reinaldo Arenas, Severo Sarduy, Mario Bellatin and Pedro Lemebel, and taking them as a means to reflect on themes such as journeys, political repression and exile that recur in the representation of AIDS in Latin America.

John O'Neill (1990) and Cindy Patton (1990; 2002) are key references when it comes to rethinking the links between AIDS and globalisation processes. Patton's strategy of mixing local knowledge and global perspectives with scientific research and personal stories in *Globalizing AIDS*, for example, has influenced our own interdisciplinary approach to visual and performative production around AIDS in different contexts in the 'global South', while Paula Treichler's famous claim that the AIDS epidemic is, above all, an 'epidemic of signification' underlies the centrality of representation and language in the case studies that we present in this text.

While Meruane does not develop the topic of visual and activist production in her book, the work of authors such as Douglas Crimp and his now classic linking of 'cultural analysis' to 'cultural activism' in the English-speaking world, and Ricardo Llamas with his diverse theoretical-activist work in Spain – both of which are mentioned by Meruane in her bibliography – are key precedents for the type of connection between visual and archival production on one hand, and activist and academic knowhow on the other, that we seek to generate through our work. The activist and theoretical work of Sejo Carrascosa, Ricardo Llamas, Javier Sáez, Paco Vidarte and Fefa Vila – members of the activist groups Radical Gai and LSD that operated from the neighbourhood of Lavapiés in Madrid in the 1990s – is essential for understanding the conditions in which the early queer movement in Spain emerged, and its involvement in the fight against AIDS and other social struggles. As part of the 2013–14 Research Residencies at the Museo Reina Sofía, former members of Radical Gai and LSD are currently participating in a project that aims to recover and re-examine the most significant issues that the two groups focused on, formulated from the space of the archive. For this reason, we chose not to explore their work further in this text and to concentrate on case studies that have been barely considered or ignored before now.

Adhering to Meruane's reasoning, we propose to consider AIDS as both a co-narrative and a counter to globalisation. On one hand, we acknowledge AIDS as the subject that best connotes the new globalised reality that appeared in the 1980s. The geographical scope of the virus, its synchronous emergence around the world, and the rhetoric of flows and communication typical of the period, reinforced the idea of the world as a network of interconnected short distances. On the other hand, we also propose to think of AIDS as the great fault in the globalisation paradigm: the fault that can point out the promises of democratic equality that the global worldsystem failed to live up to. [...]

Transition As Disruption
We first noticed the precise intersection of the visual and performative production around HIV/AIDS with the policies of the dictatorship in Spain, by way of omission rather than attention. This occurred during the project *Social Dangerousness*, co-directed by [Paul] B. Preciado as part of the 2008–2009 edition of the MACBA Independent Studies Programme (PEI), which addressed the dissident cultural production of the last stage of Franco's regime and the early years of democracy, coinciding with the first cases of HIV/AIDS in Spain (the first case was diagnosed in Catalonia in 1981 by Doctor Caterina Mieras). Our contribution was a collective research project on a group of activists and cultural producers in Andalusia who had been active in the anti-Francoist struggle and the early gay liberation movement. The research did not really manage to come to terms with the impact of the emergence of AIDS in post-dictatorial Spain, and in some sense it reproduced a historical inertia: it failed to examine the initial indifference of the traditional left towards the crisis and the early gay movement.

This oversight came to light unexpectedly, and somewhat sadly, during a filmed conversation with three of the subjects of our research: feminist researcher and activist María José Belbel, and activists and cultural producers Joaquín Vázquez and Miguel Benlloch, co-founders of the cultural production company BNV Producciones. The discussion revolved around how the construction of the official narrative of the transition to democracy had overshadowed other possible narratives, defending civil society's active resistance against the repression of Franco's regime. Suddenly, as they reminisced about the early activities of feminist and gay liberation movements, all three interviewees wistfully acknowledged that they had 'not been equal to the task' (the expression is ours) of responding to the early days of the AIDS crisis.

When news of a 'gay cancer' started reaching Spain in the early 1980s and the first cases began to be diagnosed, the gay movement was going to 'look the other way', fearing further social stigmatisation and the loss of brand new freedoms. The participants of our conversation recognised this, and one of them summed it up in a subsequent email as follows: 'Politically, one of my greatest regrets is not having fought during the time when the AIDS pandemic began. I think it was because we had already done a lot of fighting and we had built up a lot of grief.' This reference to the political and emotional fatigue involved in living in a dictatorship as a way of explaining the difficulty of organising early responses to AIDS is not exclusive to Spain, and also came up repeatedly in interviews and conversations we had in Chile. The particular forms that AIDS politics took in post-dictatorial contexts should be understood as disruptions – breaks and interruptions – in the standardised and seemingly irrefutable design of globalisation.

The intersection between post-dictatorial politics and the emergence of AIDS also raises certain questions that have not yet been dealt with in the analysis of the visual culture of HIV/AIDS, and that are key to our research: What specific performative and visual production strategies emerged in post-dictatorial Chile and Spain, to mention two examples, when they collided with AIDS? What forms of somatic resistance emerged from the collision between dictatorship and AIDS politics? How are they linked to notions of trauma, memory and affect? [...]

Document 2: Other Forms of the Political

In the past, we have occasionally used the phrase 'other forms of the political' to refer to a broad range of critical strategies of visual and performative production that opposed the policies of repression during the dictatorship and transition, both in Chile – as in the example described above – and Spain. These 'other forms of the political' appeared alongside popular culture and the early gay liberation movements. They are expressed through the potentiality of the body, quite often in a playful form. In the specific case of Spain, these 'other forms of the political' belied the argument of a 'fatigue of the political' following the dictatorship. One wonderful example of 'alternative forms' of doing politics is the work of Miguel Benlloch, an activist, cultural producer and 'performancero' (as he likes to call himself). As it happens, Benlloch is one of the co-protagonists of our second document, which was recently rescued from oblivion, and which we put forward here as the earliest existing video of an HIV/AIDS-related political-aesthetic action in Spain: an action called *SIDA DA* carried out in November 1984 by Las Pekinesas, a group consisting of Miguel Benlloch, Tomás Navarro and Rafael Villegas.

The video shows a group of people who have gathered to watch an action in the basement of the bar Planta Baja, co-founded by Benlloch, which was the epicentre of the counterculture in Granada in the early 1980s. On a stage facing the audience, three bodies wearing cardboard carnival masks – Las Pekinesas – pass the microphone from one to the other as they reel off a series of puns on the word 'sida', the Spanish equivalent of the English word AIDS which had been coined not long before, in spring 1982, by a team of epidemiologists and bureaucrats in an office at the CDC (Center for Disease Control and Prevention) in Atlanta, just as Spain was becoming the sixteenth member of the NATO Atlantic Alliance. The underground venue and the masks worn by the protagonists returned the bodies to the clandestinity that Franco's dictatorship had forced them into in the not-so-distant past.

As the historian of medicine Mirko Dražen Grmek explains in *History of AIDS*, 'when the acronym AIDS was invented, nobody paid attention to its phonetic qualities or its linguistic malleability, and, consequently, its adoption by languages other than English caused problems'. As Grmek points out, the initial diphthong is difficult to pronounce in some languages, and the two final consonants are not euphonic, which explains why the analogous acronym SIDA was created in languages such as French and Spanish. In Spain, it was only gradually incorporated into written language, and the acronym morphed as it moved from medical terminology into everyday language: S.I.D.A., SIDA, Sida, eventually reaching its current form, 'sida', in lower case, as dictated by the Royal Spanish Academy. With the specific emphasis on the phonetic qualities and linguistic malleability of AIDS, Las Pekinesas (driven by intuition rather than intention) seem to be calling attention to the textual and discursive dimension of the pandemic, five years before Susan Sontag – one of the early analysts of AIDS as a global phenomenon – formulated her critique of the use of military metaphors in medicine and declared that 'language is a virus'.

The performance by Las Pekinesas removed AIDS from the global scientific-military-media language that it came from and inserted it into the lexicon of jokes and nonsense, and into what Mignolo refers to as 'languaging': the non-alienated practice of language that produces awareness of the (colonial, patriarchal) repression and power structures that are inscribed in language. At the same time, it undermines Sontag's labelling of the body ('the sick person') that the stigma is attached to, as a position of enunciation that is always weak, 'without imagining that he, too, produces language and appropriates metaphors', as Lina Meruane points out. Through their action, Las Pekinesas appropriate the disruptive potential of language and demand the right to participate, through the body and the voice, in the mediated processes of writing and coding of AIDS. [...]

Aimar Arriola and Nancy Garín, extracts from 'Global Fictions, Local Struggles (or the distribution of three documents from an AIDS counter-archive in progress)', trans. Nuria Rodriguez, *L'internationale* (31 March 2014) (www.internationaleonline.org/research/politics_of_life_and_death/5_global_fictions_local_struggles_or_the_distribution_of_three_documents_from_an_aids_counter_archive_in_progress) [footnotes omitted].

Mahmoud Khaled
Thanks 4 the Ad/d: HIV+ Cairo//2020

In 2008, I was commissioned to work on a new piece for the 4th edition of PhotoCairo Festival *The Long Shortcut* which is widely considered to be Cairo's first arts festival (started in 2002) devoted exclusively to photography, video and film. The 4th edition was specifically the most ambitious yet, a large-scale visual arts project curatorially interested in exploring the dynamics between informal and official modes of operation which shape the social reality in Cairo and the region around it.

The point of departure for the project I started to work on was inspired by the questions activated by the curators and became more crystallised in my head when I encountered three online profiles on a gay dating website called Manjam.[1] The three profiles/accounts were for three men living in Cairo, their ages differing from young to middle age and you can tell that they were coming from different social classes, but the three of them were looking for the same thing, 'LOVE', (a lover, sex partner or a partner) which is usually the main point of signing up on Manjam. There was nothing particularly unusual to me in those profiles initially, until I noticed that each stated clearly in their self-description section the fact that they are HIV positive! This was almost my first time in Egypt to have encountered HIV infected individuals in a non-governmental context, talking personally about themselves and the virus in an objective way. The power of speaking publicly about this subject is granted exclusively to the Egyptian State and its heavy-handed institutions. These institutions produce posters and flyers and distribute them on public transportation, in schools and sport clubs, they make educational videos and TV shows to make people aware of the virus and its consequences but they end up scaring people about the virus and anything related to it because the language they use is aggressive, scary, dismissive and stigmatising of anyone or anything connected to the subject the campaign is about. The State's campaign against AIDS also included a lot of conspiracy theory to complement the political agenda of Mubarak's post-war state. For example, I remember I was ten years old when the Egyptian movie *Love in Taba* was broadcast on TV, a film about three men from Cairo who went on a trip to the town of Taba in South Sinai[2] and met three foreign girls; they clicked quickly and slept together during the entire trip until one day the three men woke up and couldn't find the girls but instead found letters from them at the reception of the hotel. The letters conveyed that the girls are Israelis and they are HIV+ women, who came to Taba on a mission to infect and destroy the youth of Egypt and to spread the virus. So in this case the virus was instrumentalised to fulfil the state's propaganda narrative against political enemies. The film took the stigma around the subject of AIDS and HIV to a totally different level.

The three Manjam profiles came from a completely different position towards the virus. They spoke objectively about it with regard to their identity, life and desires. They were also actively spreading a lot of information and knowledge about a subject that is considered a taboo locally. This was while they were technically supposed to just be looking for love anonymously online, in a city where their identity must be invisible for security reasons because of their sexuality and health status. This was also happening at a time when there was almost no open discussion about the virus even within the local gay community.

I immediately became fascinated by their choice of using this sexually charged Manjam platform to talk freely about themselves and the virus while also keeping open the door to seduction and open possibilities in the meantime. At that moment and because of the given context, I started to see the act of 'Looking for love' (not even the act of love itself) as a very political act and things became different in my head, so I started to study and analyse every word, image and element published in these profiles. To an extent I wanted to materialise them by transferring them from cyberspace to the material world. I contacted the owners of the accounts and after a few days of chatting online, I asked them if we could meet in a cafe or a bar for a drink: only one man agreed and became enthusiastic about the idea, the other two refused to meet and insisted on remaining anonymous.

His name was Ahmed, we met in a cafe in Zamalek, an upscale bourgeois neighbourhood where he lived in Cairo. I remember he was around fifteen years older than me and we chatted a lot about how things are experienced differently for our generations as gay men when it comes to issues related to security, health and sexuality. Then he started talking about the moment when he knew the results of his blood test at the beginning of the 1990s and that he had to travel to Germany to get his medication as it was very dangerous to stay in Cairo once the laboratory knows the contact details of the infected person. He was very vulnerable and preferred to hide from Cairo, that mega-city which eats us every day with pleasure and pain. The details of his stories were so emotionally heavy and I was so moved that he opened up so quickly to me and shared all this while we just met for the first time. He asked about my research and why I was interested in his profile and this subject specifically. I didn't know how to answer this since at this point I had no idea about what the final work would be about at all, I told him that I was still in the research phase and trying things out in my head. I am just keen to know as much as I can as it will help me a lot in shaping and finalising the form of the work. He embarrassed this answer with a beautiful sincere smile and said: 'I am very happy to know that there is someone who decided to work on this issue in the art scene.' We stayed in touch online during the whole process of formulating the work, I invited him to the opening of the exhibition but he didn't want to attend, later on I sent him the full documentation of the installation and he responded with a very sweet and sincere message which for me was the most beautiful and meaningful feedback I received on the work up until now.

We stayed connected on Facebook, liking and interacting with each other's posts for years but we never met in person again, as I was travelling a lot and not living in Cairo at the time.

Two years ago I came to know via Facebook that Ahmed passed away due to health issues according to his friends and family members who shared the sad news of his death on their newsfeeds. I felt so sad that I didn't meet him for one more time before his death but I am forever thankful for him. This kind Zamalek guy who materialised from an encounter with his online profile on a random gay dating website twelve years ago. He had allowed me to produce this work in Cairo at a time when we were so scared to talk about anything or do anything that might sound controversial in the social and political reality through which we were living. Now we are still scared, but with a different taste of fear for different reasons, threatened by different political powers.

The work I produced at the end for the PhotoCairo was a text-based installation, I titled it *Thanks 4 the Ad/d* which is a common phrase that used to be seen on Myspace and Facebook profiles signifying that the person with this comment has recently tried to 'ADD to Friends' someone and they accepted. The work was structured conceptually based on three elements: space, a document and an object. *The Space* is the hospital space where we mostly die and are born, where we suffer from severe pain and vulnerability and it is also where we recover and regain our health and strength. The aesthetics of hospitals and clinical spaces were what I wanted to relay and highlight formally in the installation. *The Document* is the three online profiles that inspired the whole piece. And finally *The Object,* which is the lightbox (billboard) referencing that physically gigantic form of advertising we see hanging on the highways of our cities and atop tall buildings. It is a loud form of media that is not intimate at all and has to be physically far away from our bodies in urban spaces for us to view it. Most importantly it must advertise and announce a subject that is socially accepted since it only functions and exists in public spaces. The installation mixed theses three elements together in a specially built space with an exterior and interior structure. The exterior acts like the waiting room of a clinic with a few chairs for the viewers to rest on. Then there is a small door that takes you to the interior of the installation with a hospital-like corridor that is shaped by two walls and a curtain; on one of the walls we find three printed and punched out online Manjam profiles (as if a virus has done its damage) displayed in a 100 x 70cm framed glass. The curtain opens into space with three wall-to-wall lightboxes bearing text and radiating heat into an oppressively stark carpeted environment. On each lightbox a different fictionalised profile of an HIV-infected individual is printed in black on white vinyl. The profiles provide insights into the strengths, insecurities, emotions and desires of the personas they stand for, as well as basic tabled information about their physical appearance and lifestyle. The installation borrowed a range of strategies used in advertising as powerful tools for the delivery of public communication which contradicts the taboo nature of the subject of AIDS in Cairo. The texts combine sensational language with the more persuasive testimonial-driven style of advertorials. I also wanted to complicate my references to the public sphere even further by fusing the form of the street lightbox as a public medium for communication with the space of the hospital in which public health is administered and governed.

The three online profiles remained as a specific point of departure for me, they were exposed like x-rays on light boxes. Three individuals who actively use the web as an alternative platform for communication, whether for personal exchanges or as a source of information on taboo issues still ignored by the official Egyptian healthcare system.

I don't necessarily see the work as a direct political confrontation with cultural norms. It rather focuses on the claustrophobia and silence of living with HIV in a culture where those experiencing the epidemic must remain hidden.

During the last year I casually met a couple of young HIV+ guys in Cairo in their early 20s at two different gay parties. I was quite amazed by how politicised, mature, strong and courageous they are. They were also very conscious of their rights and the complications of fighting for them, as well as fighting the stigma as an idea. I only wish I was able to introduce them to Ahmed and get his heart warmed by their strength as they did to mine, but I also hope he is in a better place now than ours.

Thank you, Ahmed,
Cairo, January 2020

1   A social networking platform which was launched in 2004, uses GPS technology and social discovery to connect mutually attracted gay and bisexual men.

2   Taba is an Egyptian town near the northern tip of the Gulf of Aqaba, and is the location of Egypt's busiest border crossing with neighbouring Eilat, Israel. Taba is a frequent vacation spot for Egyptians and tourists from neighbouring countries, especially those from Israel on their way to other destinations in Egypt or as a weekend getaway.

Mahmoud Khaled, 'Thanks 4 the Ad/d: HIV+ Cairo', a new text written for this book, 2020.

Pedro Neves Marques
Viral Poems//2019

2016 was the peak of the Zika virus epidemic in Brazil. Across the country, banners, posters and television ads were the face of a nationwide campaign against the virus, or rather the mosquito that carries the virus – *Aedes aegypti*. This is the same mosquito that carries Dengue and Chukingunya. These ads could be found everywhere, from broken, out of the way dirt roads to urban city centres. I remember standing on a subway in São Paulo, looking at a short clip playing on a monitor hanging from the car's ceiling, perplexed at how militaristic its language was. The state waging war against biology? These types of campaign are standard for countries affected by mosquito-borne diseases, but staring at the digitally animated mosquito looping on that liquid-crystal screen I couldn't help but feel there was something terrifyingly masculine about it. The thought stayed with me.

Former Brazilian President Dilma Rousseff was impeached on 17 April 2016, initiating a sociopolitical downward spiral in the country that two years later would eventually lead to the election of the fascist presidential candidate Jair Bolsonaro. During those two years, Brazil was taken over by a resurgence of neo-reactionary politics and a wave of toxic masculinity, racism, homo- and transphobia, and all around xenophobia. Friendships and family ties quickly broke down, and both outrage and fear were palpable on the streets. As a Portuguese citizen, I continued with my films and writings, but struggled with feelings of helplessness towards my friends and a place I had quickly learned to love.

Attentive to how, historically, the notions of nature and culture tend to mirror and reshape one another, providing a battleground for the inclusion and exclusion of certain bodies (both human and nonhuman), the coincidence between these two events didn't escape me.

These *Viral Poems* were my own, personal way of projecting politics onto nature and culture. I felt the need for intimacy. The reasons were multiple. I could easily answer it with my own emotional exhaustion – and, much more importantly, of those around me when in Brazil – as well as with my own feelings towards gender, non-binary spaces and feminism. But the answer is also technical. Different laboratories have recently developed genetically modified mosquitos, particularly the *Aedes aegypti*, in order to fight against viruses like Zika. The British company Oxitec has been particularly efficient, having implemented a 'mosquito factory' in the state of São Paulo and conducted field trials in the region. Inside these factories, millions of mosquitos are born daily – an army ready to be deployed across the country. News has since come out that these genetic experiments have leaked into the local ecosystems, with genetically modified genes found in 'natural' mosquitos.

In the end, however, it wasn't genetics that most intrigued me in this process, but rather a familiar gender dynamics found throughout the history of science. Only the female mosquitos carry and spread the virus by biting; but only the males are modified. A 'lethal gene' is inserted into the males, who, upon mating, pass it on to the females – the female's offspring die before reaching a reproductive and transmission stage, thus reducing the population of carrier mosquitos and the spread of the disease. What a burden for the male; the same old fate for the female. And in-between one and the other gender, a repetition of long-trodden fears.

The Militarisation of Biology

the militarisation
of biology
is
the language
of suppression

when
the state
begins
to wane

the suppression
of language
is
the biology
of militarisation

it   (he)   *–the male mosquito*
is   non-transmissive
does   not carry   the virus
does   no   harm

                                                            it (he)
                                                            is transgenic

a weapon

                                                            of toxic masculinity.

it   (she)   *–the female mosquito*
is   transmissive
carries   the virus
is   (he declares)   harmful

                                                            it (she)
                                                            is naturalised

an object

                                                            of toxic masculinity.

Epidemic

people out   on the streets
become military
sweeping   the land   like a virus
this hatred

my tears
and other more serious threats

> the suspense was killing us
> *—the virus of culture*

these times
others become more other
than they've ever been   purposely   by now
it should be clear why—

the difference   accentuated

> the violence was always real
> *—the virus of nature*

Immunology   **II**

the way

for everyone to become

immune

is for everyone to be

bitten

Pedro Neves Marques, selected poems from *Sex as Care and Other Viral Poems* (London: PSS, forthcoming 2020), with a previously published introduction by the author.

Filipa Ramos
What the Virus Wants//2020

> To write about Napoleon or a bacillus in the first person is to write fiction.
> – Ursula K. Le Guin, *Steering the Craft* (2015)

In the beginning, the virus wanted nothing. 'The virus was fine where it was. I don't think it was looking to hop anywhere.'[1] Probably this wasn't a very ambitious virus either. Unlike the rhinovirus or the picornavirus, common cold viruses who truly believe in growth and expansion, this virus wanted to go nowhere. This is probably why, once it got taken out there, it didn't know how to behave evenly on its hosts, being very discrete on some and too aggressive on others. Rhinoviruses and picornaviruses know that softness and docility lead the way to success. As a virus, if you're too aggressive, sooner than later you'll end up in a bottleneck situation and you'll be over in no time. But this virus knew little and wanted little more than to be left alone.

It was warm, dark and cosy where the virus was, probably inside a furry, warm-blooded mammal who could fly like a bird, hear like a machine, and be suspended like a fruit. Then the virus was carried away and started travelling from one body to another, attuning itself to the life it encountered. It did not travel alone. A virus is an amorphous thing that jumps from cell to cell, mutating at every step. A virus is a dynamic colony that, incapable of living by itself, needs a carrier and avoids extinction by constantly moving, changing and evolving on the way. A generation of viruses can occur in a single day; the 24-hour reproductive cycle of a virus equals a period of 25 years for a human. Copy and mutate, copy and *mutatte*, copy and *muttatte*. 'The restless exuberance of gene flow cannot be stilled.'[2]

Despite this exuberant flow, it was only in recent times that the likelihood of an animal carrier reaching a far-off location alive, of a human carrier surviving an infection from an unknown pathogen and of the animal and human carriers remaining in close contact with many more animals and humans, grew exponentially. Advanced infrastructure, medicine and communication are highly effective vectors for a virus. Accelerated transmission became the propeller of both the modern world and the modernised viruses. The virus found itself everywhere and in everything. It thrived across global population density and traffic and learned to master virality: a single individual – animal or human – is capable of spreading it to hundreds of thousands of other individuals. In a few months, the virus managed more than humans and algorithms together, which for decades have been compressing and dwarfing the planet; connecting; uniting and merging places, things and beings; calculating and reducing the degrees of separation that connect every single individual to everyone else, virtually inviting the friends of the friends to become friends.

The virus was caught into this. Now it believes that you and me and them are us. That We are the same. That you and me and them are made of the same stuff. That We breathe and speak and laugh and spit and sneeze and fever and cough alike. That We rejoice and revel and cry and suffer and love and hate alike. That tragedy, contingency, dispossession and comedy happen to all. So this virus, who was brought from its happy latency into a state of global circulation, now wants to show that you and me and them are us.

What the virus ignores is that despite being the same, We are far from being the same. Some of us are historically and genetically and politically and sexually and geographically better positioned than others in this entanglement We call existence. You and me and them and us may well be the same but We are not all equipped in the same way. We have been endowed with uneven features, powers and agencies; our capacity to act is different.

I can object you are subjected they can decide We are subjugated. (no commas separate us). The virus tries to play dumb to the world order; it ignores it, it hovers above it like an abstract anarchist, reshuffling the criteria of societal organisation. But there is a gap between what the virus wants and what the virus knows. And what the virus does not know is that the world order also has its own DNA. This DNA is a strong self-replicating material that permeates so many beings and non-beings in the planet. It is a foundational matter, so embedded into the system of present life that the virus not only struggles to break its strands, but it even gets trapped within its net. This DNA can be called many things. Extractive capitalism, Anthropocene, Chthulucene, Oilogarchy, Plantationocene, you name it, the virus won't. And even if the virus is not a life form, even if it is anti-social, asocial, unsocial, and does not participate in any of the entanglements and arrangements and divisions and classifications and taxonomies and differentiations and identities that some make to break up the We, the virus not only struggles to disrupt them but even complies with them. This is the story of a virus that fails to get what it wants, even if it gets many other things on the way.

Despite failing, in wanting to show that you and me and them are us, the virus manages to disturb the foundations of extractive, abusive, divisive capitalism. I am exposed, you are protected, We are vulnerable, they are sheltered. Except that some of the protected and some of the sheltered get badly infected and cough their way to death. Except that some of the exposed and some of the vulnerable are immune (or healthier, luckier, blessed, or whatever you want to call them), and prodigiously breathe throughout their complicated lives. And they manage to make their way beyond the logics that divest them and determine their position on the bad side of the entanglement where you and me and them and us are.

The virus is not interested in morals though. It does not care if you're on the fair or unfair side of things, on the lucky or unlucky part of life. The virus does not even know what justice is. Its rationale is another. The fact that you're privileged and you call yourself fortunate while still getting ill and the fact that you're unprivileged and you call yourself fortunate while not getting infected matter nothing to it. What the virus wants is to show that you and me and them are us. That We are the same. The virus is not affected by how some find ironic that a statesman is infected; that some find cruel that physicians fall from the cure they are trying to bring; that some find telling that the invisible remain uncounted, untested and unprotected, and that some think it is unfair that the old die alone and the young party together.

But the issue with this virus is that while being indifferent to these separations and criteria, in wanting to be rebalance such togetherness, to a large extent it perpetuates the state We live in and the logics We operate by. And sometimes it ends up reinforcing those same foundations it is aiming at. Despite the exceptions, the virus largely extends the agency of those who already have it, it makes uneven distribution even more uneven, it redistributes power to the powerful, access to the validated, wealth to the wealthy, health to the healthy. The virus wants to change everything for everything to change but for now it is changing everything for everything to stay the same. But what the virus wants and what the virus gets are two different things. And the fact that even virus finds itself trapped in the net of capitalism isn't very good news.

But some things may change. The edges and the centres are coming together. Boundaries are harder to establish. By coming from the cave, the virus turns our cities into caves. By coming from the jungle, the virus shows that the jungle is in us. The virus finds its way from the cave to the jungle, from the jungle to the trap, from the trap to the cage in a market, from the cage in a market to the floor that sticks, the hand that touches, the air that is breathed, and from the floor that sticks, the hand that touches, and the air that is breathed to the body that hosts and transports. The diffusing body, a body that is metabolically constituted by the life of the jungle, the life of the cave, the arrested life of the market and the non-life of the virus. A body that becomes bodies that becomes virus that becomes matter. A body that ingests exploitation, violence, abuse, toxicity and fear. A body that feeds on toxins, hormones, transgenes, antibiotics, herbicides, pesticides and fungicides. A body that is made of and part of the bodies that keep capitalism alive.

The bat, the civet cat, the pangolin are in us. But also the chicken the duck the gull the macaw the pigeon and the sparrow. The chipmunk the mouse the rabbit and the rat. The camel the cow the deer and the horse. The salamander the snake and the turtle. The monkey and the porcupine. All animals that gave people more than meat, heat, company and cure but also infections and diseases. AIDS anthrax bird flu brucellosis bubonic plague chikungunya encephalitis ebola influenza leprosy lyme malaria MERS rabies SARS toxoplasmosis tuberculosis zika. From my DNA to yours, without love.

We 'form a rhizome with our viruses, or rather our viruses cause us to form a rhizome with other animals'.[3] They treat us we threaten them. They feed us we kill them. They heal us we breed them. They kill us we eat them. They threaten us we treat them. They bite us we host them. With so much spillover, it is no wonder the virus finds distinctions hard to grasp. The problem, again, is that the virus has been trapped within a system that is more complex than itself. Knowing what the virus wants may help us to deal with it. Knowing what the virus knows may help us come to terms with a condition We have been trying to avoid for too long. You and me and them are indeed us. You pangolin me bat them persons We life. The old world awaits the new us.

1   Elizabeth A. Povinelli, 'Virus or Interpendence of Lives, an audio interview with Dani Blanga Gubbay' as part of the programme *Four Rooms* (3 April 2020) (https://www.facebook.com/thekhanorg/videos/151814866175052/).

2   Donna J. Haraway, *Companion Species Manifesto: Dogs, People, and Significant Otherness* (Chicago: Prickly Paradigm Press, 2003) 9.

3   Gilles Deleuze and Félix Guattari, *A Thousand Plateaus: Capitalism and Schizophrenia*, trans. Brian Massumi (Minneapolis: University of Minnesota Press, 1987) 10.

Filipa Ramos, adapted from 'What the Virus Wants', *The Contemporary Journal*, no. 3 (April 2020) (https://thecontemporaryjournal.org/issues/sonic-continuum/what-the-virus-wants).

Anne Boyer
This Virus//2020

> so violent a rudeness, untenanted by any tangible form
> – Edgar Allan Poe

It is a shame that to understand this virus, we must understand math, which to the many of us who were denied a decent math education in school, exists mostly as a phantasm: exponentiality no easier to grasp than the hand of a ghost. And now the health of many depends on a general capacity to believe in the future tangibility of the present intangibles. (An excellent review of the numbers is here, in this remarkable plea for action.)[1] We must not only now understand exponential growth, but also the difference between sly things, like the deadly distance between 1% and .1%.

In the meantime, the world's eugenicists-in-chiefs appear to lick their lips at the prospect of the deaths of the elderly, sick and poor. The vicious denialism of Trump, Johnson and Bolsanaro is the logic that also governed yesterday's every day misery, made grand to fit today's catastrophe. For a certain class, the death of what they consider 'the unproductive' comes as a messy but not unwelcome event. This is why you see that cadaverous look in these guys' eyes at the press conferences in which they stand in their bloated suits, mumbling administrative deceptions about the flu, about testing. We know to believe what they do, not what they say: finance gets emergency aid and the hospitals don't. In the meantime, CPAC (Conservative Political Action Conference) itself might have become a polo-shirt-and-pepe version of the Masque of the Red Death.[2]

These are the same types who say the only thing to fear is fear, which of course is not true, because fear educates our care for each other – we fear a sick person might be made sicker, or that a poor person's life might be made even more miserable, and we do whatever we can to protect them because we fear a version of human life in which everyone lives for themselves only. I am not the least bit afraid of this kind of fear, for fear is a vital and necessary part of love. And this fear, which I love, is right now particularly justified, because we have a pernicious virus that travels inside the healthy to sicken and kill the already fragile, and therefore requires that the healthy and strong deepen their moral commitments for the benefit of the sick and weak. We must learn to do good for the good of the stranger now. We now have to live as daily evidence that we believe there is value in the lives of the cancer patient, the elderly person, the disabled one, the ones in unthinkable living conditions, crowded and at risk.

Total misery in the coming days is not a total inevitability: we have a capacity to respond today. We can practice excellent hygiene, stop leaving messes for cleaners, disinfect our common spaces. We can try our best to get what we need to get by for a while. We can – today, right now – organise mutual aid networks among our existing social contacts, make plans to care for the vulnerable, prepare supplies for those who will get sick. We can provide shelter for the people who don't have it, offer to be a support for anyone feeling crazy from the news, promise to take care of someone's pets or kids if they get sick. We can provide important information to those who have been deceived or ignored. We can protect those who are unfairly stigmatised and discriminated against. We can sew masks and make disinfection kits to give to those who will be caring for the sick at home.

We can also go on a general strike, which now has a double purpose – stay at home, refuse to work, refuse to go to school, refuse to shop, refuse as much as possible to get sick or make others so. We can shout at the top of our lungs and demonstrate in our every action that the lives of the vulnerable matter, that the deaths of the sick and the elderly and the poor and imprisoned from this virus are unacceptable. The prisoners must be freed. The elderly must be cared for. Everyone must have safe housing. The sick must be supported without fear of losing jobs or being bankrupt by medical costs. The cleaners, health care workers, and other carers on the front line must have everything they need to stay safe. This virus makes what has always been the case even more emphatically so.

We also must engage in large scale social distancing. The way social distancing works requires faith: we must begin to see the negative space as clearly as the positive, to know what we don't do is also brilliant and full of love. We face such a strange task, here, to come together in spirit and keep a distance in body at the same time. We can do it. I am writing this because I want the good in us to break through the layers of hateful nonsense we've been drowning in. I think we can be good, but we also must prepare for an amplification of evil's evil. The time when the invisible becomes visible is at hand.

1   Ninghui Li, 'Open Letter 1 on COVID-19: The Urgent Need for Aggressive Social Distancing Actions'(9 March 2020)(https://docs.google.com/document/d/e/2PACX-1vQuHYLsCvNJuzydGL0H6hb RZhUhFeyYIku8HEg7ZIeZ9HRpzKMuJ0JpVXF46F9En466S2M5k82-Gla5/pub?from=timeline&isappi nstalled=0&urp=gmail_link).

2   Edgar Allan Poe, 'The Masque of the Red Death' (1842). Available at https://www.poemuseum. org/the-masque-of-the-red-death

Anne Boyer, 'This Virus', originally published as a mail shot to subscribers of *Mirabilary* (March 2020) (https://mirabilary.substack.com/p/this-virus).

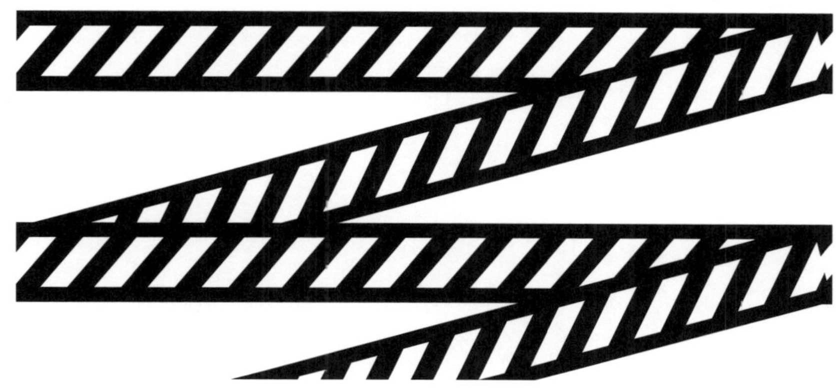

We can sew masks and make disinfection kits to give to those who will be caring for the sick at home.

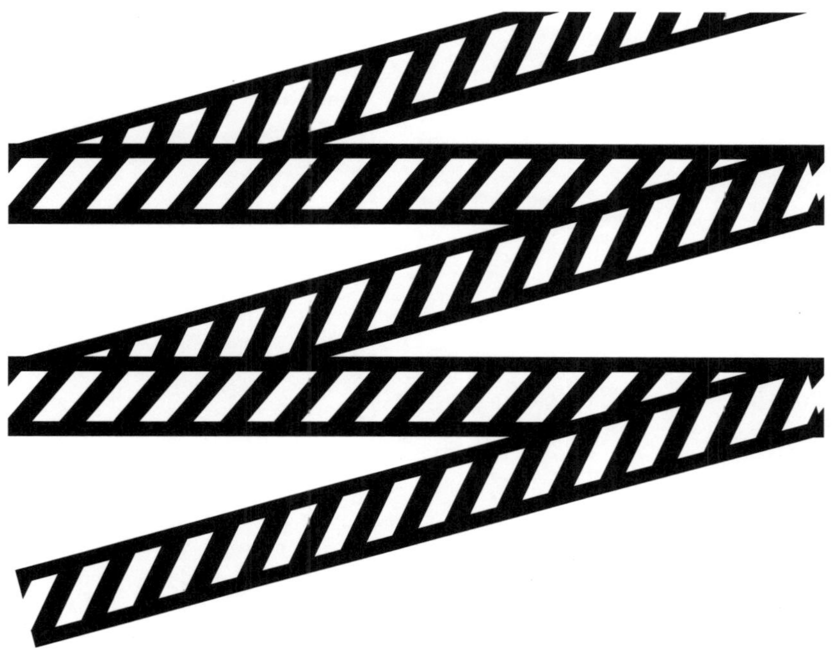

Anne Boyer, 'This Virus', 2020

Radical PSYCHIATRY, Radical POLITICS, Radical ART:

rage against the institution.

THE INSTITUTION DENIED

John Foot
Anti-Psychiatry, Critical Psychiatry, Movements and Working Utopias//2015

> There has not been only one anti-psychiatry, just as there has not been only one psychiatry.
> –Patrizia Guarnieri

> We can transform each institution – family, school, university, mental health, factory – each art form, into a revolutionary centre for a transforming consciousness.
> –David Cooper

One of the key problems in studying radical psychiatry in the 1960s and 70s is the term 'anti-psychiatry'. Words are important, and they often change in meaning; 'anti-psychiatry' is no exception to this rule. It is a strange word, toxic even, packed with power and yet often emptied of real meaning. Today, this term is bandied about, usually in a negative sense. For some it has almost become an insult, and its uses differ widely in different national and academic contexts. It is rarely defined or analysed in any depth, often identified simply with a belief in the bland assertion that 'mental illness does not exist'. Giovanni Jervis wrote in the 1970s that anti-psychiatry was 'a sign of dissent, but it isn't clear what it is against or what it denies', which could also be understood as a 'tendency, a cultural orientation, a kind of critical ferment'.

This semantic problem is compounded by the fact that most who are usually described as the 'leaders' of anti-psychiatry have denied, at one time or another, that they were ever anti-psychiatrists. There was a sense that people were already avoiding the term by the mid 1970s. Jervis wrote, 'I don't know anyone who calls themself an anti-psychiatrist'. This is a term that almost everyone (from the time) rejects, yet it continues to be used.

Take R.D. Laing, for example, who wrote this in his autobiography:

> I have never called myself an anti-psychiatrist, and have disclaimed the term from when first my friend and colleague, David Cooper, introduced it. However, I agree with the anti-psychiatric thesis that by and large psychiatry functions to exclude and repress those elements society wants excluded and repressed.

Yet Laing was the most famous anti-psychiatrist of all – 'the father and the Pope of anti-psychiatry' – despite his protestations. Or we could cite Basaglia himself, who said this in response to a question in the late 1970s:

> I would like to say that this child, anti-psychiatry, which is ten years old, does not exist – or rather exists only in the heads of people because this word has had great success from the ideological more than the practical point of view. We have never been anti-psychiatrists – we were simply employees... we worked in the real world within psychiatric institutions in order to give people who were suffering an alternative to the violence and repression of the asylum.

Basaglia added later in the same interview that 'I don't understand what anti-psychiatry or non-psychiatry actually means'. Even those who defined themselves as anti-psychiatrists, and really did deny that mental illness existed, are now suffering from the syndrome of denial.

So what are we to do with this 'child' called 'anti-psychiatry', one which causes so much anguish, and which some say does not even exist – a child that has grown up and has been disowned by its parents and former friends? In order to answer this question we need to go back to the 1960s and begin to trace the history and genealogy of 'anti-psychiatry' from its origins up to the present day.

Anti-psychiatry: Genealogy and History of a Term

> A revolution [...] is going on in relation to sanity and madness, both inside and outside psychiatry. Modern psychiatry came into being when the demonological point of view gave way 300 years ago to a clinical viewpoint. The clinical point of view is now giving way before another point of view that is both existential and social. The shift, I believe, is of no less radical significance.
> – R.D. Laing (1964)

> In the 1960s and 70s a series of tendencies which called into question the dogmas attached to traditional psychiatric 'science' were grouped together with the generic term 'anti-psychiatry'.
> – Giovanni Jervis (1975)

> *Giovanni Jervis*: 'In one sense it is very easy today to practice anti-psychiatry.'
> *Franco Basaglia*: 'No, we are non-psychiatrists.'
> – *L'istituzione negata* (1968)

In the heady atmosphere of the late 1960s, the buzzwords of 'anti-psychiatry' and 'non-psychiatry' took on a series of meanings, both for those who uttered them and for the followers of the movement. The current of thought and activity which became known as 'anti-psychiatry' (both with and without capitals and quotation marks) covered a wide range of opinions and ideas, and was identified with a number of texts, leaders and experiences in a series of countries, including those in Gorizia and then Trieste.

As a first step, then, we need to try and define what 'anti-psychiatry' was *then*, and what it means for us, historically, *today*. Put very simply, as a starting-point: *Anti-psychiatry was a critical and radical movement that emerged from within the world of psychiatry itself.* It was a political, cultural and social 'moment' in history, 'a symptom…a catalyst, and a point of convergence'. It was flexible and malleable, a state of mind, a language, a way of thinking, that is to say a way of life…not an ideal closed in upon itself or an easy to copy model but rather a perpetually renewed incitement to look beyond the appearances and prejudices that social conformism wraps us up in – at things themselves.

It can also be fixed in time. We can give anti-psychiatry a set of broad dates, for example: the 1960s and 70s. Nonetheless, the phrase 'anti-psychiatry' continued and continues to have a history even if the movement itself no longer exists in the same way (or at all).

David Cooper first coined the term in his volume *Psychiatry and Anti-psychiatry*, published in 1967, and it was used again in his introduction to the celebrated publication based on the Dialectics of Liberation Congress in London. Nonetheless, in these two books there is very little on what the term actually means. Moreover, in his final comments in *Dialectics*, Cooper warned his readers about 'false' solutions that might easily emerge from an over-simplistic or illusionary reading of some aspects of anti-psychiatry. He could already see how his words might be misused or create dangerous and false hopes, even as the term was being introduced. Was it simply a new, chic and radical label, or was it something linked to concrete and alternative forms of practice, such as in the new unit run by Cooper known as Villa 21, which he himself described as 'an experiment in anti-psychiatry'?

So what was it that held this nascent movement together (a movement riven right from the start by ideological, practical, political and personal divisions and arguments)? First, there was a *critical* approach towards traditional theories and practices of psychiatry (and the medical world in general). This critique ranged from the workings of the asylum system to bio-organic theories of mental illness, to the ways in which the mentally ill were labelled, incarcerated and treated in hospitals and clinics. Often, radical psychiatry in this period called into question traditional definitions and diagnoses of mental illness. This 'calling into question' took in a range of positions, from Basaglia's desire to 'place the diagnosis in brackets', to the denial that whole categories of mental illness really existed. Many radical psychiatrists were inspired by phenomenology and advocated forms of practice that allowed for the construction of relationships with their 'patients' on an equal footing, at least in theory. Often, the whole separation of 'patients' and 'doctors' was undermined or abolished. As Laing and his fellow authors put it way back in 1956, in their description of the Rumpus Room experiment in Glasgow, 'The barrier between patients and staff is not erected solely by the patients but is a mutual construction. The removal of this barrier is a mutual activity.' Sometimes, as in the case of the short-lived patients' movement in Heidelberg, illness was celebrated 'as a weapon'. Therefore, anti-psychiatry was a term associated with a movement that covered an assortment of positions, among which there were indeed some activists and thinkers who denied the 'existence of mental illness'.

Radical psychiatrists usually tried to understand mental illness as a social creation. What was known as mental illness, it was argued, was in some way created by social forces, inside and/or outside the family unit. This characteristic has been seen, by some writers, as the essence of anti-psychiatry. For Julian Bourg: 'Anti-psychiatry was an international radical tendency generally inclined towards viewing madness as socially constructed. It brought the spirit of anti-authoritarian revolt to the mentally ill and their caregivers.'

Sometimes, this social analysis was extended to the whole system governing mental health care, which was placed firmly within an analysis of capitalist power structures and the 'repression of deviance'. These strands of radical psychiatry brought together Marxism, forms of Maoism (as in the contestation of power structures, the Western translation of the Cultural Revolution) and new anti-authoritarian ideas coming out of 1968. Thus, anti-psychiatry was critical (and *self*-critical), social, political and cultural, all at the same time. To understand anti-psychiatry, we need to take a wide-ranging approach to the subject. As Peter Barham has argued, it was 'far more significant within a cultural history than a distinctly psychiatric one'.

It is useful to delve a little deeper into this term or label. D.B. Double further divides up the positions taken by the various 'leaders' of anti-psychiatry into a number of different strands:

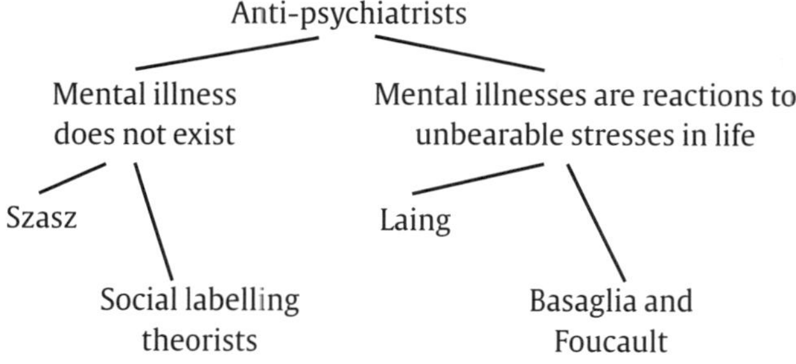

These sub-categories can be further separated in different ways. As Double argues,

> The group who recognise that the use of the term mental illness is metaphorical and, thereby, do not want to minimise the suffering of people with mental health problems can also be subdivided into two. The first would include Laing, who emphasises that reactions identified as mental illness relate to interpersonal behaviour, particularly within the family. The second subdivision, containing authors like Franco Basaglia [...] and Michel Foucault [...] emphasise that broader societal factors rather than the family are involved in presentations of mental illness.

We can also understand anti-psychiatry by what it was *against*. To cite Double again: 'The essence of anti-psychiatry derives from the sense in which psychiatry itself is regarded as part of the problem.'

Thus, in the late 1960s and early to mid 1970s, anti-psychiatry was a disparate but international political movement that aimed to reposition (in a radical way) psychiatric theory *and* practice. It was also a very broad church. Anti-psychiatry contained within its flexible borders a whole range of positions, which was part of its strength but also a clear weakness. Agreement was almost impossible. Sects and sectarianisms developed, as well as personal conflicts. Debates were interminable. Basaglia's attempts to create an organisation (Psichiatria Democratica) out of this mass of activists was commendable and important, but was paralysed at times by ongoing conflicts. The same was even truer of short-lived international umbrella organisations that attempted to bring together anti-psychiatrists.

Anti-psychiatry can also be understood as a more general form of methodology. There was, at the time, a general attempt to *overturn*, to *negate* what was already there, the structures of intellectual (and in this case medical) power. This 'anti' element was crucial to the workings of the movement. Institutional power was contested in all its forms – as encapsulated in the protagonists of this power: teachers, doctors, psychiatrists, lecturers, priests and politicians. Those with power often contested *themselves*, by denying their own authority, by stripping themselves of the symbols of power (white coats, for example, as a first step, but also titles), or by attempting to place themselves on the same level as those they were treating, teaching or giving sermons to. Radical psychiatry was part of a larger movement, and to understand it we also need to look more deeply at 1968 and the 1970s. As Fulvio Marone puts it, 'The movement of alternative psychiatry was [...] a subset of a vast movement.'

In the 1960s and 70s, the use of the term 'anti-psychiatry' was commonplace. This is true with relation to Basaglia, to Jervis and to other parts of the movement in 1968. In 1978 Ernesto Venturini also used the label in an edited book that attempted to survey the whole Italian movement. Far from being rejected by the Basaglians and others in the movement, the anti-psychiatry label was actively embraced by them for a time. [...]

Some within the movement called for the abolition of the whole category of 'psychiatry', while many others agitated within *and* against psychiatry at the same time. There were those who explored the idea of a scientific revolution inside the discipline, while others called for a revolution *against* science itself. Many anti-psychiatrists worked *as* psychiatrists in one form or another: anti-psychiatry was part of the world of psychiatry.

Moreover, it is important to distinguish between the often-sophisticated (and occasionally incomprehensible) theoretical debates among the leaders and theoreticians of the movement, and wider networks of followers and supporters. It is clear that, while Basaglia's position attempted to place mental illness 'in brackets', or suspend judgement, or avoid labelling patients, the movement as a whole often tended towards a much cruder analysis of these problems, rejecting institutions *tout court*, as well as psychiatry and mental illness. For Edoardo Balduzzi, 'Basaglia never clearly denied that there was something called "mental illness", but the decodification of his message, above all in the years of "contestation", was read in that way.'

Crude positions were often reproduced by journalists and others in their reports on Basaglian institutions and ideas. In this sense, it is possible to see how Basaglia could become 'in any case, historically, the father of Italian anti-psychiatry' despite his own frequent denials of this role in a specific sense. Jervis also underlined how extremist positions were taken up by many within the movement after 1968, a period which saw 'an unexpected process of the popularisation and vulgarisation of so-called "anti-psychiatric" themes'.

Anti-psychiatry (both as an identifier and as something symptomatic of a wider movement and new ideas) was extremely à la mode for a time, and was almost impossible to avoid. It became a kind of brand. Then, very quickly, it slipped out of fashion and was discredited and removed from the history of that period. History was read backwards, as so often happens. Even those who had tolerated the term or accepted it soon began to reject it (such as Basaglia and Laing). Its meaning also changed over time. [...]

John Foot, extracts from 'Anti-psychiatry, Critical Psychiatry, Movements and Working Utopias', in *The Man Who Closed the Asylums: Franco Basaglia and the Revolution in Mental Health Care* (London: Verso, 2015) 28–38 [footnotes omitted].

Dora García

Radical Politics, Radical Psychiatry, Radical Art:
An Introduction to the 'Mad Marginal' Project[1]//2010

I know of one Greek labyrinth which is a single straight line.
– Jorge Luis Borges, 'Death and the Compass'

Is not writing mainly about the writer continuously shunning the main subject, as if it were something too precious, and one should beat around the bush? One procrastinates about something important, about something one would like to discuss at all costs, but for the time being, one writes or speaks about something else, rather subsidiary.
– Robert Walser, 'Der heiße Brei' (my translation)

Radical politics, radical psychiatry, radical art. It all started with an insight, a conviction, and a good story. The story came from Erik Thys, a Belgian psychiatrist, who told me the fantastic tale of a certain psychiatric patients' group and of its founder. What he told me (I know now that his version was not completely accurate – but still beautiful) was that the founder of this group, a German psychiatrist, a doctor and a professor, had started a therapy group with the psychiatric patients at the university clinic of Heidelberg, in the late 60s; and that the therapeutic activities they practised included urban guerrilla techniques. Erik Thys intertwined the story of this doctor in an extraordinary way with the 'Entartete Kunst' (1937)[2] exhibition (*outsider art* being considered equivalent to *avant-garde art*, and labelled degenerate) and with the Aktion T4 program[3], which exterminated psychiatric patients and people with Down's syndrome or other disabilities in Germany, and was a sinister rehearsal for the Holocaust. This was not the end of it: Erik said there is a movement in Germany right now[4] that is calling for the Prinzhorn collection[5] (Prinzhorn himself being a Nazi sympathiser) to be moved from Heidelberg to Berlin; and for this seminal art collection to be housed in Tiergarten 4, the very place where the decision was made to exterminate psychiatric patients. Who was the man behind this contemporary movement? Someone sharing the same name as our original Heidelberg doctor, only forty years younger… a case of eternal, supernatural youth? Or a case of poetic justice?

The story of the Aktion T4 euthanasia programme is beyond horror. The story of our eternally young doctor was, from any point of view, an excellent story that I could not let go of anymore.

Radical psychiatry, radical politics. The insight and conviction was that radical psychiatry involved a profound truth about politics: that when our

Heidelberg doctor gave the patients the (courageous, radical) right to decide how to behave within the monstrous leviathan of the institution, something very close to justice took place.[6]

What does radical mean? Believing or expressing the belief that there should be great or extreme social or political change. Relating to the most important parts of something or someone; complete or extreme (Cambridge Dictionaries Online).

What is an institution? The best definition for me came from Franco Basaglia: *that which resists change.*

It was clear, then: radical and institutional are mutually exclusive. *Radical psychiatry, radical politics, radical art*: rage against the institution. But also, and here comes insight again: an uncompromising idea of truth.

To reveal the truth, to dismiss ideologies that prevent the disclosure of truth. Psychiatry, politics and art are ideologies[7], and ideologies conceal truth, deform vision, dogmatise the response to a certain situation[8]. A radical position must reveal the truth about psychiatry, about politics, about art. Is psychiatry part of medicine, is it even a science at all? Is anyone being cured in psychiatric hospitals? Is there such a thing as psychiatric illness? The truth about psychiatry casts doubt on the very fundaments of psychiatry: *What is psychiatry? (Che cos'è la psichiatria?* [9]). A remark of David Cooper's[10] supports this: 'If psychiatry is one day to be an effective force, it will be thanks to a transformation which will earn it, for a time at least, the name of anti-psychiatry.'[11]

Radical politics. The truth about politics. The psychiatric patients' group we are talking about, and one of its possible after-effects, the politically radicalised RAF, was made up of Germany's finest youth, the gifted children who demanded that the truth about the West German state be revealed.

In Guy Debord's late film *In girum imus nocte et consumimur igni* (1978), the camera lingers at a certain point on two photographs: the exterior of the Stuttgart-Stammheim maximum-security facility, where the first generation of the RAF committed suicide (and, incidentally, where ███████ was imprisoned in solitary confinement from 1973 to 1976), and a press shot of the leftist militants Andreas Baader and Gudrun Ensslin on trial in 1968. 'La plus belle jeunesse meurt en prison', reads the narrator. *The flower of youth dies in prison.*

Radical politics. The truth about politics. To quote Thomas Elsaesser's 'ANTIGONE AGONISTES: Urban Guerrilla or Guerrilla Urbanism? The Red Army Faction, Germany in Autumn and Death Game':

The RAF was the resistance that German citizens had never managed to organise when it mattered, for instance, resisting the Nazis or opposing the persecution of the Jews. The RAF was in this precise sense not the 'return of the repressed', but involved in a situation of *Nachträglichkeit*, engaged in making up for something that had been omitted in the past, desirous to assume a role, across a historical gap, that was marked by shame, guilt, self-hatred. Under these circumstances, speaking of 'mutual symbiosis', as does Delius, may not quite strike the right note, although it recognises that something other than pure antagonism played across the confrontation between the state and the terrorists. The RAF was not only attacking the state: it was also 'addressing' it, their mode of address being that of 'symbolic identification'. That such an awareness was even shared by some of those thus addressed is attested by security chief Horst Herold's remark 'I loved Andreas Baader'.

Or, to quote Carmen Roll in the interview I conducted with her in Trieste, June 2010:

Basaglia had very strong anti-fascist positions. He said to me sometime in 1978, 'You are the girl who has reconciled me with the Germans'. […] [T]he process of democratisation in Germany, for left-wing Italian intellectuals, was a point that deserved primary attention. And the ■ had a lot to do with it, you have to realise that the radicalisation of the ■, I remember… when the Minister of Culture for Baden-Württemberg, in the Baden-Württemberg Parliament, with the proceedings broadcast over the radio, said: '■ ist die Gebährmutter des Radikalen, Unkraut' (■ is the womb carrying the radical offspring, bad seed), and this was what Hitler said about the Jews, the Gypsies… they used the same language! We started to study our enemies, and our enemies were people who were fifty years old then. A guy who was fifty in the 60s, and who was a university professor teaching psychiatry, where was he in the 40s? It was not Klaus Dörne and all these professors who started investigating the connection between psychiatry and concentration camps, the elimination of handicapped people, Gypsies, homosexuals; it was the ■. And when we started to talk about this, we made enemies. Because in Germany, it was very difficult to be a university professor and have it discovered that as a young doctor you had worked in a concentration camp, or in a psychiatric hospital that was known for having deported people, handicapped people, to concentration camps. It was hard to be a university professor during the student movement, which was profoundly anti-fascist. And we uncovered them: very important, very powerful people. And we made real enemies, and the Italians liked us for that. That was the position of the ■, of my friends and me at least: we will never tolerate this (the Fascists still in power). Our parents did this, and we will never do it.

Radical art. The truth about art. The 'Entartete Kunst' exhibition forever sealed the profound and complex connection between modern art and outsider art.

'*Wahnsinn wird Methode*', 'Madness becomes method'[12], was one of the slogans depicted on the gallery walls. The 'Entartete Kunst' exhibition was designed to inflame public opinion against modernism, as elitist, incomprehensible, praising ugliness – the arguments against the avant-garde have hardly changed since then.

The truth about art. A term such as 'outsider art' deserves some reflection. Outside of what? Obviously the term 'outsider' implies exclusion, exclusion from something. Whether at the forefront (the avant-garde) or outside, this art is clearly not an insider. It is not at the centre.

The counterculture! A term again very precisely defined by Basaglia: *the culture of the deviant.*

Whatever meaning we give to *outsider art* – art made by psychotics; art made by non-professional, untrained artists; art made by the socially marginalised; art that is not art because it was never conceived as art; art made spontaneously, that is, without knowledge of what art is supposed to be; art that is defined as art *by other people* (insiders) instead of its maker (an outsider) – whatever meaning we give to *outsider art*, it says much more about *mainstream art* than about whatever is outside it.

Logically speaking, then, 'mainstream art' (or art *tout court*?) should be made by sane people; trained and professional people; socially successful people; mainstream art is art that has been art since the moment of its conception; un-intuitive art, that is, art made with well-grounded knowledge of what art is supposed to be; art that is defined as art by its maker (an insider).

No wonder then that the truth about art might sound like: radical artists profoundly mistrust the ideology of art.

One could speak here of Artaud, and his refusal to use the term 'artworks' for the artworks he had made in the asylum. Instead, he greatly preferred to call them 'documents'.[13] One could speak here of Robert Walser, and his ruthless, bitter satire of the well-established literati. We could speak here of the idioms so often used by filmmaker Jack Smith: 'mouldy aesthetics' and 'plaster art'.

Radical politics, radical psychiatry, radical art. As in the quote from Robert Walser, perhaps this is not really what we want to talk about, perhaps this is only the subsidiary subject we are using to 'beat around the bush'.[14] That might it be, then, the real bird we are seeking?

<hr>

1   The 'Mad Marginal' project was initiated by Dora García in 2009 at the invitation of Andrea Viliani from Galleria Civica di Trento (I). The almost accidental discovery of the writings by Franco Basaglia (by pulling the *fil rouge* of the ■) lead to a very ambitious, tentacular project about marginality as an artistic position, the concepts of the mainstream and counterculture, anti-institutional movements, and the notion of outsider art. This project has enjoyed the generous support of Hogeschool Sint-Lukas, Brussels, Belgium.

2   The 'Entartete Kunst' exhibition, normally translated as 'Degenerate Art', opened in Munich on 18 July 1937, and is still one of the most successful art exhibitions ever: after touring eleven German cities, it had received over two million visitors.

3   Action T4 (German: Aktion T4) was the code name for the euthanasia program in Nazi Germany that officially spanned from October 1939 to August 1941, but continued unofficially until the demise of the Nazi regime in 1945 and even beyond; during it, physicians killed thousands of people specified in Hitler's secret memo of 1 September 1939 as suffering patients 'judged incurably sick, by critical medical examination', but described in a denunciation of the programme by Cardinal Galen as long-term inmates of mental asylums 'who may appear incurable'.

4   Cameron Munro (1964) and Artur Hojan (1973) founded the 'Tiergartenstrasse 4 Association' to research Nazi crimes. Between 2005 and 2009, the association researched Nazi euthanasia in the Wielkopolska region (Warthegau). Some of the results of this study were published in *The Chronicle from Dead Places* (2005) and *Opfer der NS-Psychiatrie* (2007). The Tiergatenstrasse 4 Association was founded in 2005 as a private international association in Poland. It has sixteen members from all over the world.

5   Hans Prinzhorn (6 June 1886–14 June 1933) was a German psychiatrist and art historian. In 1919 he became Karl Wilmanns's assistant at the psychiatric hospital of the University of Heidelberg. His task was to expand an earlier collection of art created by the mentally ill, started by Emil Kraepelin. When he left in 1921, the collection had grown to over 5,000 works by about 450 'cases'. In 1922, he published his first and most influential book, *Bildnerei der Geisteskranken* (Artistry of the Mentally Ill), richly illustrated with examples from the collection. While his colleagues were reserved in their reaction, the art scene was enthusiastic.

6   According to Carmen Roll in the interview she was kind enough to grant me: '████ was a doctor at the psychiatric polyclinic of the University of Heidelberg. When people were in distress, police brought them to the polyclinic. And one of the tasks of the doctors working at the university polyclinic was to select which of these people would go to the psychiatric hospital in Wiesloch, where there were two thousand patients, and which could remain as patients at the polyclinic and get therapy, psychotherapy. Because it was obvious that at Wiesloch there was no psychotherapy. So ████ said at a certain point, "I will not do this (send people to Wiesloch), because Wiesloch is a concentration camp. I just met you (the patient) today, you tell me your story of suffering and distress, and then I have to judge where to send you... But how do I judge? If you are dirty, you are jobless, you have nothing, then I say: Wiesloch. If you are well dressed, you have three friends with you, your mother is calling, you father is on his way, you are a good student, you have a good social background, and everyone will help you get out of your crisis, then I say: you can stay at the polyclinic". So ████ decided not to send anyone to Wiesloch anymore, and everyone stayed at the polyclinic. But they could not afford that; there was a waiting list at the polyclinic. In this new group at ████s polyclinic, there was not just you (the nice family girl), but people from the "lumpenproletariat", jobless, stinking, with bad clothes. And to avoid the waiting list, ████ started to do group therapy with all of them. And he worked from ten in the morning till two the next morning, you could have a therapy appointment with him at ten in the evening; and this drove the other doctors out of their minds. So ████ went into the waiting room and said, "Who among you is a really urgent case?" and everyone went: "Me! Me! Me!" and he said, "Ok, then, discuss it among yourselves, and then I will

discuss it with you". So instead of just waiting in the waiting room, people started to talk, and then ███ went to join them and did therapy, which was called "group agitation". Because Heidelberg was a student city, many of these young people in distress were students. And when ███ got into trouble, students led the protests along with the poor, sometimes so-called chronic people whom ███ had saved from Wiesloch. So we were a mixed group of students and working-class chronic youth. We were a very young group, none of us were over forty. So it was a class composition that was characteristic for this place, and this was in 68 or 69; the student movement was at its peak. So the ███ was a natural outcome of a sort of social setting. And then ███ sent his nurse to the doctors' meetings. Every morning at the psychiatric university, the doctors had this meeting at eight o'clock to discuss the different cases; and ███ decided not to go and to send his nurse instead. And the other doctors took offence. And the whole thing got started as a natural development of things that could only have happened in Heidelberg. I went to Heidelberg in 68 because I was a militant in the student movement; Heidelberg, Berlin and Frankfurt were the centres of the student movement in Germany. Because in Heidelberg and in the other places, there were American army bases, and this during Vietnam.'

7   Ideology: a theory, or set of beliefs or principles, especially one on which a political system, party or organisation is based (Cambridge Dictionaries Online).

8   To quote Franco Rotelli in the brief interview he was kind enough to grant me: 'Ideology is the falsification of reality. Basaglia tried to understand what was happening. The mental hospital was an ideology. Basaglia said, "This is an ideology, which tries to hide a reality, saying that someone can be cured here, saying that the hospital is a necessity, saying that there is an illness and a doctor to treat this illness. But I don't see any doctor and I very much doubt that there is any illness to be treated here, and certainly no one is being cured. This is ideology; I don't believe in this pseudoscience" – that is what Basaglia said. And he also said that the mental hospital is made just for poor people. Therefore there is a class problem here. And this is not my ideology, this is what I see. And this class vision, you don't find it in Cooper, you don't find in Guattari, and you don't find it in any of the other so-called anti- psychiatry movements.'

9   Franco Basaglia (ed.), *Che cos'è la psichiatria?* (Parma: Amministrazione Provinciale di Parma, 1967).

10   David Cooper (b. 1931, Cape Town; d. 1986, Paris) was a British psychiatrist, noted theorist, and leader in the anti-psychiatry movement, along with R. D. Laing, Thomas Szasz and Michel Foucault.

11   Octave Mannoni, 'The Anti-Psychiatric Movement(s)', *International Social Science Journal*, vol. XXV (1973).

12   Incidentally, 'Turn your illness into a weapon' (AUS DER KRANKHEIT EINE WAFFE MACHEN), was the most celebrated slogan of the ███.

13   I owe this quote to Nicola Valentino.

14   'Beat about/around the bush' – the meaning of this idiom is: to prevaricate and avoid coming to the point. The figurative meaning we have for this phrase has evolved from the earlier meaning, which was more literal. In bird hunting, some participants roused the birds by beating the bushes while others caught them in nets. So 'beating about the bush' was the preamble to the actual capture.

Dora García, 'Radical Politics, Radical Psychiatry, Radical Art: An Introduction to the "Mad Marginal" Project', in *Mad Marginal Cahier # 1, From Basaglia to Brazil* (Milan: Mousse Publishing, 2010) 11–20.

R.D. Laing
Knots//1970

The patterns delineated here have not yet been classified by a Linnaeus of human bondage. They are all, perhaps, strangely, familiar.

In these pages I have confined myself to laying out only some of those I actually have seen. Words that come to mind to name them are: knots, tangles, fankles, *impasses*, disjunctions, whirligogs, binds.

I could have remained closer to the 'raw' data in which these patterns appear. I could have distilled them further towards an abstract logico-mathematical, calculus. I hope they are not so schematised that one may not refer back to the very specific experiences from which they derive; yet that they are sufficiently independent of 'content', for one to divine the final formal elegance in these webs of *maya*.

April 1969   R.D.L.

[…]

It is our duty to bring up our children to
love,
honour and obey us.
If they don't, they must be punished,
otherwise we would not be doing our duty.
If they grow up to love, honour and obey us
we have been blessed for bringing them up properly.
If they grow up not to love, honour and
obey us
    either we have brought them up
properly
    or we have not:
if we have
    there must be something the matter
with them;
if we have not
    there is something the matter with us.
[…]

She feels
    he is asking too much (greedy)
    to expect her,
    not to feel he is asking too much
(greedy)
    to expect *her*
    not to feel he is mean and greedy
    to feel she is mean
    to feel he is greedy
    to feel *she* is mean
    to feel he is mean
    to feel she is mean
    to feel he is greedy
    to feel she is greedy
when all *she* wants is that
    he be more generous in his judgement
about her
namely, not to feel she is mean
to feel he is mean
    to feel she is greedy
    to feel he is mean
    to feel she is mean
    to feel he is mean
    to feel she is greedy
    to feel he is mean
to want her to be more generous in her
judgement about him namely,

[...]

One is inside
then outside what one has been inside
One feels empty
because there is nothing inside oneself
One tries to get inside oneself
    that inside of the outside
    that one was once inside
    once one tries to get oneself inside
what
    one is outside:

        to eat and to be eaten
to have the outside inside and to be
        inside the outside
But this is not enough. One is trying to
get
the inside of what one is outside inside,
and to
get inside the outside. But one does not
get
inside the outside by getting the outside
inside
for;
although one is full inside of the inside of
the outside
one is on the outside of one's own inside
and by getting inside the outside
one remains empty because
while one is on the inside
even the inside of the outside is outside
and inside oneself there is still nothing
There has never been anything else
and there never will be
[...]

R.D. Laing, extracts from *Knots* (1970) (London and New York: Routledge, 2006) 2–3, 56–7, 86–8.

Martin Herbert
Undivided Attention: On the Art of Luke Fowler//2012

Luke Fowler's *All Divided Selves* (2011), a 90-minute film centring on the once-notorious 'anti-psychiatrist' R. D. Laing, divides documentary filmmaking against itself. Assembling archival footage of Laing, his critics, and his freewheeling treatment sessions, the Glasgow-based artist offers an intricate composite of clashing opinions and incompatible filmic registers, weights and counterweights. For seemingly every clip of Laing calmly unpacking his thoughts on, say, schizophrenia and the military-industrial complex to a (typically hostile) interviewer, there's a fusty mainstream psychiatrist spewing scorn. If a stretch of footage features Laing's patients taking a sanctioned ramble through mazy verbal abstractions or getting thumped on the back of the head by a group-therapy leader – Laing advocated such protocols in lieu of medication or conventional therapeutic methods – there's also a dazed woman consulting a conventionally tweedy shrink. He exhorts her to take her medication until she says, in a defeated monotone: 'OK, I'll take the lithium.' Laing is a visionary; he is an idiot. His methods ease suffering; no, they don't.

But even though the vintage footage is pieced into a linear chronicle of Laing's darkly picaresque life (moving from the streets of Glasgow, where he was born, to London, where he founded his live-in therapy centre in the 60s, to even-handed depictions of his later questionable forays into advice columns and poetry LPs), it is also intercut with another, non-archival kind of filmmaking. Culled from 16mm rushes shot by the artist over the course of two summers, this light-suffused secondary footage hews ardently to the natural world. Bugs struggle in soupy algae; sun dances on streamlets and on a wrinkled polyethylene bag in the back seat of a car. The stamens and pistils of plants shine greenly; bright colour washes over the screen in intermittent abstract bursts. Occasionally, the images chime cleanly with Laing's own on-screen pronouncements and the film's consideration of alternative approaches to mental illness. We see a cow being branded as Laing talks about how social 'laws' are implanted in individuals, and after glimpsing a page of a book about communism that a girl is reading while sunning herself on some rocks, we're shown a swath of billowing red cloth. The presence of Fowler as filmmaker is emphasised: more than one shot features him, Bolex viewfinder pressed to his face, reflected in a rear-view mirror. But most of these interlaid vignettes are close-ups, magnifications of the richly changeable, sumptuously colourful texture of reality. It is hard to imagine how Fowler could more forcefully convey sheer presence and sensual immediacy – qualities in tension with, if not directly opposed to, the historicising impulse of documentary – via cinematic means. Affect and cognition collide.

In their collaborative 2008 work, *B8016: Draw a Straight Line and Follow It*, Fowler and sound artist Lee Patterson shot footage and made field recordings on a highway cutting across the isle of Islay in the Scottish Inner Hebrides, splicing the results into a contemplative 16mm film. In notes about the piece, the pair write that the project 'shares concerns that are at the heart of both our practices: the art of observation – looking beneath the surface – and the art of collecting – reclaiming the undesired and overlooked'. The tension between these two concerns or, perhaps more precisely, the effort to bring them into some kind of consonance, however glancing or tenuous, is palpable in *All Divided Selves* and is crucial to Fowler's larger ambit. For him, 'the undesired and overlooked' is a category that enfolds, and puts into improbably meaningful conversation, a certain kind of historical figure and the minutiae of the physical world, which Fowler views with a naturalist's attentiveness.

Fowler made his first film on Laing in 2001, when in his early twenties. Titled *What You See Is Where You're At*, it offers a look at the broken residents of an East London community centre used by Laing and others as a commune-like asylum for the schizophrenic. Ever since that project, the artist has been an inveterate comber of the celluloid and videotape archive. The snippets he collects have found their way into a number of works that focus on denizens of the political, cultural or social margins, with an emphasis on the problematic protagonists of the long 60s. [...]

It's important to note that romantic nostalgia is not the common denominator of these forays into the recent past. If anything, an ingrained anti-romanticism informs Fowler's work. In an interview with Redler in 2000, he said: 'First and foremost I was drawn to [Laing's] experiment[s] because of personal circumstance, i.e., my own experiences of contemporary psychiatry [...] disillusion with the way in which my father was treated by the system, and an overall healthy, cynical attitude towards institutions.' Beyond this hint of personal investment, one might say that Fowler's interest here, as in much of his work, is in a group, a community – in this case, the mentally ill. While each of his films has a charismatic individual at its core, they are not lone heroic *Rückenfiguren*. Each is embedded in an improvised and often threatened microsociety. [...]

One senses that for Fowler there's a meaningful parallel between the micro-communities of his films and the micro-communities he himself is part of. Far from being merely an interested, *Wire*-browsing observer, Fowler has been a long-term participant in an experimental music scene that brings him into proximity with Jones and to Cardew's living colleagues. He has been in two bands, Rude Pravo and Lied Music, and has run the small label Shadazz for more than a decade. He has also made films and installations with sound artists such as Patterson and Toshiya Tsunoda. Other projects, meanwhile, trace links within the particular microculture of Glasgow – climatically harsh, creatively nurturing, Fowler's hometown as well as Laing's. The Glasgow footage in *All Divided Selves* flips between grainy shots of the city as it was in Laing's day and contemporary images – we see the exteriors of old tenements and their relatively cleaned-up contemporary interiors, including what is presumably Fowler's office, with its slimline Mac. We could – and the film seems to imply we should – map Laing himself onto the same network that connects Fowler to the four subjects of his quartet of 16mm shorts, *Tenement Films* (2009), which were shot in an apartment building that Fowler lived in for eight years. [...] One way to understand his appearances in his own films as a filmmaker, camera in hand – in *All Divided Selves*, for example, or in several shots in *Tenement Films* – is as instances of reflection on what Fowler calls 'our relationships together'. [...]

Martin Herbert, extracts from 'Undivided Attention: on the Art of Luke Fowler', *Artforum* (October 2012) 241–7.

Pedro Reyes
Nine Tenets of the Sanatorium and Sanatorium Manifesto//2015

Nine Tenets of the Sanatorium

VOLUNTEER-RUN
Most Sanatorium therapies wouldn't necessarily yield best results if conducted by a professional. Our intention is not to put down existing methods, but to create an alternative space where everyone can help each other, regardless of their credentials. By being volunteer run, we aim to access society's untapped human capital.

INTIMATE STRANGERS
Encounter is a face-to-face exchange between two people, both willing to understand and adopt the perspective of the other person's reality to shed new light on their own experience. When the right procedure is offered, you can have the most insightful conversation even with (or perhaps, thanks to) a complete stranger.

SALUTOGENESIS
Health is not the absence of disease. It's a state in which we know that life is manageable and meaningful; it's how we retain our ability to keep going when facing changes internally and externally. These therapies are an extensional device to enhance your present state, to help you find your sweet spot.

ROLE PLAY
Even though the Sanatorium is a horizontal organisation where the public's status is as important as that of the therapists, we play roles, using props such as lab coats to free us from the one-dimensional labels society assigns to us.

SECULAR MAGIC
When we say that the Sanatorium is a delivery system of placebos, it's important to explain that medical environments have an aura that helps us believe that we as patients will be cured. We use this clinical 'packaging' to stage small rituals, which are often only accessible to those who subscribe to a system of beliefs. The Sanatorium takes these rituals out of their ethnographic specificity and makes them available to everyone.

PLAY DRIVE
To achieve a mental state where we have the confidence to produce changes, we need a warm-up process. That's why the light-hearted spirit of play is so useful. To tap into our creativity, we need to train our spontaneity, which is a way of meeting the moment, of responding as the present situation requires.

ALL ARE WELCOME
The Sanatorium is not intended for one specific audience. It's a place you can visit in different groups: with friends, classmates, co-workers, family, on a date, etc. Inspired by the notion of sociatry, its ultimate goal is to leave the sphere of art to provide a cost-effective service to restore sanity in stressed communities.

STRANGE/FAMILIAR
The Sanatorium is primarily a work of art. The pretence of being a Sanatorium allows people to play with the idea of sharing their problems, while its status as a work of art lets us test innovative techniques. This ambiguous nature also helps us get a fresh perspective on our world. Art can make the normal look strange (challenging the arbitrariness of the status quo), as well as the opposite process, to make the strange normal (paving the way for the acceptance of new ideas).

SPECT-ACTOR

The most important work at the Sanatorium is that done by the patient. They are spectators that become actors. In that sense, the therapist is not doing the therapy. He is allowing it to happen. Although it may appear that the therapist is doing something to or on someone, this is not the case. The therapist is doing something with the other person.

Sanatorium Manifesto

SANATORIUM	takes	PSYCHOSOMATICS
	out of	BIOLOGICAL INTERPRETATION
	and into	A DELIVERY SYSTEM OF PLACEBOS

SANATORIUM	takes	SHAMANISM
	out of	ETHNOGRAPHIC SPECIFICITY
	and into	INSTRUCTION BASED ACTIVITIES

SANATORIUM	takes	CURATORIAL PRACTICE
(The Museum of Hypothetical Lifetimes)	out of	THE SYSTEM OF ART OBJECTS
	and into	NARRATIVES OF THE SELF

SANATORIUM	takes	ANGER MANAGEMENT
(Vaccine against Violence)	out of	12-STEP PROGRAMS
	and into	SOCIAL CATHARSIS

SANATORIUM	takes	WORSHIP
(Ex-Voto)	out of	RELIGION
	and into	SECULAR MEANINGFULNESS

SANATORIUM	takes	SORCERY
(Goodoo)	out of	THE GLOOM
	and into	RATIONAL INTENTIONALITY

SANATORIUM	takes	PROXEMICS
	out of	ANTHROPOLOGY
(The Great Game of Power)	and into	WARM-UP ROUTINES

SANATORIUM	takes	SOCIAL PSYCHOLOGY
	out of	DIAGNOSTICS
	and into	TACTICAL IMPLEMENTATION

SANATORIUM   takes   ONTOLOGY
(Ontological Algebra)   out of   PHILOSOPHY
                    and into   THE OCCAM'S RAZOR OF ALGEBRA

SANATORIUM   takes   CONFESSION
(Citileaks)   out of   THE ECONOMY OF GUILT
                    and into   INNOCUOUS HEARSAY

SANATORIUM   takes   SYNESTHESIA
(Synesthetic Test)   out of   POETICS
                    and into   EXPERIMENTAL METHOD

SANATORIUM   takes   ORACLES
(Philosophical Casino) out of   ESOTERISM
                    and into   MAIEUTICS

SANATORIUM   takes   BODY LANGUAGE
(Mudras)   out of   LOCAL CULTURAL SYNTAX
                    and into   A GRAMMAR OF MINDSETS

SANATORIUM   takes   VISUAL MNEMONICS
(Heraldry Mint)   out of   ICONOGRAPHY
                    and into   SELF-MADE MANDALAS

SANATORIUM   takes   WORD GAMES
(Anagrams)   out of   LANGUAGE POETRY
                    and into   A SELF PORTRAIT

SANATORIUM   takes   MEDITATION
                    out of   SPIRITUALITY
                    and into   AN AESTHETIC PURSUIT

SANATORIUM   takes   COUPLES THERAPY
(Compatibility Test for Couples)   out of   COUNSELLING
                    and into   PRACTICAL JOKES

SANATORIUM   AIMS TO BE A TOOL
                                IN THE ADVANCEMENT
                                OF SOCIATRY

Pedro Reyes, 'Nine Tenets of the Sanatorium and Sanatorium Manifesto', in *Pedro Reyes: Sanatorium Operations Manual* (Geneva: Geneva University of Art and Design and London: Ridinghouse, 2015) 18–21.

Simone Leigh
Free People's Medical Clinic//2016

I was born to a family of missionaries. My father is a Jamaican Nazarene minister who was assigned to a church on the South Side of Chicago. By the time I was ten he had established ten Head Start programs across the city (part of a federal initiative to promote the health and early education of young children from low income families), as well as a home for delinquent boys. We moved to a large house in a black, middle class, white flight neighbourhood, where other missionaries from the Global South – most of whom hailed from countries where the church was their only source of education and advancement – stayed with us as they prepared for service.[1] On a good day you could say this work was based in liberation theology.[2] However, the effects of the colonised mind, sexual repression and the apparent self-hatred expressed in the biblical doctrine of 'washing yourself white as snow in the blood of the lamb' formed the more visceral experience I was left with. I went to college and never looked back. So, my answer to the question 'Are you a public servant?' is fraught with personal history, as I thought I had turned my back on the mandate to spend my life doing 'good works'.

The old-time black American expression 'Race Woman' best describes the role I have in relation to my community. Today, in my work, I am concerned with uncovering unknown histories and moving the concerns of black women from margin to centre. That has always been my mission, and I would feel that urgency whether or not I was an artist. I don't feel like a public servant – I would never describe myself as anyone's servant because I'm a black woman and part of the history of free forced labour that this country is built on. However, I do feel that I have a particular responsibility to my community because of who I am and where I live.

Inspired by the Black Panthers' community-based healthcare efforts in the 1960s, 70s and 80s, 'Free People's Medical Clinic' converted the Brooklyn home of the late Josephine English – the first female African-American ob-gyn [obstetrician-gynaecologist] to have a private practice in New York – into a temporary clinic offering free medical care. After two years of planning and community meetings, for four weekends in 2014 the clinic offered a range of programmes and services to the public, from HIV screenings and counselling to lectures on herbalism. I was invited to develop the clinic by Rashida Bumbray, who was guest curating 'Funk, God, Jazz, and Medicine' for Creative Time. Rashida and I had worked together several times before, and the level of mutual trust we have encouraged me to try this type of project, despite my scepticism of social practice. During the years I was developing my art practice while raising my daughter and teaching children in New York, I had become familiar with funders and their emphasis on results and sustainability. I doubted whether I could accomplish my work with integrity under the pressure to produce certain outcomes.

I still think that there are a lot of great ideas that may not be sustainable but should still happen; sustainability is a very inappropriate mandate for art. I work very hard in my studio practice to maintain the possibility, even the expectation, of failure. Also, I believe that some good ideas need only be realised once. And yet the clinic is a project that needs to exist over a period of time, because giving care is based on trust and relationships. I would love to continue the project through monthly weekend workshops for young black girls, with one major change: we would have very little visibility. Whereas most artists seek the most visibility possible for their projects, especially those that engage the public, I would like to continue this work underground. One of the most significant antecedents for the clinic is the United Order of Tents, a secret society of black nurses that has operated continuously since the time of the Underground Railroad, taking care of each other and performing good works in the community. I believe that, unlike groups that broadcast their projects to the public, underground organisations like this one offer the ultimate modality of self-care for marginalised people.

At every point in the development of 'Free People's Medical Clinic', we uncovered histories of self-reliance. We didn't need to bring anything new – the goal was to make more apparent the work of practitioners who were already working to meet the needs of the community. Yet I also looked to practices outside of our community for inspiration, such as the *muthi* market in Durban, South Africa, an open-air pharmacy where you can get medicine to stop your mother-in-law in her tracks or to treat a headache or a wound. These kinds of markets are a source of knowledge for African diasporic communities, for whom there's more of a blur between medicine for the mind, body and spirit. The clinic also tried to address Western medicine's lack of concern for preventative care. For instance, we offered holistic and therapeutic services like acupuncture and massage, which are considered basic healthcare in certain parts of the world, despite being deemed luxury treatments in the United States.

The original Black Panther clinics focused on sickle cell anaemia (a disease that disproportionately affects black people), so advocacy was at the core of their community engagement. Our focus was on empathy. In American healthcare, and American society at large, there is a widespread lack of empathy for black pain. As we planned the clinic, a new study emerged that demonstrated that even black people have become less empathic to black pain.[3] We sought to address the disruption between self and body through dance, yoga and classes on Afrocentering – which aims to literally raise black women's awareness of their own bodies – led by Aimee Meredith Cox. In addition to being an experience of physical healing, the practice is also meant to be emancipatory. If you increase funding to the state or to hospitals to support more interventions in the community, but you haven't addressed the lack of recognition and empathy for black people who are in pain, most of those patients will still go away without adequate care. For centuries the task of suturing this gap in empathy has been accomplished by black nurses who have over-served an underserved population.

One facet of the clinic was a publication called *Waiting Room Magazine*, which collected texts by black women authors on various histories that have been overlooked or suppressed. Robin Coste Lewis contributed a poem about her discovery of a black ancestor who owned slaves. We included a piece on the Tuskegee syphilis experiment by sociologist Alondra Nelson[4] and an essay by Vanessa Agard-Jones about how pesticides in the Caribbean affect gender and sexuality. Naomi Jackson wrote a piece about Esmin Green, a Jamaican woman who had a life experience that most Caribbean residents of Crown Heights can identify with – she was working three or four jobs to send money home. In the summer of 2008 Green was forcibly admitted to the psychiatric emergency department of Kings County Hospital Center in Brooklyn and subsequently died while waiting in the hospital for twenty-four hours without receiving help. A surveillance video revealed that after she collapsed, she lay on the floor for more than an hour before her body was removed. In its coverage of the story, the *New York Times* suggested that 'waiting may have killed her'. I struggle to imagine the fortitude required to sit and wait for your own death. Black people, often black women, are participating in our own oppression by being obedient.

Waiting rooms are really abject. I have always felt that they manifest the darkest aspects of our culture, and a major reason they are so inhumane is the long wait. To address that problem, in 'Free People's Medical Clinic', we tried to translate what was happening in the private rooms into performances in the waiting room. We offered free dance classes at the clinic, but also free Pap smears [a form of smear test for cervical cancer], so the division between public and more private, intimate space was complicated. A lot of the clinic's services, like massage therapy for example, couldn't be revealed to anyone. I wanted to resist the idea of display, but what would the art audience see, and what would we show them? In the waiting room we held public activities like black folk dance classes based on the Katherine Dunham technique and acupuncture demonstrations that were designed to demystify the process for those who hadn't done it before. I also wanted to create semi-private safe spaces for certain communities. We organised a queer-only class led by niv Acosta and a South Asian-only yoga class led by Mona Chopra.

The importance of this kind of safe space and collective resilience was reinforced on the last day of the clinic. Two doctors who had worked in the Black Panther Party's clinics visited and explained that the BPP had been so embattled by the police that they were forced to barricade their clinics' façades with sandbags – more like a bunker than a hospital. At every step, I felt that to understand strategies of self-determination, we had only to work to understand the culture that had developed underground – the methods that were already there.

1   'White flight' refers to the movement of white people, especially middle-class whites, from inner-city neighbourhoods undergoing racial integration to the suburbs.

2   Liberation theology is a movement in Christian theology that emphasises liberation from social, political and economic oppression as an anticipation of ultimate salvation.

3   See Matteo Forgiarini, Marcello Gallucci and Angelo Maravita, 'Racism and Empathy for Pain on Our Skin', *Frontiers in Psychology*, vol. 2, no. 1 (2011), available at http://www.ncbi.nlm.nih.gov/pmc/articles/PMC3108582/; and Sophie Trawalter, Kelly M. Hoffman and Adam Waytz, 'Racial Bias in Perceptions of Others' Pain', *PLOS.One* (November 2012), available at http://journals.plos.org / plosone/article?id=10.1371/journal.pone.0048546

4   The Tuskegee syphilis experiment was a clinical study conducted between 1932 and 1972 by the US Public Health Service to analyse the natural progression of untreated syphilis in African-American men in rural Alabama. The study's participants, who were told that they were receiving free healthcare from the US government, were never informed that they had the disease nor were they treated for it. The abuses of this experiment led to the establishment of federal laws and regulations for ethical oversight of clinical research.

Simone Leigh, 'Portfolio: Simone Leigh', in *Public Servants: Art and the Crisis of the Common Good*, eds. Johanna Burton, Shannon Jackson and Dominic Willsdon (Cambridge, MA: The MIT Press, 2016) 222–7.

Mary Walling Blackburn
XOXO Insanity, Institution//2011

Mental Institution

In the annals of the Arkansas Lunatic Asylum, the very first patient arrives several days before the facility – a multi-storied, Victorian brick edifice – officially opens in March 1883. The state's first and only public zoo is built next to the asylum in 1926, and at first it houses exactly two animals: an abandoned timber wolf and a circus-trained bear, whose calls carry into the asylum at night.

The bear and the wolf. We're suckers for things coming in twos, for not forging ahead alone. But every mental facility has its first patient: an Adam, an Eve, or an Adameve, stepping or pushed singular into the void of a space still unmarked – without vibration, without community. There were instances in which there was no singular first; in nineteenth-century Canada, inmates from one mental institution were borrowed to provide the necessary labour required to build another. Once the building had been completed, these same patients were secured in a structure of their own making but not their own design.

What does it mean to make an institution? To toil unpaid within a mechanism that is not your own? The inmates of one North American ward crushed excess grapes for a wine they could not drink. Despite the fact that the asylum operated without currency, this communally-built site – replete with hallucination and its own harvest – did not equal a hippie paradise. From a distance, this place could be perceived as inherently progressive, but its patients and staff shared an internal narrative, one that ideologically frames a form without horizons. For the patients, this institution appeared to have no limits. To exit institutionalisation seems impossible if one cannot configure from within it how one lives without it.

What is repressed in artists' exploration/flirtation with both undoing and rethinking institutions? Here, I have placed the mental institution at centre, but if the mental institution is an impossible material when it comes to the labour of artists that harness the sociological imagination to tread against and away from bureaucracy's material organisation of power, what is revealed by the unsuitability of the mental asylum as artists' supply?

In nineteenth-century North American psychiatric facilities, labour was often compulsory and unpaid, the facilities were overcrowded, and patients were held without consent. But what would consent have felt like within any institution? What forms of self-organisation would be adopted by those who have loosened their relationship to a fixed social reality, by those who have been forced into the institution for demanding another social reality? In the history of madness, who has sanely asked to be let into an institution, to be held without touching? And yet, more often than not, one finds the patient ceding his or her self over to it, whether it be a mental ward, a prison, a school, or a museum. Especially for Americans, the institution has become as natural as sky, land, and empire; nothing else exists. Or rather, we fail to imagine how we will fruitfully exist without imperial institutions.

When an empire is lurching to a halt at its very end, it might be the moment when it begins, or is forced, to re-imagine its relationship to a national insanity. 'The institution is ill', said Dr. Jean Oury, mentor of Félix Guattari and founder and director of La Borde – an experimental psychiatric hospital in France that opened in 1951, just before the Algerian War, while France's colonies were dispatching their 'Gauls' during the Indochina War. If the institution is ill, the logic is that it can be repaired; but does Oury refer to one or to all – to the prison, to the mental ward, to the school, to government at large? If these forms couple, the recombinant hybrids can both reinforce and undo the former instrumentalisations of its wards in unpredictable ways. But the real, unanswered question here concerns whether, in forms singular or doubled, formal institutions can operate outside of state structures? La Borde comprised an attempt. Oury and his doctors dismantled the architectural separation between patients and administrators by placing the offices within the wards and inviting patients to be administrators (but not doctors?). Finally, the rhythm of La Borde did away with the capital economy of speed; Oury waited for fifteen years for one female patient to smile – and that fifteen-year smile was reportedly satisfying. Does the smile occur long after France has lost its colonies? He does not tell us.

It is worth considering that the fifteen-year smile – or the treatment that brought it about – might have been bankrolled by the raw materials generated within the colonies occupied by the very same state that supported La Borde. Allow me a partial fantasy: a French businessman trades in West African gum arabic, in peanuts, in fabric, and in gold. Regardless of his successes, his daughter is comatose. Nothing moves her. The businessman will try anything, but his capitalism cannot revive her. But perhaps a site like La Borde can use his business capital to fund its experimentation with a power structure that is not completely aligned with state policy. But once the 'daughter' has left the asylum, calibrated, why would the millionaires continue to shell out? Potentially, state and corporate powers sanction and support the creative destruction of the institution – on a micro-scale – because such labour distracts revolutionaries and troublemakers.

Each institutional form organises its errant citizens by making them captives, because they effectively disorganise communal life when left to their own devices. In the southern wilderness of France, an experimental educator named Fernand Deligny lived with autistic boys that his colleagues had disregarded, dubbing them 'unmanageables'. Deligny referred to them as 'radical others', and he asks how we (unradical others?) can move near and with the radical other. In this instance, autistic space (as Deligny coins it) is generated and maintained by the unmanageables, marking a field of difference within a familiar landscape, within the geographical and ethnic boundaries of a singular nation. It is here that unradical others might enter and negotiate neurologically atypical forms of communication with the castoff sons and brothers of their fellow countrymen; it is where the mental institution and its architecture have been shed, but the state remains.

According to one interpretation of psychiatric history (informed by Fanon and driven by Foucault), colonial empires utilised mental wards in order to negotiate the least mitigated symptoms of native resistance. During the British occupation of Zimbabwe, one mental institution patient refused to call Europeans anything but 'Eskimo'. His explicit naming of their foreignness momentarily amplifies their difference – in geographic relation to Zimbabwe, he has identified the colonisers as being from the edge of the planet and beyond reasonable proximity. By using a surreal means of exposing the colonisers' excessive foreignness, the patient indicated that although he is a 'guest' within the institution, he is neither a guest nor a foreigner within the land.

His illogic is a logic in the illogic of his incarceration, specific and national. To reverse the fact of being proclaimed foreign in one's own land. It is a refusal of the guest status of insanity within one's own culture. In the women's quarters of the same mental ward, the higher-functioning White patients are serviced at the 'Fair Lady Salon', where they receive their traditional 'Eskimo' hairstyles.

The institution hallucinates. It hurls itself both toward and away from the society at whose threshold it is placed. The terms 'Eskimo', 'Foreigner', 'European' and 'Fair Lady' all get swapped – not because they are interchangeable, but because each is a smokescreen used by exterior forces to force themselves across a border. I imagine that there are patients in contemporary American psychiatric wards who have begun to call all of the doctors and their staff 'terrorists'; would these patients then be patriots? In this psychiatric imaginary, the authorities are 'radical others' – but they are not the same as the patients. Neither feels that they can pass from one type of radical other to another, or that this passing would be advantageous; after all, such a swap would still not take the doctor and the patient outside of monstrous structures. [...]

Soft Institutions

But inside of institutions, whether asylum, prison, juvenile hall, army or college, my finally-White and never-rich kin were not and are not repaired. Will an artists' temporary institution do the necessary psychiatric trick? After all, who gets to experiment with their mental liberation outside of hierarchies? How do we visualise passing as it applies to race, class, or a combination therein, and in a way can that alter the institution? Despite the 'new beginning', these Adameves have not yet forged or found an institution capable of repairing them: no prison or juvenile hall, hospital, military base, college or museum can do it. Some will simply enter formal institutions and artist projects as White people, unrevolutionary and undone.

Which overarching governing forces heal whom, and which class of people are they meant for? Are we returning to Oury's premise that institutions do not repair their citizens when the 'institution is ill'? When the Supreme Court ruled in 1954 that segregation in schools was unconstitutional, the lawmakers of Sheridan, Arkansas bypassed the ruling by forcing all Blacks to reside outside of the town, effectively making Sheridan's schools White-only. Cauleen Smith's sculptural video work, *Remote Viewing* (2011), is built around this incident. Following this forced migration, a hole was dug in front of the town's former Black school, and the building was pushed into the hole and buried. Town zoning stretched laterally and not vertically, and Smith points to the double construction of interior and exterior crypt, reconstructing the moment when the town engineered its own psychosis. The school bell begins to ring as the building tips over. It seems to be an utterance, but it is not Smith's. She is careful to assert: 'That story does not belong to me. It simply infected me, and the film was a way to burn off the fever.' Here the artist heals herself of an institutional infection. When the institution chooses amputation, she chooses recovery.

The artists who make pretend institutions (temporary schools, fake agencies and so forth) rarely set out to invent little prisons or workable nuthouses that serve real people – really crazy, really violent. It is possible that artists are not equipped. Artists are comfortable making objects that document institutions, and they make objects (relational or otherwise) that perform the liberated institution. Another manifestation is the object that is liberated by abandoning the institution, just as there is the object that believes it can liberate the institution. As I do, these artists flirt with soft institutions, playing with the remains of madness – touching it lightly, quickly, and then moving away. In Paul Thek's notebook he scrawls: 'Institutions were formed for lack of spontaneous love.' To dilate his line of thought, we could move counter-current to the institution, not by forming another organisation, but by saying, as Thek does: Let me nurse you. Let me defend your body and your spirit. Let me bathe and bury you.

The Institute of Racial Passing. The Bureau of Escape (or is it a museum?). It's an impossible organisation: archaic, unfunded, and unspeakable. It's a space that moves with those who stand at the threshold of race and class and gender. It asks how deeply the invention of an institution can move and whether making art – relational or material, professional or amateur – can attend to the insanity of passing? The artist who plays with institutions won't touch this false storefront. But as artists recast the institution in the loving throes of utopic impulse – rhizomatic, perennial, untrammelled, and operating in some self-modelled notion of the future perfect – I still want to know whether the wake of their efforts reaches a margin, an unattractive demographic, a space unutterable. I'd like to see the articulation of an institution that traces or excavates the shared political dimension of radical others and passing, that considers the application of insane measures toward producing another social reality.

Mary Walling Blackburn, extracts from 'XOXO Insanity, Institution', *e-Flux Journal*, no. 26 (June 2011) (www.e-flux.com/journal/26/67957/xoxo-insanity-institution/) [footnotes omitted].

When the
sick rule
the world,
mortality
will be

sexy

NARRATING ILLNESS

Susan Sontag
Illness as Metaphor//1978

Illness is the night-side of life, a more onerous citizenship. Everyone who is born holds dual citizenship, in the kingdom of the well and in the kingdom of the sick. Although we all prefer to use only the good passport, sooner or later each of us is obliged, at least for a spell, to identify ourselves as citizens of that other place.

I want to describe, not what it is really like to emigrate to the kingdom of the ill and live there, but the punitive or sentimental fantasies concocted about that situation: not real geography, but stereotypes of national character. My subject is not physical illness itself but the uses of illness as a figure or metaphor. My point is that illness is not a metaphor, and that the most truthful way of regarding illness – and the healthiest way of being ill – is one most purified of, most resistant to, metaphoric thinking. Yet it is hardly possible to take up one's residence in the kingdom of the ill unprejudiced by the lurid metaphors with which it has been landscaped. It is toward an elucidation of those metaphors, and a liberation from them, that I dedicate this inquiry.

Two diseases have been spectacularly, and similarly, encumbered by the trappings of metaphor: tuberculosis and cancer.

The fantasies inspired by TB in the last century, by cancer now, are responses to a disease thought to be intractable and capricious – that is, a disease not understood – in an era in which medicine's central premise is that all diseases can be cured. Such a disease is, by definition, mysterious. For as long as its cause was not understood and the ministrations of doctors remained so ineffective, TB was thought to be an insidious, implacable theft of a life. Now it is cancer's turn to be the disease that doesn't knock before it enters, cancer that fills the role of an illness experienced as a ruthless, secret invasion – a role it will keep until, one day, its etiology becomes as clear and its treatment as effective as those of TB have become.

Although the way in which disease mystifies is set against a backdrop of new expectations, the disease itself (once TB, cancer today) arouses thoroughly old-fashioned kinds of dread. Any disease that is treated as a mystery and acutely enough feared will be felt to be morally, if not literally, contagious. Thus, a surprisingly large number of people with cancer find themselves being shunned by relatives and friends and are the object of practices of decontamination by members of their household, as if cancer, like TB, were an infectious disease. Contact with someone afflicted with a disease regarded as a mysterious malevolency inevitably feels like a trespass; worse, like the violation of a taboo. The very names of such diseases are felt to have a magic power. In Stendhal's

Armance (1827), the hero's mother refuses to say 'tuberculosis', for fear that pronouncing the word will hasten the course of her son's malady. And Karl Menninger has observed (in *The Vital Balance*) that 'the very word "cancer" is said to kill some patients who would not have succumbed (so quickly) to the malignancy from which they suffer'. This observation is offered in support of anti-intellectual pieties and a facile compassion all too triumphant in contemporary medicine and psychiatry. 'Patients who consult us because of their suffering and their distress and their disability', he continues, 'have every right to resent being plastered with a damning index tab.' Dr. Menninger recommends that physicians generally abandon 'names' and 'labels' ('our function is to help these people, not to further afflict them') – which would mean, in effect, increasing secretiveness and medical paternalism. It is not naming as such that is pejorative or damning, but the name 'cancer'. As long as a particular disease is treated as an evil, invincible predator, not just a disease, most people with cancer will indeed be demoralised by learning what disease they have. The solution is hardly to stop telling cancer patients the truth, but to rectify the conception of the disease, to demythicise it.

When, not so many decades ago, learning that one had TB was tantamount to hearing a sentence of death – as today, in the popular imagination, cancer equals death – it was common to conceal the identity of their disease from tuberculars and, after they died, from their children. Even with patients informed about their disease, doctors and family were reluctant to talk freely. 'Verbally I don't learn anything definite', Kafka wrote to a friend in April 1924 from the sanatorium where he died two months later, 'since in discussing tuberculosis...everybody drops into a shy, evasive, glassy-eyed manner of speech.' Conventions of concealment with cancer are even more strenuous. In France and Italy it is still the rule for doctors to communicate a cancer diagnosis to the patient's family but not to the patient; doctors consider that the truth will be intolerable to all but exceptionally mature and intelligent patients. (A leading French oncologist has told me that fewer than a tenth of his patients know they have cancer.) In America – in part because of the doctors' fear of malpractice suits – there is now much more candour with patients, but the country's largest cancer hospital mails routine communications and bills to outpatients in envelopes that do not reveal the sender, on the assumption that the illness may be a secret from their families. Since getting cancer can be a scandal that jeopardises one's love life, one's chance of promotion, even one's job, patients who know what they have tend to be extremely prudish, if not outright secretive, about their disease. And a federal law, the 1966 Freedom of Information Act, cites 'treatment for cancer' in a clause exempting from disclosure matters whose disclosure 'would be an unwarranted invasion of personal privacy'. It is the only disease mentioned.

All this lying to and by cancer patients is a measure of how much harder it has become in advanced industrial societies to come to terms with death. As death is now an offensively meaningless event, so that disease widely considered a synonym for death is experienced as something to hide. The policy of equivocating about the nature of their disease with cancer patients reflects the conviction that dying people are best spared the news that they are dying, and that the good death is the sudden one, best of all if it happens while we're unconscious or asleep. Yet the modern denial of death does not explain the extent of the lying and the wish to be lied to; it does not touch the deepest dread. Someone who has had a coronary is at least as likely to die of another one within a few years as someone with cancer is likely to die soon from cancer. But no one thinks of concealing the truth from a cardiac patient: there is nothing shameful about a heart attack. Cancer patients are lied to, not just because the disease is (or is thought to be) a death sentence, but because it is felt to be obscene – in the original meaning of that word: ill-omened, abominable, repugnant to the senses. Cardiac disease implies a weakness, trouble, failure that is mechanical; there is no disgrace, nothing of the taboo that once surrounded people afflicted with TB and still surrounds those who have cancer. The metaphors attached to TB and to cancer imply living processes of a particularly resonant and horrid kind. [...]

Susan Sontag, extract from *Illness as Metaphor* (New York: Farrar, Straus and Giroux, 1978) 3–9.

Jo Spence
The Picture of Health?//1988

Four years ago I was diagnosed as having breast cancer. Like so many women before me I submitted myself to the medical machine, going along with the treatment so far as to have a lumpectomy performed. The feelings generated in the circumstances surrounding this were so totally negative that I felt, come what may, that I had to get off the medical orthodoxy's production line. The article 'Confronting Cancer' shows how I felt at the time.

Confronting Cancer
When I was a young woman, living still in the parental home, I became aware that I was Waiting for Something to Happen. Years later, when it had apparently

already happened without my even noticing, I regretted the loss of this feeling of expectation. Even later, I realised what it had been – the desire that comes with wanting to fall in love, wanting to be told you are loved, by that special Other. Recently, I realised that the feeling had come back. Not (sadly) in relation to love, but to illness and hatred.

This preamble is by way of approaching a difficult subject. Last Christmas, having recently completed three years' study as a mature student, having earned my first-class degree with honours, now utterly exhausted and wondering what the hell it had all been about, I had to go into hospital. Suddenly.

Dutifully, so as not to waste time, I took with me several books on theories of representation, a thin volume on health and a historical novel. One morning, whilst reading, I was confronted by the awesome reality of a young white-coated doctor, with student retinue, standing by my bedside. As he referred to his notes, without introduction, he bent over me and began to ink a cross onto the area of flesh above my left breast.

As he did so a whole chaotic series of images flashed through my head. Rather like drowning. I heard this doctor, whom I had never met before, this potential daylight mugger, tell me that my left breast would have to be removed. Equally I heard myself answer, 'No'. Incredulously; rebelliously; suddenly; angrily; attackingly; pathetically; alone; in total ignorance. I, who had spent three years (and more) immersed in a study of ideology and visual representation, now suddenly needed another type of knowledge; what has come to be called 'really useful social knowledge'. Not only the knowledge of how to rebel against this invader, but also of what to do beyond merely reacting negatively. I realised with horror that my body was not made of photographic paper, nor was it an image, or an idea, or a psychic structure…it was made of blood, bones and tissue. Some of them now appeared to be cancerous. And I didn't even know where my liver was located.

This peculiar disjuncture in my knowledge of the physical world caused such total crisis in my thinking and activity that it is only now, some six months later, that I am beginning to realise what has happened to me. So began a research project on the politics of cancer, with a fervent desire to understand how I could begin to have a different approach to health in which there would be less consumerism, more medical accountability, more social responsibility, more self responsibility.

Ever since I can remember I have tackled extreme forms of adversity by becoming ill. Usually after the event, I have manifested asthma, hay fever, eczema, colds, flu, bronchitis, depression, lumps and tumours…whatever. I am now convinced that these came about because, within the class I belonged to, I had been socialised to neglect myself, materially, environmentally, economically, psychically, even (dare I say it) spiritually. Now I am taking the toll as I approach my fifties of having tried so hard for years to give too much, to perform too much, to be too involved in too much…often for the wrong reasons and with the wrong people.

I was aware in my hospital bed, as I took the first step towards defiance of the medical orthodoxy, that it would be a long and lonely confrontation. It took an immense amount of courage initially to say no, that I didn't want to be mutilated (beyond the three vivid slashes that now adorn my breast), or to be radiated or drugged (what in warfare are called 'hack and burn' methods). The recollection that, at 28, I had had an ovarian tumour removed because of the side effects of early steroid treatment for my asthma, and that, now, I could lose first one then another breast, terrified me beyond all reason, beyond anything that had ever happened to me before. The realisation that I also had months of waiting whilst I was screened to find out if I was now clear of active cancer equally terrified me.

I took the coward's way out and became a vegan. I tackled my diet first. In five months (following the integrated regime of the Bristol Cancer Help Centre) I have lost four stone in weight merely by eating healthily. I sought out therapists in order to find out how to help make my life more balanced without giving up struggling. I took up co-counselling and learnt how to be assertive rather than aggressive. I regularly visit 'my' psychiatric social worker who has steadily worked through endless problems with me, patiently unravelling my closed off system of logic, my repressed desires. And I found myself a delightfully bolshy socialist feminist naturopath. Now I can begin to hear myself ticking over again. No miracles, no racing motor, no rejuvenated going off into the sunset… it's just that I can begin to hear my inner voices speaking to me in ways I didn't realise were possible.

Beyond that, I can still call upon the social knowledge of all the theoretical and political work I have encountered across the latter years of my life. I can again begin to feel solidarity in political struggles, in spite of the total loneliness of defying the medical orthodoxy. No longer am I engulfed with guilt about not working hard enough, not putting on a good enough performance, whether I occupy the correct political position or not, whether this or that latest theory can be lived without. I have had to face the fact that I am totally vulnerable, able to die, to feel terror, to be terrorised… but able to fight back with the help of others. Thank you, I learned a lot.

First published in City Limits, 22 July 1983

In the system of medicine for which I finally opted (Traditional Chinese Medicine – TCM), the patient is encouraged to begin to take some responsibility for getting and staying well. At the very least this means more work for the patient, and the necessity to make informed decisions; at its best, it means the shattering of lifelong habits in relation to food, drugs, exercise and breathing, and the awakening of the knowledge that the body cannot deal forever with a completely unharmonious relationship with her psychic, spiritual, social, economic, living and loving conditions. In plain English, I learned to love myself better and get more in touch with my actual needs and feelings so that I could start to try to change things wherever possible. It is my belief that TCM offers me the best chance of survival as a cancer patient, or at least a better quality of life. It does not pretend to offer me a 'cure', but is a way of managing the illness, putting it at bay, and perhaps slowing it down.

My TCM practitioner is Yana Stajno, whose partner David Lurie prescribes herbs to me on a weekly basis, taking account of my total condition when he prescribes. I see Yana as a traditional female healer, in that she uses her hands, her medical skills and counsels me whilst she attends me. We have a totally professional relationship, yet within it we discuss ways in which I treat her as a surrogate parent while she encourages me not to be too dependent on her. I have experienced love and care from them both which is without parallel in my years of medical treatment by general practitioners and hospital personnel. They charge me on a sliding scale at their lowest fee as such medicine is not available on the NHS. Traditional Chinese Medicine is either picked at as a medical commodity (e.g. acupuncture), or else is sneered at by western cancer specialists, who display an alarming degree of ignorance (and racism) in their belief that their recently evolved treatments are superior to thousands of years of cumulative healthcare within TCM. In China both traditional and orthodox treatments are available for cancer, and patients can (in theory at least) have access to either or both systems.

The regime for rebalancing my whole body and my psychic life is as follows:
- Long term change to a macrobiotic diet with occasional organic white meat or liver, plenty of fruit and vegetables, some nuts and seeds, fresh sprouted seeds and beans and freshly juiced fruit and vegetables
- No sugar, salt, gluten, dairy or animal products, no preserved, tinned or processed food
- Daily Qi Gong exercise, a routine part of cancer treatment in China, to help circulation, breathing and energy distribution, as well as strengthening the body
- Twice weekly acupuncture
- General healthcare through Chinese medicine
- Occasional lymphatic massage
- Daily megadoses of vitamin C and mineral supplements

- Herbal intake daily (brewed up from raw dried Chinese herbs in my kitchen)
- Monitoring of stress levels
- A loving relationship and reciprocal counselling sessions with David Roberts, my partner in life
- Plenty of cuddles and bodily contact with others

Because I am a photographer, I began to ask myself questions about the way disease and health are represented to us. Given that women are expected to be the object of the male gaze, are expected to beautify themselves in order to become loveable, are still fighting for basic rights over their own bodies, it seemed to me that the breast could be seen as a metaphor for our struggles. The fact that we have to worry about its size and shape as young women, its ability to give food when we become mothers, and its total dispensability when we are past child-bearing age, should be explored through visual representation as well as within healthcare. The two should not be separated out in any way, as our concept of sexuality and our social identity stem from both lived experience and the imaginary self we carry in the mind's eye. Just as the female body is fragmented and colonised by advertisers in the search for new markets for products and is fetishised and offered for male consumption through pornography, so it is similarly fought over by competitors for its medical 'care'. There are no departments of 'whole body' medicine in any hospitals I have ever attended. The concept is quite alien at any institutional level, although individual doctors and nurses exist who are interested in such medicine.

Even while I was in hospital, I began trying to represent to myself what was happening to me by using my camera. But how to represent myself *to* myself, through my own visual point of view, and how to find out what I needed and to articulate it and make sure I got it – ultimately wanting to make this visible to others? How to deal with my feelings about myself and give them visual form?

I realised that a major absence in my own family history was any knowledge of what had happened to other members of my family in terms of mental and physical illnesses. Family photographs hide any evidence of illness or ageing, since photographic conventions encourage us to 'smile for the camera' and the lack of clarity in small images prevents us seeing fine detail. I finally made up a health chart of my own life placing banal snapshots against details of diseases and treatments. This led to a decision to visually document my struggle for health and to try to see how that allied itself to campaigns in other fields, in particular, peace campaigns.

I believe it should be everybody's right to take photographs inside all state institutions. So I photographed a lot of what happened around me in hospital. Using my delayed action shutter I was able to include myself in the picture, but

I never had the nerve to photograph anything happening to me directly, least of all my appalling treatment at the hands of consultants, which in any case would have warranted a video camera with sound. Terry Dennett and Maggie Murray photographed me at the hands of the NHS and undergoing TCM.

A meeting with Rosy Martin in 1983 led to our involvement in photo therapy, which means, quite literally, using photography to heal ourselves.

In sessions with Rosy, I began to work on what I came to call my mind/body split. It had become clear that in documenting my physical progress, I had entirely left aside questions of how I experienced my illness. Through photo therapy, I was able to explore how I felt about my powerlessness as a patient, my relationship to doctors and nurses, my infantilisation whilst being managed and 'processed' within a state institution, and my memories of my parents. Later the work moved towards body image, emotional eating and the way parental control worked through diet and feeding patterns. This led on to a visual exploration of the mother and daughter relationship, as a result of which my mother ceased to be the monolith of my imagination and began to exist on many different visual planes, each linked to my memories of her at different periods in her life. The ability to have a dialogue with my imaginary mother (now dead) encouraged me to 'parent' myself better.

In 1985 I enlarged an image/text critique of orthodox medicine which had been exhibited at the Camerawork gallery into a touring show called 'The Picture of Health?'. The documentary work by myself, Terry and Maggie and the photo-therapy work by Rosy and myself was contextualised by Jessica Evans' work on orthodox medicine, in which she foregrounded the myth of the doctor as hero through images from medical text books, film stills and staged photographs.

Once the exhibition was on the road I felt I could relax – until I decided it might be useful to use it to talk to people within orthodox medical circles. I have now begun a new journey which is taking me to health conferences, women's groups and into direct encounters with medical students. To stand in a lecture theatre in a major London teaching hospital, explaining my experience as a patient and the contradictions between ways in which the medical profession controls women's bodies and the 'imaginary bodies' we inhabit as women, was most exhilarating. Learning new and more subtle strategies, beyond aggression and dogmatism, has delighted me and shows me I am moving in a more healthy direction.

Jo Spence, 'The Picture of Health?', in *Putting Myself in the Picture: a Political, Personal and Photographic Autobiography* (London: Camden Press, 1988) 150–171.

Eve Kosofsky Sedgwick
A Dialogue on Love//1999

It's hard, this part. In the new diaries I'd undertake for the first few days of every January when I was a kid, I'd shipwreck on the need to introduce all the *dramatis personae* at once. My older sister Nina was good at that, though. So this is from her 1958 diary: 'I'm an 11-year-old girl called Nina Kosofsky. I weigh 75 lbs., and I have dark hair and dark eyes. Quite

> often I am a
> bit short-tempered. Yours truly
> enjoys reading, dolls,

dancing, writing stories, poems, and plays. Hiking is also in my line.

'Buttons is our almost-7-year-old cat. She is very fat and everyone always thinks that she is about to have kittens. (She can't, though, she's been spade.) She is very unfriendly with other cats of both sexes. She is all black, grey, and white striped, except for her orangey stomach.

'David is my 4- going on 5-year-old brother. He looks quite a lot like me. David is very cute when he wants to be (and that's almost always), and he knows it. He doesn't talk babytalk or lisp, except that he sometimes changes j's to d's and th's to v's.

'Mommy.

> My mother's name is
> Rita Goldstein Kosofsky,
> and she's 36.

She also looks a lot like me. Mommy is *very* even-tempered. Unlike a lot of mothers, she (almost) always likes, and usually uses, new ideas. I love her very, very much.

'Daddy. Leon J. Kosofsky, my father, is 38 years old. He is not fat, but just big. He is mostly bald except for some hair around the edges of his head. He is sometimes

> rather short-tempered
> which I think is my fault, but
> usually he

is *very* kind and understanding. Daddy can sometimes look almost exactly like Yul Brynner. I love him very much.

'Eve, my sister, is 8 years old. She has light hair and freckles. She is *really* a "book-worm". I guess that that must be part of the reason for her being old for her age. Eve is quite plump (she outweighs me by 4 lbs.). I

> seem to remember
> her being even-tempered,
> more when she was young,

although she is still very easy-going.'

In fact it comes readily enough, the task of scene-setting. There's no pleasure to me at this point, only dread, in invoking a Kosofsky world in this or any space. But I discover that to tell something to *Shannon* – in fact, to tell anything to Shannon – makes a wholly new motive I all but shamelessly indulge.

No, the harder part is in telling it now; choosing now to thread the viscera of the labyrinth of

> what I didn't know
> and when I didn't know it,
> and what *that* felt like,

not to know things; I don't even mean big things, but the most ordinary ones.

'The canonical areas, love and work – those are weirdly good for me. I mean, of course there are problems, some big ones, but it doesn't seem as though those areas are where The Problem lives. Assuming there is such a thing as The Problem.'

'"The Problem"...?'

'Oh, I guess...the ontological problem. What's the Matter with Eve.' Why she and life seem to refuse each other. Because after all

> it isn't that things
> for me don't *work*. They do! They
> do, in many ways,
>
> so beautifully:
> if anything, *that* scares me
> because if things change

(and I need them to change), wouldn't it likely be for the worse?

I expect there are tears here. Not copious tears, but seeping ones: I think of them contemptuously as the tears of privilege.

'It's frightening to feel so little attachment to a life that's so full of the things other people long for – rightly long for, I think: a lot of intimacy, enough money, peace and privacy, intellectual stimulation, plenty of recognition, time for my own work, no violence, both parents living, mostly good health, a long, tender relationship with my fella, oodles of terrific friends... . It's not that these things don't seem miraculous. They do: when I was a kid I certainly didn't expect to have most of them. It almost seems miraculous, being a woman, just never to have been raped or battered or had an unwanted pregnancy. I've the most acute sense that things not only could be infinitely worse, but actually are for most people. Though I can't imagine why that's supposed to be a cheering realisation!

'But somehow the goodness of these good things doesn't find its way inside me. I go after them purposefully enough, but when they arrive it's as if I didn't know how to reach my hand out and pull them in.'

There's a Christian hymn with lines I'm fond of,

For the beauty of the earth,
For the beauty of the skies,
For the love that from our birth
Over and around us lies

– maybe perversely fond of, because what I like them for is the pathos of how the beauty and love are described as being everywhere in the world but inside us.

I *was* a morbid,
sentimental kid, I'm sure
of that, and the thought

of dying young was
a good friend to me often.
Sure it sounds funny,

but to think of death
brought me a sense of safety.
Rest. Of being held.

'Another form it maybe took, though, is that I never, ever wanted to have children of my own.'

'Do you have any?'

'No! Never *have* wanted. The friends who've known me longest say it was always true. What I mostly can remember about that is a long, bottomless draught of reproach against my parents for having made me be born. And, oh, I remember thinking – thinking it in so many words, maybe I was eight, maybe eleven – "I could never stand for *any*one, for any

child I had borne, to
feel this unanswerable
reproach against *me*."'

TALKING ABOUT HER WISH TO DIE OR NO LONGER BE, OCCASIONED BY HER FINDING A LUMP ON HER NECK WHICH IMMEDIATELY HAS HER THINKING ABOUT CANCER. SHE TOLD ONLY HUSBAND AND ONE FRIEND. WHAT SHE DOES NOT TELL IS HER EXCITEMENT AT THE POSSIBILITY OF CANCER AND DYING, WHICH SHE NURSES AND WHICH HAS NUMEROUS FACETS – GUILT OVER A 'WICKED' THOUGHT, SOME RELIEF, SOME ANXIETY, ETC. WHAT STRIKES ME IS THE PASSIVITY AND THE SENSE OF BEING RESCUED BY DEATH. SHE RESONATES TO THE RESCUE – BEING SWEPT OFF BY DEATH LIKE BEING TAKEN OFF BY SOMEONE ON A WHITE HORSE. MENTIONS ASSOCIATIONS OF LAWRENCE OF ARABIA, *AT THE BACK OF THE NORTH WIND* – THE IMAGE IS ONE OF LOSS OF BOUNDARIES AND A MERGING WITH SILENT FIGURE NOW MALE BUT MAYBE NOT ALWAYS. IT IS IN CONTRAST TO THE IMAGE OF HAVING TO ESTABLISH HER SELF IN INTERACTION W/ AN OTHER. THESE BOTH ARE DISTINCT FROM THE IMAGE OF A WARM, LOVING, CARING RELATIONSHIP W/ FRIENDS – WHICH HOWEVER STILL SEEMS A MATURE EVOLUTION OF THE RESCUE FANTASIES. [...]

Eve Kosofsky Sedgwick, extract from *A Dialogue on Love* (Boston: Beacon Press, 1999) 13–17.

Khairani Barokka
medusozoa, neuropathic pain//2017
rest stop//2019

medusozoa, neuropathic pain

in kalimantan, a lake so inland in exile
that jellyfish there have no sense
of sting; divers swim at ease,
brushing legs against ghosts.

evolving out of our sense
of poisoning tentacles is possibility;
breathe this. the world is dying,
yet holds both my enduring
corpus and animals whose limbs
have wept away all hurt.

this is blessed plurality of sense.
this a many-tentacled neuron
diversity, this. a synapse in
coelenterate could tell it not
to kill us. a synapse in ourselves
could try to, fail to, fall wet.

rest stop

body reminds me to love thyself
with a harpsichord of crowing nerves

and so

the beats

for rest

and so

reminds

alive alive

and now with medicine (finally)
body a kinder weathervane:

*body is everything underneath and between the weather. the weather is what,
everything, it withstands. and so not a droplet of hate for body since breaking began
in it, only, when called for, infernos of: weather.*

laughingly, I realise that this is what's meant by "under the weather" (for me).

by "weathering".

pain—imprint of and on unique bodymind—crackles, stutters within

and so

the beats

for rest

and so

"Ma'am, what is productivity unit of self"

is not *alive alive*

dear body, one body, slight body, ephemeral mass.

i hum not to weather, to rush of lost seeking, to abled assumptions spoonfed to
the mob—

timeticking markets of stock at the altar of rainforests used as pawns this is not
the song—

to body goes humming
goes all the hum.

Khairani Barokka, 'medusozoa, neuropathic pain', *And Other Poems* (3 November 2017) (https://
andotherpoems.com/2017/11/03/two-poems-by-khairani-barokka/); and 'rest stop', *Westerly*,

Patrick Staff and Catherine Lord
Script for *Weed Killer*//2020

The following text is a series of excerpts of artist, writer and historian Catherine Lord's memoir The Summer of Her Baldness *(2004) arranged to be used as the script for Patrick Staff's video* Weed Killer *(2017). Included below are facsimiles of the strike-throughs, notes and addendums used by Staff and their performer Debra Soshoux to adapt the written text to spoken monologue.*

Is ~~chemo~~ **it** horrible she asks?
~~Why, I wonder, is it unnerving to weep in front of a student? Even a graduated one? Even a slightly older one? Even a dyke? What would be the matter with a fair exchange? Their work, my tears. Why is weeping in a classroom, though we have all felt like it, more of a threat to the mortar that holds together the bricks than stupidity or hatred or ignorance?~~

You feel like shit, I say, face wet. Of course Deirdre hugs me. This is not quite right – the shit part, that is, not the hug part. ~~Kristeva aside,~~ I don't actually <u>feel</u> like a turd. Turd is a leap I cannot make. Nor ~~do I feel~~ **does it feel** like I have the flu, though the comparison is <u>often</u> volunteered. No, Flu feels like something is <u>borrowing</u> from your body for nourishment. You don't <u>want</u> to make the loan **[pause]** but you can. ~~Chemo~~**This** is different. Something has broken <u>into</u> your body **[pause]** and it has murder on its mind.

~~Chemo is~~ **It's** medieval, enough poison to make you crazy miserable but not enough to put you <u>out</u> of your misery.[1] your skin is not only too tight but much too thin, every pressure point on your body hurts, ~~and so does your entire skull. The soles of your feet burn, everything going into your mouth, even the water that you must drink because you are desperately thirsty and because if you don't the drugs will sit in your bladder and corrode it from the inside out, everything feels like a bad idea.~~[2]

Piss like a racehorse, the nurses tell you, and when you do, it comes out <u>red</u>. ~~Though food on the face of it does not appear to be your friend you need~~

~~something in your stomach besides water because when your stomach is empty you feel it beginning to consume itself.~~ Nothing is funny, you can't read, you can't watch tv, you can't sleep and you <u>cannot get the poison</u> out of you because you have swallowed a <u>pill</u> that overrides the better instinct to vomit which you must avoid **not do** ~~because you might seriously damage the lining of your stomach and esophagus. There are women who have described finding sheets of tissue in their puke.~~

~~Chemo is~~ **It's** like mainlining <u>weed killer</u>, which is what, to invoke the perversely feminised metaphor oncologists prefer,[3] my particular 'recipe' sounds like. **Adriamycin** and **Cytoxan**[4]: they fit <u>right in on the pesticide shelf.</u> ~~You're not sure, however, whether you want to be picked for Team Crab or Team Bermuda and you would have much preferred to spend the entire game on the sidelines.~~

Chemo dosage is calculated by skin area. I have 1.7 square meters of skin. ~~Morgan Fisher once happened upon the same chart my oncologist keeps in his desk drawer. Morgan used it to calculate his own skin area. He painted the rectangle exactly his size on a sidewalk in downtown Los Angeles and called it a self portrait. to the best of my knowledge, Morgan has never had chemo.~~

~~There is in addition the matter of chemo brain, a phenomenon announced a few days ago by canadian researchers. chemo brain cases moderate to severe cognitive impairment, including memory loss, difficulty in concentration and reduced logical function. Cancer patients have complained about chemo brain for decades, but doctors had only recently bothered to consider what weed killer might do to human brain cells.~~

~~On your worst days, you think that turds have it better, which is only to say that depressing is one of the biggest side effects of chemo, it being difficult, lets face it, to keep up the chin, or the pecker or the spirits, whichever you prefer, when you feel like a weed and perhaps after all not so far from a turd. you have episodes of wondering why your sweetheart is spending two hours at the supermarket and here all your friends have gone and why your mother won't behave like a mother for once in her life and just get on a plane and why your therapist has forgotten to call and why even your cat has decided you are so boring she would rather sleep by herself.~~

The need for contact is voracious. After a <u>week</u>, you answer <u>yes</u> to every question on those checklists of symptoms to see whether you are A Depressed Person and ~~should get~~**need** professional help. ~~Finally the legs get back to the energy to~~

~~climb out of the hole but the white blood count continues to drop. it does so for another two weeks, after which, all going well, it crawls back to a more or less normal level.~~ You do in fact feel better in the short run, much better, but you also know that the side effects could be in your future: heart attacks, kidney failure, intestinal parasites, collapsed veins, loss of sexual interest, sores in the rectum, skin so thin it splits, weight loss, weight gain, extreme fatigue, ditto vaginal dryness, olfactory hallucinations, severe skin burns, permanent hair loss and, of course, the stress induced by waiting for the ~~advent of~~ any of the above.[5] you begin to wonder: is this how the end begins? the body, betrayed, no longer has confidence that what it takes in might nourish. food doesn't fire the muscles. it saps them. you want to <u>penetrate</u> the envelope of your skin. **[pause]** no feasting. no fucking.

~~on the same day you feel really and wonderfully human again, back to your old self, and happy, for a change, to be that old self,[6] you're ready for the next round. chemo works by killing all the fast-growing cells, of which cancer is only one kind, the kind that cannot repair itself, or so the theory goes. that is to say, while other fast-growing cells repair themselves after chemo, cancer cells cannot. but when you stop to think about it, the difference between killing your fast growing cells and killing you is a matter of splitting hairs and you are not in possession of hairs to split. this is what people are describing when they say chemo brings you to death's door.~~

[break]

Question: Is hair as unnecessary a profusion[7] as a dick in most social circumstances? Conversely, is hair as much fun as a dick in most social circumstances?
Question: If the penis is located between the legs, and the phallus is located between the ears, where is a lesbian's hair when it is not on her head?

~~Question: If a straight women rushes to the wig store — get it ready, get it in advance, have it waiting so it will be there when you need it — what should a lesbian do? Wigs are tight. Wigs itch. Wigs are about passing. Or are wigs like lipstick? Get over it, apply the signifiers, hit the road?~~

Question: How come men <u>OWN</u> not only dicks but baldness?[8] In the year of the fabulous dude and fag, how does a dyke lay <u>claim</u> to baldness outside of her own home?[9]

10

[break]

Baldness is a scar. **[pause]** I want my scar. **[pause]** I want to be able to put my hands on it, and have the wind touch it, to rub comfrey **soothing** salve into it and to feel the rises and hollows of my skull without hair scratching and skidding under my fingertips. I don't want to shop to cover my scar, which will at any rate fade and heal, just as the ones on my breast and under my right arm are doing so.[11] I do not want to pass. I do not want to get gently back in to the world of people **[pause]** who are afraid of looking into the eyes of someone whose chances of dying in the near future are better than theirs **[pause]** by a long shot, **[pause]** or so they believe. ~~Baldness becomes me, in a literal sort of way.~~

~~You bond with women who are going through the same thing. I know, for example, susie's disability started two days ago. i know that she decided to shave off the final wisps of her baby orangutan hair last week and she hates looking in the mirror in the morning because before she looks, when she wakes up next to the guy she just married after living with him for seventeen years, she isn't a person with three more rounds to go. i know that naomi, who progressed from pate to fuzz, speaks from experience when she tells me not to worry about my blood count because whatever happens there is a drug that will take it up again. i know that glenda is going through chemo six today, and that her sister has come out from georgi because it was so bad last time that glenda's heart almost stopped and her ten year-old daughter had to race for the nurse to take the drip out. even though i dont really know glenda i sit here writing and hope that she got back home safely and i will see her next week.~~

[break]

'How do you get through depression?' I asked my group last night. you just do, they say. people call you up. people bring you things. people take you out. you let people help. you let them do it now because they'll get bored with you later. there's a name for it. it's called compassion fatigue.

you weed, said suzie, even if it's only for ten minutes. you just go out into the garden and weed.

1   Difficult phrasing.

2   Cut in edit

3   Cadence

4   Rehearse pronunciation with Debra.

5   Rhythm

6   Cadence

7   nb profusion/protrusion

8   What shifts when we ask these questions as trans ppl?

9   Cat and mouse.

10   Lament.

11   What scars do we have?

Patrick Staff and Catherine Lord, 'Script for *Weed Killer* (2017)', edited by the artist for this book, 2020.

Naomi Pearce and Alice Hattrick
Lucy Beech: *Pharmakon*//2016

Lucy Beech's new film *Pharmakon* (2016) explores health anxiety and self-diagnosis in an era of mass communication. The film engages with marginal communities that seek support via online networks. 'The Healing Grapevine' provides care and conversely intensifies its users' symptoms. Here, connectivity is poison and cure. These support groups are stereotyped as women who collaborate in their sickness through a shared discourse.

Diagnosis similarly involves a collaborative exchange between clinician and patient. Beech invited writers Alice Hattrick and Naomi Pearce to correspond via email about the film, in order to mirror this dynamic, as well as the structure of these online networks. They were given a set timeframe of two weeks in which to write and edit the correspondence. This text continues their ongoing project 'Under the Influence', the first instalment of which was produced in association with Women's Art Library, London, in November 2015.

On 5 June 2016 at 11:33 Naomi Pearce wrote:

Dear A,
Lucy was worried this complex ecology she'd been nurturing might stop functioning – turn toxic.

Documentary meets re-enactment becomes fiction. Whatever this film is, it feels invasive. A series of interrogations, repeated voluntary and involuntary acts which breach borders; hands learn to frisk, doctors run tests, a woman describes unknown fibres breaking through her skin.

...So again, we are writing to each other about women under the influence.

FB (Female Bouncer) is our protagonist and the face we look at the most. Christa manages 'The Healing Grapevine'; a support group cum online quackery offering natural remedies for those suffering from 'unknown infestations'.

Lucy gave Christa a name and with it agency.

Christa manages pain into product – doing emotional labour all the time – tapping into her own traumatic experiences as resource and securing customers through identification: 'I know many of u have doubted yourselves, as I did.' Christa won't give u a cure but she will give u access to another way of surviving: community.

Have you seen *The Passion of Joan of Arc*? FB has the same suffering look depicted on Renée Falconetti's face. See the way her scalped head tilts back, jaw gesturing to the left, eyes searching, transfigured. Rumour has it *The Passion's*... director was a sadist, inflicting pain in order to capture it. More sad female biography: Falconetti suffered from mental illness throughout her life, eventually committing suicide in 1946.

It's a silent film, Falconetti has no words. And yet, diagnosis relies upon our ability to give appropriate narratives to the body, to find the right words.

Unlike disease – which doctors tell us we 'have' – illness is a feeling, something inward, only accessible to the patient, an 'underworld of experience'.

I've been looking back through our old emails, not the good ones, the ones from after we spent those nights together. Something is clearly misfiring. It's as if all the physical closeness short-circuited our discourse, we stopped encountering one another in ways we could understand. Maybe this new-found bodily knowledge broke our brains.

Last week we crushed so hard on Maggie Nelson. Eating dough sticks and drinking white wine, your words ran through me. I took this transfusion. On the tube home writing notes on my phone, revived and nourished, high from the encounter of our thoughts. Sometimes when we talk it's physical; concepts become shapes moving in space, words wrestle to become arguments as our minds lock together.

Love always,
Nx

On 6 June 2016 at 14:21 Alice Hattrick wrote:

N,
I've been in bed all day. Unclean hair unclean skin. Under my arms sticking to themselves. A bad smell coming from the rotting tulips she gave him for his birthday. Storm coming. The tightness in my chest making me aware of my body. Just like perfume makes me aware of the air surrounding it and inside it, air in its mixed and threatening form mixing up inside me, contaminated air. Toxic. I thought about my Mum when I read that essay Lucy sent us:

> 'you will find it institutionally, in the form of welfare disputes or dismissals from employment; interpersonally in the breakdown of trust and respect in a marriage; psychologically in the self-doubt and depression of an ill person who lacks an approved way of deciphering the way they feel in their body'.

(failed marriage followed by endless series of failed relationships, failed/late education, signed-off work, passed-on 'illness' to her daughter, probably about to be fired for being ill, etc. etc.)

She thinks sick, lives a sick life.

THE PRESENTATION SCENE: I remember mum and I went to one about this magical new form of therapy for ME when I was a teenager at the Quaker meeting house in Brighton. It was about tailored forms of therapy, but it was all a secret so no one could just do it themselves. It was presented by people in 'recovery', who had got better enough to stand up and persuade people it could work for them too. Anyone else would be untrustworthy, right? As far as we could tell it was basically CBT with stuff like graded exercise thrown in (before CBT was prescribed by the NHS, if you can wait long enough). Mum and I were sceptical. I think we only went to call it out as bullshit. Mark ourselves out as different from all the crazies on forums all day and not leaving the house and sending hate mail to anyone who said ME wasn't a real illness. We were not the only mother/daughter couples at the Quaker meeting house that day (the family home as site of contagion). We were alone together. She takes her to-do lists with her to her (subsidised) therapist she sees now. Signed off work. New drugs. Don't act agitated.

No one trusts doctors, but this mistrust is reflected back onto the patient. They start to distrust themselves. They lose words. FB has a good face.

Her inputs: mites, videos online, special water... No outputs (pain is language destroying).
A xx

On 6 June 2016 at 22:33 Naomi Pearce wrote:

A,
What makes a sick life? A lifestyle, a diagnosis, a frame of mind? Bad luck or the influence of 'bad people'? With my arthritis – which has always just been *there* – distinctions have never been made. Health is abstract when pain is an everyday nuisance rather than total debilitation. It is always about managing and I don't mean 'just about managing', I mean more a case of organising, like a to-do list: 'take painkillers, don't sit still too long, exercise etc.'

You drew a heart on your copy of *The Argonauts* next to the line: *They seemed to make a fetish of the unsaid, rather than simply letting it be contained in the sayable* Is this what Lucy's film does? FB's disembodiments – her physical out-of-jointness – destroy her language? I think I do the opposite, writing to articulate sensations, a fumbling around to give form to feeling, if only that I might know it better, feel it stronger.

This film has many containers and they slot into each other like tupperware. The glass house hosts all: healing plants, volunteer gardeners, yogis and 'The Healing Grapevine' meetings.

The smallest of non-movements betrays FB's relaxedness: a quick crick of her neck on the door of the club, she's struggling to contain what's going on inside.

There's a scene in the glasshouse where FB turns away from the stretching yoga bodies, she rejects this kind of embodiment. She attempts to understand her physicality – to meet it as Kathy Acker says in her writing on bodybuilding – through the distancing meditation of her iPhone. Earphones go in, hands cup the screen, FB becomes immersed within a community who forgo presence to encounter one another online: 'The fibres have made a home in her face'

Christa by contrast is poised throughout. As she prepares to film a vlog post she asks her volunteers to fuss over her body, check her hair, her makeup. All the surface stuff.

Women find safety in numbers.

The final scene: FB gulping down energy medicine in the form of branded bottled water. Communities provide containers.

Replace the 'i' in illness with 'we' and get wellness. Influence – as you know – is such a messy and unrestricted process, like the way germs spread. 'The Healing Grapevine' enables women to collaborate in their sickness through a shared discourse, this 'we' gives a special kind of access: permission for total introspection.

This form of collective care seems incredibly nourishing. Is it the exchanging of money or its delusional foundations that make it toxic?

Lucy considered opening the film with an abortion. What could demonstrate bodily alienation more clearly than a woman rejecting her 'nature'? Brain overriding, no home here.

Instead we have the beautiful looking word Pharmakon. It's stamped across the lush and vital green of the opening scene.

The pharmakon is at once what enables care to be taken and that of which care must be taken. Simply: a poison and a cure. Its power is curative to the immeasurable extent that it is also destructive.

Love always,

Nxxx

On 7 June 2016 at 14:21 Alice Hattrick wrote:

N,
Lucy's film was going to start with an abortion, well so did my 2016.

I took the test an hour before people came over for dinner for NYE. I painted a beautiful writer's fingernails gold, had feelings in what felt like a different body (medicated, pregnant). Mouth shut praying NO ONE ASK ME ANYTHING ABOUT ME. Later his friend told me not to fuck up again and I walked off before I could say anything back. Don't worry, I don't want to keep it.

I looked at the scan of it even though you're not supposed to. I liked the drama of the record. I even liked going to first appointment. It felt nice, to be cared for, and about. Do you have any questions? etc. Later, less so. There was lot of pain for such a tiny thing. But you've read that text already.

Now I have to re-write a book proposal (again) to make it more about psychosomatic illness and perfume, or, even, just about my mother. I'm thinking about good/bad objects, projection/introjection, to feeling unreal, to being/not being good enough, to the binaries contained by 'pharmakon' (and Pharmakon).

Have decided to write quickly as you can probably tell (you think too much for the both of us). Will write more about 'thinking sick' next time.

Love always

A

On 7 June 2016 at 21:17 Naomi Pearce wrote:

A,
I so wanted you to have a baby even though it didn't make sense.

Maggie writes that even before we can speak 'our mothers police our mouths'. It's this care that instils in us the conviction to continue living. Back in January, it was hard enough convincing yourself.

I'm still on the pharmakon because (if it's ok) I want to keep talking about having or not having babies.

Lucy tells me to read Bernard Stiegler: 'He's written a lot about it'. In *What Makes Life Worth Living* Stiegler opens with a passage about Donald Winnicott, apparently 'the transitional object' is the first pharmakon.

The transitional object is a teddy bear or a blanket, something that allows the child to split from the mother and safely enter the world. Beneath this piece of cloth holds something that is neither an exterior space, nor simply internal to either the mother or child. It's the border to both:

The transitional object is the point of departure for the formation of a healthy psychic apparatus, and yet [...] dependence becomes harmful, that is, destructive of autonomy and trust. The care that the mother takes of her child necessarily includes protecting them from this object: eventually she will have to teach them to let their blanket go.

Maggie describes her love affair with her infant son: 'A buoyant eros, an eros without teleology.' This purposeless love writes alternative narratives on the body, it isn't exactly yours anymore.

In her book *On Immunity: An Inoculation* Eula Biss writes: 'My son's birth brought with it an exaggerated sense of both my own power and my own powerlessness.'

Watching now as my mum attempts to recalibrate (empty nest) having performed the role of host and carer since the age of 22. Four children and more decades later she is anxious, frustrated: 'I used to be able to do things.'

Filmmaking can be thought of as a form of care, one that questions and antagonises

FB often looks frightened. Her job is to police and protect other bodies. What about her own?
Love always,
nx

[...]

Naomi Pearce and Alice Hattrick, extract from 'Lucy Beech: *Pharmakon*' (Liverpool: Liverpool Biennale and FACT, 2016) 1–7, revised by the authors for this book, 2020.

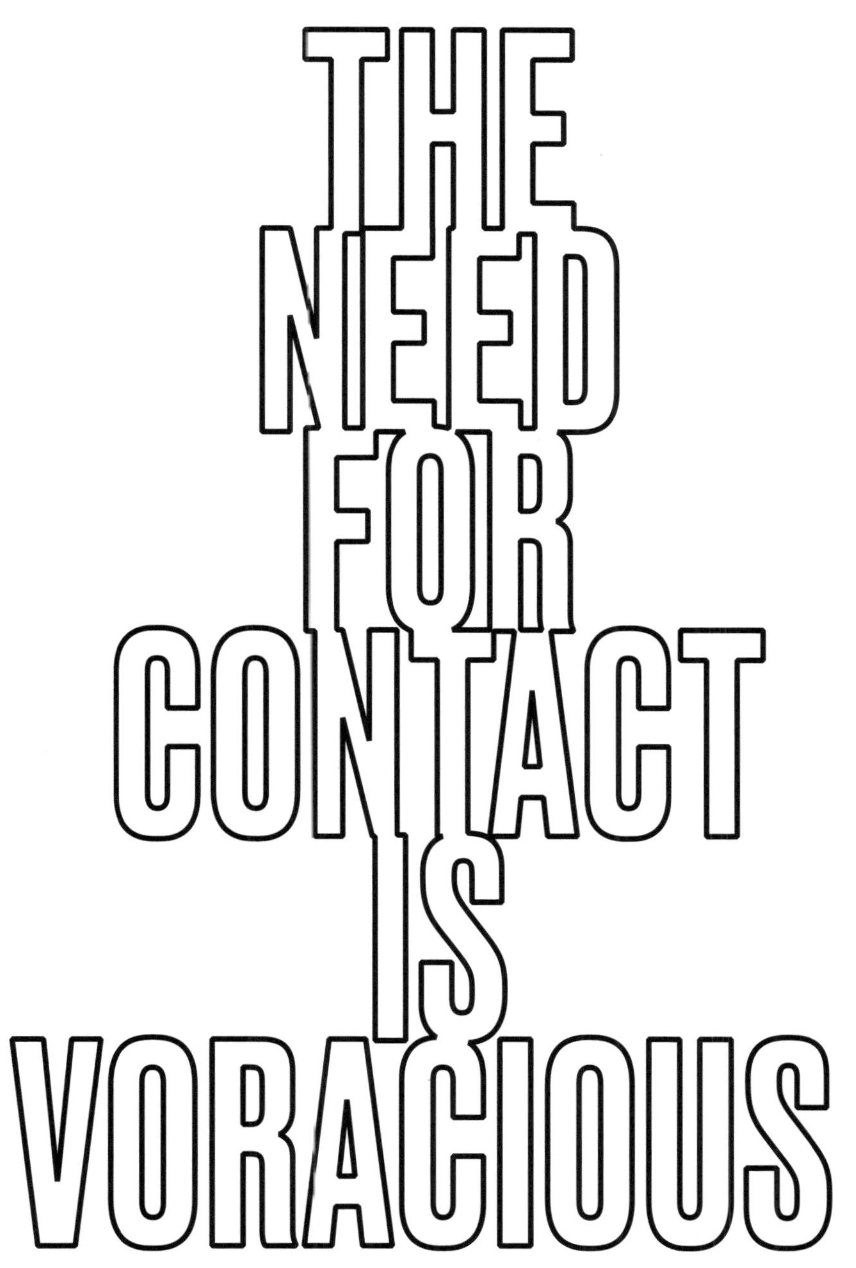

Catherine Lord, 'Script for *Weed Killer*', 2020

Dodie Bellamy
When the Sick Rule the World//2013

[...] The sick rinse their bodies with vinegar and dry off with a blow-dryer to prevent mould growth. The sick travel in used cars which they sell to one another, cars that have never been detailed, that have been aired out and cleared with activated carbon felt blankets and zeolite. Behind their used case the sick pull teardrop-shaped trailers made from steel and non-fragrant wood.

The sick will create new families based not on blood but affinity of symptoms. The sick will travel in packs commandeering porcelain-lined fragrance-free buses. The well will no longer delete the email of the sick. When the sick rule the world hotel rooms will be obsolete, airplanes will be obsolete, new cars will be obsolete. All existing new cars will be remaindered and shipped to Cuba. When the sick rule the world fragrance-free auto shops will keep the old cars running smoothly. All service stations will be full service, the well filling the tanks for the sick. Mechanics and gas jockeys who do not wear gasmasks will soon themselves become sick. The sick refer to people who do not wear gasmasks as 'breathers'. [...]

When the sick rule the world roses, gardenias, freesias and other fragrant flowers will no longer be grown. On Valentine's Day the sick will give one another dahlias and daisies to say I Love You. The sick should have sex as often as possible because it's good for the immune system. The sick should lie on their backs and receive rather than deliver the fucking. When two sick bodies come together their desperate hearts open, it is lovely to watch them, the thin iridescent haze of sickness flowing across their skin, when two sick bodies fuck their hazy genitals sparkle and frizzle. The sick and the well should never mingle. The sick latch onto the genitals of the well like carnivorous plants, milking the well of their life force, but the well are too rich, too funky, neurotoxic deodorant off-gassing from pores, the sick's iridescent haze curdles, congealed vinegary bits clinging to sweaty torsos, the sick spasm with so little pleasure, turn away sickened with remorse. [...]

Sex partners of the sick must wash their hands carefully before sex and avoid touching the genitals with a hand that has contact with the anal area. For lubricants, synthetics may be problem; experiment with butter or vegetable oils made from foods the sick are not sensitive to. Incense and perfumes cannot be used to set the mood, but good music, videos or other approaches can work. Organic cotton bedding can reduce coughing and other less romantic symptoms. Muscle spasms and cramps from pesticide exposure may be immediate or delayed by as much as three days up to six weeks. If fatigue or pains are problems, the sick should remain passive and their partners should assume the positions that require the most energy. Fresh air and improved environmental controls will help the sick gain vigour. Be creative, patient and persistent. The sick must always empty their bladders shortly after sex. The sick should never be kissed on the lips, as lip-kissing transmits bacteria and viruses.

There is no such thing as a hypochondriac; there are only doctors who cannot figure out what is wrong with you.

When we eat in a restaurant we take in the energy of those who cook and serve it, and their energy is bad energy. When the sick rule the world there will be no restaurants. When the sick rule the world Calvin Klein will design aluminium foil window dressings and our porcelain walls will be decorated by Limoges. Gas masks will be sexy, the envy of every Paris runway. […]

Wary of money, the sick use credit cards whenever possible. Upon returning home they empty their pockets of any coins or bills they may have accumulated and immerse them in a bowl of zeolite crystals, which absorb dangerous residues. Placing the crystals outside in the sun will recharge them. When the sick rule the world the well will be servants, and all the well will try to become sick so they too can have servants. Pretending to be sick will be a capital offence. When the sick rule the world the limbs of the well will be chopped off in the middle of the night, the well one still alive, flailing and screaming. The limbs of the well will fetch exorbitant fees on the black market, sold to sorcerers who will dry the limbs and grind them into magic powders to be placed into amulets to ward off blindness and toxins. These amulets will bring prosperity to their owners. […]

When the sick rule the world mortality will be sexy. When the sick rule the world, all writing will be short and succinct, no paragraphs will be longer than two sentences so we can comprehend them though the brain fog the well bring to us daily. […]

Dodie Bellamy, extracts from *When the Sick Rule the World* (Los Angeles: Semiotext(e), 2015) 30–31, 32–3, 34, 35, 36.

CARING
FOR MYSELF
IS NOT
SELF-
INDULGENCE,
IT IS
SELF-
PRESERVATION,
AND THAT IS
AN ACT OF
POLITICAL
WARFARE.

Audre Lorde, 'Epilogue', 1988

SELF CARING

Audre Lorde
Epilogue//1988

Sometimes I feel like I am living on a different star from the one I am used to calling home. It has not been a steady progression. I had to examine, in my dreams as well as in my immune-function tests, the devastating effects of overextension. Overextending myself is not stretching myself. I had to accept how difficult it is to monitor the difference. Necessary for me as cutting down on sugar. Crucial. Physically. Psychically. Caring for myself is not self-indulgence, it is self-preservation, and that is an act of political warfare.

Time in this place is speedy, rich and stark. My days are a thirsty atonal combination of the mundane and the apocalyptic. Mingling without much warming. Moving without missing a beat from the report of peritubal metastases (Does that mean escape into the abdominal cavity?) to estimates for constructing my workspace in St. Croix. Drastic life-changes laced together with the eternal ordinary.

My aim is to move more easily between the two, make transitions the least costly, approach a student's completed manuscript and the medical reports and the house estimates in some open-hearted way, with a sense of proportion. I order a perfume from Grenada called 'Jump Up and Kiss Me'.

I try to weave my life-prolonging treatments into a living context – to resist giving myself over like a sacrificial offering to the furious single-minded concentration upon cure that leaves no room to examine what living and fighting on a physical front can mean. What living with cancer can teach me. I go to Germany this fall for further mistletoe treatment. I look forward to working with the Afro-German Women's Group.

I believe that one of the ways in which cancer cells insure their own life and depress the immune system is by creating a physiologically engendered despair. Learning to fight that despair in all its manifestations is not only therapeutic. It is vital. Underlining what is joyful and life-affirming in my living becomes crucial.

What have I had to leave behind? Old life habits, outgrown defences put aside lest they siphon off energies to no useful purpose?

One of the hardest things to accept is learning to live within uncertainty and neither deny it nor hide behind it. Most of all, to listen to the messages of uncertainty without allowing them to immobilise me, nor keep me from the certainties of those truths in which I believe. I turn away from any need to justify the future – to live in what has not yet been. Believing, working for what has not yet been while living fully in the present now.

This is my life. Each hour is a possibility not to be banked. These days are not a preparation for living, some necessary but essentially extraneous divergence from the main course of my living. They are my life. The feeling of the bedsheet against my heels as I wake to the sound of crickets and bananaquits in Judith's Fancy. I am living my life every particular day no matter where I am, nor in what pursuit. It is the consciousness of this that gives a marvellous breadth to everything I do consciously. My most deeply held convictions and beliefs can be equally expressed in how I deal with chemotherapy as well as in how I scrutinise a poem. It's about trying to know who I am wherever I am. It's not as if I'm in struggle over here while someplace else, over there, real life is waiting for me to begin living it again.

I visualise daily winning the battles going on inside my body, and this is an important part of fighting for my life. In those visualisations, the cancer at times takes on the face and shape of my most implacable enemies, those I fight and resist most fiercely. Sometimes the wanton cells in my liver become Bull Connor and his police dogs completely smothered, rendered impotent in Birmingham, Alabama by a mighty avalanche of young, determined Black marchers moving across him toward their future. P.W. Botha's bloated face of apartheid squashed into the earth beneath an onslaught of the slow rhythmic advance of furious Blackness. Black South African women moving through my blood destroying passbooks. Fireburn Mary[1] sweeping over the Cruzan countryside, axe and torch in hand. Images from a Calypso singer:

The big black boot of freedom
Is mashing down your doorstep.

I train myself for triumph by knowing it is mine, no matter what. In fact, I am surrounded within my external living by ample examples of the struggle for life going on inside me. Visualising the disease process inside my body in political images is not a quixotic dream. When I speak out against the cynical US intervention in Central America, I am working to save my life in every sense. Government research grants to the National Cancer Institute were cut in 1986 by the exact amount illegally turned over to the contras in Nicaragua. One hundred and five million dollars. It gives yet another meaning to the personal as the political.

Cancer itself has an anonymous face. When we are visibly dying of cancer, it is sometimes easier to turn away from the particular experience into the sadness of loss, and when we are surviving, it is sometimes easier to deny that experience. But those of us who live our battles in the flesh must know ourselves as our strongest weapon in the most gallant struggle of our lives.

Living with cancer has forced me to consciously jettison the myth of omnipotence, of believing – or loosely asserting – that I can do anything, along with any dangerous illusion of immortality. Neither of these unscrutinised defences is a solid base for either political activism or personal struggle. But in their place, another kind of power is growing, tempered and enduring, grounded within the realities of what I am in fact doing. An open-eyed assessment and appreciation of what I can and do accomplish, using who I am and who I most wish myself to be. To stretch as far as I can go and relish what is satisfying rather than what is sad. Building a strong and elegant pathway toward transition.

I work, I love, I rest, I see and learn. And I report. These are my givens. Not sureties, but a firm belief that whether or not living them with joy prolongs my life, it certainly enables me to pursue the objectives of that life with a deeper and more effective clarity.

August 1987
Carriacou, Grenada
Anguilla, British West Indies
St. Croix, Virgin Islands

1   Ex-slave who led a workers' revolt in St. Croix in 1848.

Audre Lorde, 'Epilogue', in *A Burst of Light and Other Essays* (New York: Ixia Press, 1988) 130– 33.

Anne Charlotte Robertson
Five Year Diary//2014

85+ reels, approximately 26 minutes each,
Super 8mm and video
Begun November 3, 1981, in Boston, Massachusetts, USA

I present my life in multimedia: film (1st visual source), sound from film (when possible, depending upon finances; 1st audio source), audiotape dubbed diary (2nd audio source), on-stage live introduction to each reel (milieu setting, perspective giving, autobiographical storytelling: 2nd visual, 3rd audio, source), live narration from within the audience (4th audio source), amid a surrounding environment (as much as is possible to bring to a screening; 3rd visual resource), with myself usually available to the audience during intermissions, as the primary source/resource of information and perspective on my life.

This diary is a constant work-in-progress, as is every life. It is a matter of collection rather than pre-visualisation of scenes; I try to take a documentary approach to life events and my surrounds, rather than moulding my life into a theatrical artifice. Despite the multitude of information offered to the audience via multimedia, the result is not a barrage, but a view into complexity, and themes of personal change. Making my diary has literally saved my life; it is an inspiration to others, that 'examining one's life can help make life worth living'.

I am a 50-year-old woman, single, with a vow to poverty. The title *Five Year Diary* refers to the little blank books with locks and keys, that allow only a few lines to each day's notation; the audience is invited to be my brother and sister, and see what a life can yield. My present and future hope is to leave a full record of a woman in the twentieth century. I have been a diarist since I was a child; likewise I have kept visual records, and artefacts. My training in schools and by myself has been in writing, crafts, theatre, photography, psychology and film. During the past 17 years I have added audio recordings to my diary accumulation, thus approaching the utilisation of all the senses that art can present of memory. My work in film is entirely self-produced (except for laboratory processing and technical processes such as video/sound transfer); I am the sole artist, camera, editor, lights and sound.

All that surrounds and interests me would disappear in an apocalypse, as surely as the film image disappears after projection. I take as many personal artefacts as possible with me to screenings, to create a 3D environment, so that even the intermissions are alive for the audience.

I am an organic gardener also, someone who has deliberately chosen to leave the city after many years, to live among trees; gardens can be planned to a certain extent, but intensive planting calls for spontaneous crowding, work of art that is similar to my own growth as an artist in multimedia. I am a diarist, a visual artist, a performer, and a storyteller, with my films 'at the mouth of the cave', telling you all that we are not merely shadows, we are all complex beings needing nurturing, and change, and the acknowledgement and acceptance of changing ourselves.

A Short Affair (and) Going Crazy

(video available)
(1982/1996; Super 8mm film, narration and audio tape)
(running time 24 minutes)

This is Reel 22 of my Super 8mm opus *Five Year Diary*. It covers the period 23 August to 1 September 1982. Within is documented a compulsive paranoid manic depressive psychotic breakdown, following a brief love affair.

Synopsis: Introduction; a vegetarian dinner; the lover sleeping; sorting garbage; ex-lovers' art; friends and cocaine; moon; composting sable brushes; the kitchen sink; wine; eating with my hands; the kitchen table; self-portraits; construction machines; hiding behind the curtains; morning glories at dusk; dinner with my mother: the drawings in the hall, yoga and the goddess rap; calling the lover: saying goodbye; carnival rides; street scenes: weeping; flowers and bees: shadows on the carpet and empty rooms; esoterica sign language: sorting the compost: walking through Boston, hunting for clues; finding him in a fountain: my favourite statue: the slug incident; paranoia about plastic; putting everything in garbage bags: the construction site outside; calling the lover.

A Breakdown (and) After the Mental Hospital
(video available)
(1982/1991; silent/colour Super 8mm & tape & narration)
(running time 26 minutes 04 seconds)

This is Reel 23 of my Super 8mm opus *Five Year Diary*. It covers the period 1 September to 13 December 1982. Within it are documented a paranoid manic nervous breakdown, a description of a mental hospitalisation, and the subsequent recovery period. Sound is of wild tape of the breakdown, and a hidden tape recorded psychiatric session; the second soundtrack is narration from 1991.

Synopsis: Introduction: paranoia about root vegetables; esoteric sign language; searching for hidden significances; crush on Tom Baker ('Doctor Who' from BBC Television); my cats Amy and Buddy; vegetarian cooking: the compost heap: my mother and her house; driving into Boston; unemployment: television hypervigilance; hiding inside; exorcism with tea and mirror and lamps; too much wine; my friend the painter Susan Brown: the movie *The Turning Point*: experiences in a mental hospital: psychiatric session recording; autumn street and garden scenes; the mental day –hospital; domestic still-lives; binging; self-Gestalt-therapy; school: groceries; winter; my garden: a series of self-portraits.

This is Reel 23 of my Super 8mm opus, *Five Year Diary*. It covers the time period 1 September to 13 December 1982. Videotransfer was made in 1991, pro bono, by Bob Brodsky. The second track of narration dates to this later time.

I was sitting in on classes at Massachusetts College of Art, and had just been accepted to graduate school there, in filmmaking. But a loan had been refused, and I had no money to attend. It was summer vacation; I had just registered for classes, but knew it was futile.

My father had died this year. I see this now as one of the precipitating causes of the paranoid nervous breakdown. Also, a technician at school had threatened to call the police to retrieve my borrowed Nizo silent Super8 camera, which I had damaged this summer. And a new lover had turned out to be both bisexual, and about to return to his school across the country. I was losing everything; even my dream of film school was vanishing.

I carried the camera everyday. This is the actual record of eight days before I was put into a mental hospital for three months. I went to a friend's house, hoping to be safe. There I 'exorcised Richard Nixon' and descended into madness. In the morning I left my camera, walked across the street, and lay down in a sandpit, hoping to be buried alive. I was 'put away' promptly.

I refused to take medications in the mental hospital. I was beaten, overdosed and nearly raped. Finally I was threatened with the courts, and took the drugs. After surviving a bout of pneumonia, I returned home.

It was nearly winter. My garden had been killed. I sat in on classes again, and recovered my equilibrium at home.

My nervous breakdown had been characterised by paranoia, and massive manic delusions of being the Goddess of the World. I had been afraid of root vegetables, plastic and aluminium, and put all my belongings into plastic bags. I had eaten food with my fingers in front of the camera, 'since God told me to do so.' I kept an audiotape diary of my delusions; this is one of the soundtracks. (The recovery period has a tape of a hidden recorded psychiatric session.)

My diagnosis was manic depression. Now I saw the psychiatrist every week and was also soon in family therapy. I ate beets again, so I must have been sane. Yet I had gained fifteen pounds in the mental hospital, and was bingeing on food again at home. I felt extremely fragile after having been locked-up inside for three months.

The camera was my saving grace. I could not afford to process the film for several more years, and kept 200 rolls of film in my refrigerator in plastic bags. Yet I used the camera everyday, thus enabling me to capture every mood. Even a mad woman can make art. And art itself is one of the best therapies.

Anne Charlotte Robertson, extracts from 'Five Year Diary', in *Five Year Diary*, eds., Ben Cook & Bárbara Rodríguez Muñoz (London: LUX and Anxiety Arts Festival, 2014) 17–19, 22.

Park McArthur
What is Collectivity, Conviviality, Care?//2017

On 13 August 2011, which was a Thursday – no, the calendar says it was a Saturday – I bought a notebook. Inside it I wrote: 'a space to process care collective stuff – be open with myself – in combination with what I'm reading about dependency and care with or vs. justice. "Collective" feels like using a language adopted – a language I am trying to learn – as I learn how to operate in a collective in general. A collection of people. A collective.' The week prior to 13 August was my first experience participating in a care collective: a group of nine people helping me shower, change my clothes, and get into bed each night. Nine individuals – at least one person and sometimes two or more helping each night of the week, with two additional people occasionally swapping in when needed – made and sustained this collective.

Throughout the fall of 2011 and the winter of 2012 I wrote in this journal almost daily, so regular was my need to write about these initial experiences receiving care in this way. Outlined here is what was established and what continues to be created. This account seeks to describe the form of collective care as well as the relations that formed it and were formed by it. Unevenly descriptive, this incomplete narrative also seeks to frame the questions I have concerning care's obligations and desires. In an effort to think about interpersonal care on a social scale, I map my experiences of dependency onto the queer theorist Jasbir Puar's outline of 'convivial' relations, proposing that debilities and capacities function like 'categories such as race, gender and sexuality [which act] as events – as encounters – rather than as entities or attributes of the subject'.[1]

Care and Access

The first time I received care from a rotating group of people who were neither my family nor people I hired was as an attendee at the 2010 US Social Forum in Detroit. Five or occasionally six friends shared a hotel room for the weeklong event. Our group did not formalise a schedule of how and when to provide care but kept in close touch with one another, trading on anticipated jobs: helping me in and out of bed and the bathroom, meeting up for meals. The labour of care was not distributed equally among the people sharing the hotel room; friends I was closest to emotionally shared their time with me more frequently and most regularly, and I felt most comfortable with them.

Across the city of Detroit, in the Wayne State University dorm rooms, organisers of the conference's Disability Justice Track created a care-shift collective called Creating Collective Access (CCA), begun during the Allied Media Conference. CCA – whose organisers invited individuals to pool their resources, skills and abilities and needs – was envisioned as 'a community-built-and-led collective access network of crips and our comrades, wanting to help create access in ways that also build community, care, crip solidarity, solidarity with non-disabled comrades and is led by crips!'.[2]

Care girded the structure of CCA, and it determined the pace of living together in Detroit. Each person's daily care needs were folded into each day's rhythms and activities. CCA attempted to keep care self- and group-determined: asking questions about the ways in which a self is social.

Organisers of the US Social Forum as a whole – like many groups using a one-to-one customer service approach to accessibility – provided handouts and hotlines for questions concerning structural access: which buildings and forms of public transportation were available to people getting around on wheels; where to locate roomy elevators and all-gender bathrooms. Access needs were addressed through the circulation of information to people perceived or self-described as benefitting from this information. But CCA – and lived experiences of disability and debility – enliven and trouble the common denominator of structural access, foregrounding the care needed to complete structural accessibility's proposal. How does one use public transportation if maps are illegible and directions difficult to remember? Who will be there to make transfers to the toilet safe within the ADA-compliant bathroom? If the forum's convention centre houses thousands of people – along with their noise, their motion, their activity – who will be a calming counterpart? These questions of touch and weight, relationality and recognition, interrogate the psychosomatic, phenomenological, and haptic fields and feedback loops of life. They are questions often ignored in public spaces and that go unaccounted for within formulations of just societies. They are questions that do not end at the end of the workday. They are not answered by the hiring of a sign language interpreter for a half hour of programming – they involve and allow for intention and consent, dependency, safety, exploitation and abuse, translation and effect. In the United States partial answers to these questions have been historically situated and bound to private family life and the state. Such questions are concerns of people who receive-give-need-want care. They animate the relational, intrapersonal, asymmetrical, nonreciprocal, non-recuperable parts of life.

The work of people who receive-give-need-want care outlines an ontology of care. To acknowledge the tenuous, collapsible relationship between debility and capacity – within disability and non-disability alike – proposes an ontology of care not yet theorised but always lived, much in the way that the philosopher

Laura Hengehold writes, 'our bodies should always be better than the societies we currently have'.[3] Without ignoring the importance of the societies we currently have or could have, this statement flips the assigned metaphors of disabled fire alarms and paralysed systems of an insane marketplace for a world in which every disabled, paralysed body and insane mind is already better than the conditions we take to be their linguistic approximation – setting aside a body politic, in order to be our bodies and minds that always exceed a politics.

Care is a plastic term. Care studies' acceleration as an academic trend does not mean that people necessarily want to identify as 'needing care' or as 'care workers'. Campaigns led by care providers, for example, talk about how the term can be used to exploit workers by placing an emphasis on work by a 'family member' rather than the work of an employee for her employer. In campaigns for disability rights, the term *care* is often understood to be infantilising and antithetical to struggles for self-determination. Unpaid care work done by friends isn't a more socially or economically progressive alternative to paid care work but lives within economies of care presently in need of wage protection, wage increases and job security.

In CCA, as in many kinds of kinship networks, the question of two or more bodies in correspondence with one another – care receiver and caregiver – pushes access further afield from its traditionally understood legislative base of equality, anti-discrimination policy, and structural access, toward generative grounds of communal commitment, collective affinities, identities, labours and desires. Articulated and theorised as 'access' in addition to 'care', CCA lays bare the relationship between them. When care is access, access is made to be a communal effort and constitutive goal of personal and group care.

Relation

I did not participate in CCA but heard about it, read about it, witnessed it, admired it, and compared it to my own hotel room version of group-provided care. I think about it now.

Seeking regular care from places other than biological family, monogamous partner, government agency, or private business means reaching out to people beyond those with whom I live, beyond professional home health agencies. In my effort to meet people who might want to try this out with me, I sent a series of emails, Facebook messages, and listserv announcements describing my care needs to friends, acquaintances, and strangers, offering to compensate people helping me through an exchange of fifteen dollars an hour and/or work that I could provide in return. Seven friends replied, saying they would participate for free, and two people I didn't previously know also joined.

Collective care providers are connected to one another in ways unrelated to me. Also crucial to collective care's hybridity are the people I live with, who provide me with regular care and work my care needs into their daytime and evening schedules. My care is a collective endeavour insofar as seven people make the week's seven days, but we do not spend time all together; some participants have yet to meet each other. We haven't yet made decisions collectively. A number of participants work multiple care jobs; many people are in additional care collectives. For others, this group is the first time they've cared this way – as it is also the first time I have.

Across this spectrum of caring labour vibrates a charged interest in what possibilities exist or are created in the ways we relate to one another. The relational events we engage cross and recross divides of nakedness and coverage, emotional closeness and reticence, attention and bored inattention – manifesting as actions that look like embracing, making dinner, drinking alcohol, cutting hair, falling asleep, reading poems and essays, watching YouTube, massaging limbs, recounting stories. These activities ornament the basic goals of showering, changing into pyjamas, and getting into bed, and, for my friends, going home, often late at night. My own commitment to these relational modes scales time and space – from the shapes our bodies make during a lift and transfer to the alternative commitments we decline in order to meet at the same time and place.

Collective, then, is likely a misnomer, a pseudonym for something else finding its form, its routine and sway within sequential, differently shaped chains of day-to-day, one-on-one-on-two pairings. Care collective situates my care requirements centrally, around which additional needs, desires and force fields orbit and pull. As we gather, couple, and link ourselves to one another through particular movements and ways of being together, the ways in which we feel with one another, and the ways in which we feel one another, change each night of the week. Processes of unravelling and restabilising occur as we make ourselves vulnerable to one another while working to deliver our bodies safely from platform to platform, surface to surface. The strain of someone's body lifting mine; my body's strain in keeping myself upright; learning how we work our mutual instability together. I observe and am given this open materiality: I describe how I want my shirt to be lifted over my head and experience my care partner's translation of these directives into motion and pull. I say I will be home at 9:25 p.m., and I am late. Someone waits for me, or I wait for her.

Conviviality

A playing out of what adult peers do together notates this care. Conviviality, as a potential ground for group formation, expands collectivity's categorising, its distribution of skills and identifications assumed to be even, similar, self-contained, and consensus-based. Again thinking through Puar's essay 'Prognosis Time: Towards a Geopolitics of Affect, Debility, and Capacity', care based in dependency invites or, more specifically, requires inequivalence and asymmetry to produce uneven relations, events, and also the place from which I write: the squeeze. There is the squeeze, and there is the mandate. There is the loop of two arms anchored at my lower back, legs on either side or in between mine and a charged space, a space somatic but not exclusively sexualised, smooshed breasts and chests, arms that change with the days but come back within a week (and sometimes within an hour). And then there is what is compelling about something useful and something ordinary. To share something I can't make sense of: I write from the squeeze, but I also write from my anticipation of the squeeze, a readying. I write from its release too.

Care collective will change its current state and has already. It may disperse entirely or reproduce itself in other ways. Dispersal and dissolution are the promise of convivial relationality. As Puar writes, conviviality is open to its own 'disruption and alteration of the conditions of its own emergence such that it is no longer needed – an openness to something other than what we might have hoped for'.[4] This is true for the group as a whole, for participants' relationships with one another, and for my relationship with each person. In its togetherness, conviviality feels like a thesis – not a conclusion or even a proposition worked out, but an old definition of the same forcefully sonic word: a thesis as hands or feet keeping time. Not counting but counting down. 4, 3, 2, 1, hit it.

Postscript III
A version of this writing, intended as an essay and titled 'Sort of Like a Hug: Notes on Collectivity, Conviviality, and Care', was presented at the conference 'Cripples, Idiots, Lepers, and Freaks: Extraordinary Bodies / Extraordinary Minds' on Friday, 23 March 2012, at the Graduate Center of the City University of New York (CUNY) as part of the panel 'Cripping Community', moderated by Dr. Akemi Nishida. It was previously published in the *Happy Hypocrite*, no. 7, 'Heat Island' (2014), edited by Mason Leaver-Yap, and was translated into French by Noura Wedell and included in the exhibition *Juices* at Forde Geneva, curated by Maud Constantin, Tatiana Rihs and Ramaya Tegegne. A further edit of the text Mason and I worked on was shortened and reshaped here for the catalogue published alongside *Question the Wall Itself* curated by Fionn Meade and Jordan Carter for The Walker Art Center; in lots of ways this writing is mostly a postscript.

In other ways it is also an epilogue to future plans. Is a dream a plan? What if there were a building with apartments where residents both give and receive care; where everything about care that is invaluable is felt. Where entanglements occur, including those tangles that must become disentangled after some time. In thinking about this building as a place, this text is a placeholder as we continue to talk about (and plan for) what we want and need.

1   Jasbir Puar, 'Prognosis Time: Towards a Geopolitics of Affect, Debility, and Capacity', *Women and Performance: A Journal of Feminist Theory* 19 (July 2009) 168.

2   'Creating Collective Access: Practicing Crip Solidarity and Love', Creating Collective Access (http:// creatingcollectiveaccess.wordpress.com/).

3   Laura Hengehold, *The Body Problematic: Political Imagination in Kant and Foucault* (Pennsylvania: Pennsylvania State University Press, 2007) 300.

4   Puar, op. cit., 169.

Park McArthur, 'What is Collectivity, Conviviality, Care?', in *Question the Wall Itself* (exh. cat) (Minneapolis: Walker Art Center, 2017) 248–53.

Johanna Hedva
Sick Woman Theory//2016

[...] The Sick Woman is an identity and body that can belong to anyone denied the privileged existence – or the cruelly optimistic promise of such an existence – of the white, straight, healthy, neurotypical, upper and middle-class, cis- and able-bodied man who makes his home in a wealthy country, has never not had health insurance, and whose importance to society is everywhere recognised and made explicit by that society; whose importance and care dominates that society, at the expense of everyone else.

The Sick Woman is anyone who does not have this guarantee of care.

The Sick Woman is told that, to this society, her care, even her survival, does not matter.

The Sick Woman is all of the 'dysfunctional', 'dangerous' and 'in danger', 'badly behaved', 'crazy', 'incurable', 'traumatised', 'disordered', 'diseased', 'chronic', 'uninsurable', 'wretched', 'undesirable' and altogether 'dysfunctional' bodies belonging to women, people of colour, poor, ill, neuro-atypical, disabled, queer, trans, and genderfluid people, who have been historically pathologised, hospitalised, institutionalised, brutalised, rendered 'unmanageable', and therefore made culturally illegitimate and politically invisible.

The Sick Woman is a Black trans woman having panic attacks while using a public restroom, in fear of the violence awaiting her.

The Sick Woman is the child of parents whose indigenous histories have been erased, who suffers from the trauma of generations of colonisation and violence.

The Sick Woman is a homeless person, especially one with any kind of disease and no access to treatment, and whose only access to mental-health care is a 72-hour hold in the county hospital.

The Sick Woman is a mentally ill Black woman whose family called the police for help because she was suffering an episode, and who was murdered in police custody, and whose story was denied by everyone operating under white supremacy. Her name is Tanesha Anderson.

The Sick Woman is a 50-year-old gay man who was raped as a teenager and has remained silent and shamed, believing that men can't be raped.

The Sick Woman is a disabled person who couldn't go to the lecture on disability rights because it was held in a venue without accessibility.

The Sick Woman is a white woman with chronic illness rooted in sexual trauma who must take painkillers in order to get out of bed.

The Sick Woman is a straight man with depression who's been medicated (managed) since early adolescence and now struggles to work the 60 hours per week that his job demands.

The Sick Woman is someone diagnosed with a chronic illness, whose family and friends continually tell them they should exercise more.

The Sick Woman is a queer woman of colour whose activism, intellect, rage, and depression are seen by white society as unlikable attributes of her personality.

The Sick Woman is a Black man killed in police custody, and officially said to have severed his own spine. His name is Freddie Gray.

The Sick Woman is a veteran suffering from PTSD on the months-long waiting list to see a doctor at the VA.

The Sick Woman is a single mother, emigrated, without documents, to the 'land of the free', shuffling between three jobs in order to feed her family, and finding it harder and harder to breathe.

The Sick Woman is the refugee.

The Sick Woman is the abused child.

The Sick Woman is the person with autism whom the world is trying to 'cure'.

The Sick Woman is the starving.

The Sick Woman is the dying.

And, crucially: The Sick Woman is who capitalism needs to perpetuate itself.

Why?

Because to stay alive, capitalism cannot be responsible for our care – its logic of exploitation requires that some of us die.

'Sickness' as we speak of it today is a capitalist construct, as is its perceived binary opposite, 'wellness'. The 'well' person is the person well enough to go to work. The 'sick' person is the one who can't. What is so destructive about conceiving of wellness as the default, as the standard mode of existence, is that it *invents illness as temporary*. When being sick is an abhorrence to the norm, *it allows us to conceive of care and support in the same way*.

Care, in this configuration, is only required sometimes. When sickness is temporary, care is not normal

Here's an exercise: go to the mirror, look yourself in the face, and say out loud: 'To take care of you is not normal. I can only do it temporarily.'

Saying this to yourself will merely be an echo of what the world repeats all the time.

I used to think that the most anti-capitalist gestures left had to do with love, particularly love poetry: to write a love poem and give it to the one you desired, seemed to me a radical resistance. But now I see I was wrong.

The most anti-capitalist protest is to care for another and to care for yourself. To take on the historically feminised and therefore invisible practice of nursing, nurturing, caring. To take seriously each other's vulnerability and fragility and precarity, and to support it, honor it, empower it. To protect each other, to enact and practice community. A radical kinship, an interdependent sociality, a politics of care.

Because, once we are all ill and confined to the bed, sharing our stories of therapies and comforts, forming support groups, bearing witness to each other's tales of trauma, prioritising the care and love of our sick, pained, expensive, sensitive, fantastic bodies, and there is no one left to go to work, perhaps then, finally, capitalism will screech to its much-needed, long-overdue, and motherfucking glorious halt.

Johanna Hedva, extract from 'Sick Woman Theory', *Mask Magazine*, no. 24, eds. Hanna Hurr & Ripley Soprano (January 2016) (www.maskmagazine.com/not-again/struggle/sick-woman-theory).

Mujeres Creando
In Conversation with Max Jorge Hinderer Cruz and Pablo Lafuente//2018

Mujeres Creando is a collective formed in 1992 in La Paz, Bolivia. It operates in several fields – from provision of legal aid and social programmes to radio broadcasting and artistic-political interventions – always with an activist approach and from an anarcho-feminist perspective. This conversation took place on 20 and 21 March 2018 in La Paz, with three members of Mujeres Creando: Danitza Luna, María Galindo and Yolanda Mamani, at La Virgen de los Deseos (Our Lady of Desires), the house from which Mujeres Creando operate in La Paz.[1]

The House
Danitza Luna   La Virgen de los Deseos is the heart, the refuge, the place of rest for Mujeres Creando. It's also its political centre. Many debates happen here, and we try to encourage people to circulate, discuss and think. Many people have taken refuge here.[2] Here, there is a feeling that, 'I can say what I think and

nobody will stop me from doing so.'

Yolanda Mamani   For me the house is a space for learning, a space for freedom. When some of us – domestic workers – first arrived, we didn't know how to use computers, but we have experimented and explored with the available machines and the internet. It's also a place to meet comrades, to discuss thoughts and to exchange ideas, where you feel free but also accompanied, because you're not alone. That's the nice thing about being in the house, having comrades who will be with you at all times.

Luna   Sometimes you have to go to the outside world, which might be shitty. When you return you remember why you do what you do. Today I was thinking this after returning from a debate at the art school in El Alto.[3] Coming back here is an ideological and affective recharge – then I can go out and fight again. For me it's life, like breathing.

María Galindo   The house must be around 13 years old. If we were in the sixteenth century it'd be a convent, where we'd take refuge to escape a very cruel world. But it could also be a quilombo, created by those who escaped from slave plantations. In Bolivia there are many social movements, and I have always wondered what a social movement is. For me it's a language you write, but also a practice of everyday life. It can't just be a set of demands addressed to the state; it must have its own life, an autonomy from the state and its apparatuses, from the parties. A social movement is the capacity to construct a language, a theory, a proposal – to develop a set of political practices, but also a set of daily life practices. A social movement without daily life is weak. Its strength comes from the ability to create a solid daily fabric. The house is the proof of this. I can say that I'm autonomous, and you may or may not believe me. But the house is the proof that this is possible.

One of the things that happens in the house and creates this daily life is Radio Deseo (Radio Desire). It wasn't our initial idea, but Mario Castro's, a famous radio journalist who, in his old age, called me to say we had to have a radio station. 'We don't have money or time', I replied. But he said 'everything you do is important, and the radio is a speaker for people to hear what you do. I'll help you find the money and teach you everything'. Because we knew nothing. 'This is a microphone, if you hold it you can't shout.' And I continue to shout. We paid for the radio, but not for his idea, for his generosity.

Max Jorge Hinderer Cruz   I'd like to make a small list of all the things that have taken place in the house since it opened. Would you like to? There is the crèche, the café and the restaurant...

Luna   The café and the restaurant with affordable prices...

Galindo   Café, restaurant, library, photocopier and office materials, also a grocery and affordable pharmacy. There was a moment of extreme crisis in the country during the first half of the 2000s, and one of the members began to gather medicine and distribute it for free. We also sold food at cost price, at a time of hunger and general lack of food, before the arrival of Evo Morales.[4]

Another thing that happens in the house is Mujeres en Busca de Justicia (Women in Search of Justice), a legal advisory service that deals with cases of male violence against women, from fathers not fulfilling their legal obligations of care to gender-based violence. We have created a sort of court where we summon the man to speak, while women remain mostly silent. When he lowers his guard and signs an agreement, we take it to an official court and have it legally sanctioned, in case he changes his mind. The legal service continues today, the pharmacy and grocery don't.

It's great that Danitza and Yola are able to say how they feel about the house, as it existed before they joined Mujeres Creando. Each of the new members has changed the house so much.

A Bit of History

Hinderer Cruz   Could we map the generations of Mujeres Creando? When did the movement begin?

Galindo   It began in 1992. We were three women. It had a rough start here in La Paz because we were aware that in Bolivia neoliberalism had achieved social consensus since its arrival in 1985. It was the peak in a period in which women were being used as cushions to absorb the effects of neoliberalism, working for almost no money and fighting for the subsistence of their families. Men were more politicised, perhaps because of their contact with the workers' movement. The neoliberal trope of instrumentalising women in gender empowerment propaganda also appeared then. We came into the picture questioning the role that was assigned to women. We also find our origins in the critique of the party, Che Guevara and missionary model of traditional leftism that thinks it knows what the people need. We started the movement on our own, isolated – also because of homophobia, as I've been out as a lesbian all my life. Since then, there have been many different moments; we are talking about twenty-six or twenty-seven years.

Hinderer Cruz   How is this history evidenced in the life of the city, in its politics?

Galindo   We have worked a lot with graffiti, in four Bolivian cities – La Paz, Santa Cruz de la Sierra, Cochabamba and Oruro. Now graffiti is a common communication tool, but in those days it was unusual. We also had a grocery at the periphery of La Paz, and built seventy greenhouses in Villa Fátima and Las Delicias. We made natural drinks as food supplements and traditional remedies.

Pablo Lafuente   So already from the beginning you combined pedagogical and social intervention activity with activist propaganda, in the form of graffiti.

Galinda   We never considered graffiti to be propaganda. Another action we always engaged in was to make the life of NGOs impossible, as we did at the last 8 March (International Women's Day). It was fun to go to their events and do awful things, eat all the food, act like a plague. We very much enjoyed this, it was like a pastime, but it became almost like a legend. […]

Galindo   It was the La Paz 'art week', so there were a lot of female artists in the room, and none of them expressed solidarity with us, because the bourgeois notion of art in Bolivia is too strong. 'Art gives you prestige, art is for the elites, art is for the cultured.' In truth, it was very funny. I think that is a very important element, joy, because if your daily life is the activist struggle, this struggle needs to give pleasure, because otherwise it's unsustainable. This also means turning the notion of immolation, of struggle as sacrifice, as a final goal that you never reach, upside down.

Hinderer Cruz   That is, precisely, a sentence printed on one of the T-shirts you made. What does it say, exactly?

Luna   'Nuestra venganza es ser felices' ('Our revenge is being happy').

Artists and Non-Artists
Hinderer Cruz   I'd like to ask, Yolanda, how you, who don't participate directly in the artistic projects, see the artistic work within the movement. What relevance does it have for you?

Mamani   I think art is a good way to reach people, especially because Mujeres Creando practises street art. I work more on the radio, and when I do the interviews they ask if it's 'Radio Deseo, of the crazy women'. Some people have a lot of respect for Mujeres Creando because of all those actions, not only as art but also the direct actions with Mujeres en Busca de Justicia. Even though we sometimes create discomfort, they know us, they know we are confrontational, that we won't be shut down. If it was made for enclosed spaces, in the south zone, women like me wouldn't have the chance to see it.[5] I think it's good to take art out of the museum, so people who are passing by see it and try to understand it. [...]

Luna   I don't claim the position of the artist; it's a position that doesn't give me anything, I'm not interested in it. The term 'art' is so broad, so undefinable, so light and so heavy at the same time. As a political movement I don't think we are interested in being part of that context.

Lafuente   Could we say that the radio and the projects developed for the art system are parallel communication tools, with different languages, that communicate the same series of ideas and narratives in different places and to different groups? [...]

Galindo   We have a single rule for the radio: nobody can speak in the third person. So, for example, if a group of students proposes to do a programme on prostitution, they can't unless they work as prostitutes. In the case of domestic workers it was also very clear, because in Bolivia there is a habit of class domination and colonising the words of others. The other never speaks for herself – you say what they feel, think. Radio Deseo, from its small scale, is trying to break with this.

Luna   Women's personalities in this part of the world are very quiet, but it's not a submissive silence, it's a silence that carries a lot of pain and impotence, and learning this within the movement is important. It's like a school, something that is built internally, extremely powerful and fertile.

Mamani   Experts are used to talking about domestic work or indigenous women or indigenous people. The media, almost always, have victimised domestic workers, or take the time to call us thieves or unprofessional. We used to also victimise ourselves. It was the easiest thing to do. But we began talking about what we'd like to say, the things that are news for us. Now, when they invite me to universities to talk about my work, the students sometimes ask me how I improved my voice, if I have a 'radio voice'. I don't, I have the voice that I have. The important thing is to know how to communicate, to say what you feel and think, and for that it is not necessary to have a beautiful voice; you need to be willing to denounce injustices.

Lafuente   It's a similar strategy to that used in *Espacio para abortar* (Space for Abortion),[6] a project that functioned in an artistic context, in which abortion is discussed...

Galindo   ...in the first person...

Lafuente   ...from the body, in the voice of women who went through that experience.

Galindo   For us the word delivered in the first person is a political, philosophical premise. And women are the first to say, 'I don't have anything to say', as we've been silenced. The extreme case of speaking in the first person in Radio Deseo is the programme on femicides, because the daughter of Helen Álvarez, the host, was murdered. Every Monday since her death she talks about femicides: her voice breaks, and she continues to speak. It is fascinating to hear a woman who knows femicide so closely and with such coherence talking about it. It moves, a lot. It moves consciousness.

Hinderer Cruz   Mujeres Creando includes in her name the notion of creation. We can say the creative act relates to aesthetic experience, but also to the creation of simple, material things, with a social or communitarian basis. One of the things I was most impressed by, when I visited La Virgen de los Deseos in 2005, was the night crèche, something I had never seen in feminist centres before. I believe what is shared by artistic production and the grassroots work is creation. Creation of a way to express yourself.

Lafuente   ...and to intervene... […]

Feminisms Against the State

Galindo   Mujeres Creando has no mandate, no goals, no objectives. It is important that it doesn't become a missionary endeavour. If one day a group of women from rural contexts want to connect with us and work on rural contexts, we would respect that, but it hasn't happened. Everything we address is in relation to the street and the city as political scenarios. We are not working with rural collectives, even though many of the comrades who come to the city from that context bring in much information, much anguish that results from leaving behind a logic where it is very difficult to act, to transgress or to rebel. […]

Mamani   In this sense, I very much like the Encuentro de Mujeres Trabajadoras (Meeting of Working Women) we organise every year, a two day meeting with workshops. When I was part of the union, I did workshops on labour rights or the topics that worried us at the time, but now I'm running a workshop on how to be a *chola*, even questioning our being *cholas*, our own identity. I'm tired of intellectuals who use so many words that you don't understand, and speak from a desk, in a way that is so different from speaking from your own being.

Hinderer Cruz Mujeres Creando thinks of itself as an anarchist movement, an anarcho-feminist movement. Bolivia has a strong anarchist tradition, related to industrial and mining proletariat and to Aymara originary organisations. Since 2006 we have a government that claims to be from the Left. Why is anarchism important in Bolivian politics today?

Lafuente Or to put it another way: did that political change in 2006 imply changes in Mujeres Creando too? As you mentioned, Mujeres Creando is created in response to a neoliberal context, but there was a regime change then.

Galindo I'd say it's not true that Bolivia passed from a neoliberal to a post-neoliberal regime. The neoliberal regime is as strong as it used to be, even stronger, as it has an ideological camouflage as leftist and indigenous. It's a neoliberal *extractivist* national regime that co-opts social movement leadership and employs mafia dynamics. Women are a sexual trophy, a projection of the macho power of the leader. We are one of the few resistance movements, even if it might sound arrogant. Our anarchist approach makes sense as a way to avoid being bought, to avoid being seen as an extension of the state.

It's important to also consider that the state apparatus in Bolivia is small, it doesn't give access to healthcare, education or a functioning administration. In a regime like this, being anarchist makes a lot of sense, for example, supporting the 'informal economy', which generates a subsistence network run by women without which Bolivia wouldn't work. [...]

1   We, Max and Pablo, have previously worked with Mujeres Creando in various contexts; for example, as curators in: 'The Potosí Principle: How Can We Sing the Songs of the Lord in an Alien Land?', Museo Nacional de Arte Reina Sofía, Madrid, 2010; Haus der Kulturen der Welt, Berlin, 2010; Museo Nacional de Arte and Museo Nacional de Etnografía y Folklore, La Paz, 2011; and 'How to (...) Things that Don't Exist', 31st Bienal de São Paulo, 2014.

2   Translator's note: the pronoun 'nosotras' (the feminine 'we') is pervasive among responses from Mujeres Creando members. This is unusual as Spanish, unlike English, does not allow for the subject to be easily omitted.

3   El Alto is a city contiguous with La Paz.

4   Evo Morales was elected president of Bolivia in 2005 and assumed office in 2006, after massive popular and social movement mobilisations that lasted from 1999–2005.

5   The southern part of La Paz, 'Zona Sur', is known for its wealthy, exclusive neighbourhoods and commercial and financial areas.

6   *Espacio para abortar* (Space for Abortion) is a project presented in the 31st Bienal de São Paulo. It consisted of light cylindrical structures, conceived as 'uteruses', in which visitors could listen to accounts of women who had had an abortion, a practice that is illegal in Brazil. The women were convoked through a contact process with women's organisations in the centre and at the periphery of São Paulo.

Mujeres Creando, extracts from 'To the Last Consequences: Mujeres Creando in Conversation with Max Jorge Hinderer Cruz and Pablo Lafuente', *Afterall*, issue 46 (Autumn/Winter 2018) 54–65.

Sarah Sharma, Lynx Sainte-Marie and Lauren Fournier
Antinomies of Self-Care//2017

Selfie-Care and the Uncommons
Sarah Sharma

Self-care is a strategy of survival, 'an act of political warfare' for bodies neglected and worn down by the intersecting nodes of capitalism, patriarchy and white supremacy.[1] Self-care is distinct from the *selfie-care* found in glossy, neoliberal, post-feminist magazines, where women are instructed to recharge in order to re-enter currents of patriarchy/capitalism/white supremacy. The self *taking care of itself* has become a photo op, one that too often parades the individual as the most important unit in political struggle. This co-opting of the radical necessity of self-care speaks to neoliberal feminism's ignorance of how gender is mutually raced and classed. Neoliberal feminism is a privileged by-stander often complicit with the regime of violence that leaves so many uncared for.

The self-care/selfie-care political spectrum is easy to plot. #Selfiecare is a photo of a pair of feet floating in a pool of sudsy water being worked on by the repetitive motions of the manicurist at the nail factory. On the other end of the spectrum you might find people engaged in communal forms of reproductive labour so others can eat, sleep and rest. Care in the commons is not so digitally noteworthy – this is a type of care that the medium cannot capture and quickly brandish via a hashtag. Selfie-care comes by way of online self-diagnostic quizzes, clickbait lists and BuzzFeed tips. Selfie-care lists things one must do: Dance, Eat, Breathe, Hydrate, Touch a Tree, Send a Nice Email.

I suspect those things take on extra special significance in contemporary culture because they can't be taken care of by a technological device or through the labour of another. Selfie-care makes the commons not only a regime of productivity and efficiency, but also one of overdetermined scarcity. The left is not immune from selfie-care. The list, like the selfie, reorients self-care away from an act of refusal toward a momentary retreat, supposedly excusable in this moment of Trump. Self-care becomes a lifestyle choice for a productive, healthful life, whether you are an activist or a capitalist. Sadly, there is no #selfcare list that says: get high, call in sick, watch Netfix all day, punch a bigot or a Nazi, and then enjoy a loaf of bread. Ultimately, #whocares if it's a kale smoothie or loaf of bread – that's a matter of #selfiecare.

The radical potential of self-care is impeded by the need to document it, publicise it, enclose it in a list. Unlike selfie-care, self-care isn't about the private domain of the self, but about the maintenance of the conditions of possibility for people to be cared for in common.

The Endless Possibilities of Our Limitations[2]
Lynx Sainte-Marie

I've spent the last several years presenting, performing, facilitating, lecturing and consulting in spaces all over this colonised land commonly known as Canada. Recently, my focus has been healing justice and disability justice, challenging individuals and organisations to move away from *self care* as an absolute rule – where the onus of care is on the individual – towards a *community care* practice and politic. Healing justice takes much of its teachings from disability justice, borne of sick and disabled, queer, trans, gender non-conforming, Black, Indigenous, People of Colour (BIPOC) communities who prioritise the bodies, leadership and genius of the most marginalized.[3] Both of these intersectionality-centred frameworks – disability justice and healing justice – ask questions like: How can we move towards liberation together? Are we not only giving, but also asking our communities for what we need, and holding them accountable? Communities that heal together resist better together. And sustainability is key. The imperialist white supremacist capitalist cishetereopatriarchy knows it runs more efficiently when we're separated, outnumbered and alone.

What oppressive systems teach us about the kind of support we should value is poisonous and insidious. It means that people are reluctant to see the everyday, practical things they do as care work. As if, like building muscle, when you're not wincing from the tearing of tissue, you're probably not doing it right. Disabled activists who organise online feel the brunt of these ableist narratives every day, even though our arthritic fingers hurt with every hashtag. BIPOC care workers and cultural workers, particularly those of us with multiple intersections of oppression, are paid less than our white/white-passing/lighter-skinned peers, and are often asked to work for free, or not asked at all. Many of us struggle to take care of ourselves, while those of us with more privilege and resources are taught that the people we should be supporting are out there somewhere. So, we volunteer at crisis lines four hours a week, while the emotional labour we engage in with loved ones is scarce. We work with disabled youth, yet the struggles of our chronically ill friends go unnoticed. Couple this with all the self-care we should be doing, but aren't, because the world needs saving, and it's no wonder so many of us deal with burn-out and compassion fatigue.

But the ways we can and do take care of ourselves and of each other, with whatever we have at our disposal, are valuable. Now, when I think about the care I want to cultivate with others, I think of the range of things we are able to do for ourselves with the support of our folks. I think about celebrating our self-determination and striving for interdependency. I think about the time they moved carefully beside me down the street, without questions and accusations, watching me as I cautiously took my first neighbourhood walk in a year. And the crowdfunder that he, she and they created on my behalf for the medical device I use for my pain. Or when we promised to check in with one another and spoke about boundary-setting as intentional pathways to each other's hearts. I think about the capacity I have as a sick and disabled person, and how the Medical Industrial Complex describes my capacity as 'limited'. But, when we centre disability, our limitations become endless care strategies and possibilities. We're powerful on our own, no doubt, but all of us working together – as multi-issue people with complex bodies, histories, relationships to this land, and stories, holding our most marginalised while still getting the care that we need – this is the kind of care that, I believe, will set us free.

Sustaining Our Selves, Collectively
Lauren Fournier

Self-care is ambivalent. On the one hand, *care of the self* has been reclaimed by intersectional feminists as a politicised act of autonomy by which those whose lives have been rendered precarious uphold the value of their lives: in hostile circumstances, survival becomes resistance. Johanna Hedva articulates an ethos of agency for those living with chronic illness[4], while Audre Lorde and Sara Ahmed champion 'self-care as warfare', emphasising how taking care of the self, particularly when that self is marginalised, is necessary for sustaining resistance to social, political and economic structures that work against us.[5]

On the other hand, to *take care of the self* is a neoliberal imperative that has been criticised for removing responsibility from the state, displacing the onus to the individual. Think, for example, of debates about publicly funded health care and privatisation, where right-wing politicians frame questions of 'access' to healthcare in terms of 'customers' and the right to purchase, rather than in terms of citizen rights.

Alert to how capitalism swallows resistance movements with such ease, or at least tries to, we must approach 'self-care' critically, especially in light of the current context of neoliberal capitalism, with its privileging of the individual *self* above all else.

In my curatorial project 'Self Care for Skeptics' (2015), artists, writers and activists troubled self-care through intersectional feminist, queer and BIPOC frameworks. Some contributors acknowledged the desirability of self-care practices – it's important to look good and feel good, for example – even as they critiqued the patriarchal, neoliberal, capitalist and ableist ideologies that scaffold the notion of self-care. Others moved away from self-care and embraced new conceptions of collectivity, opting for an ethics of collaborative care that places renewed emphasis on community.

In 'The Sustenance Rite' exhibition, which is part of 'Take Care', artists engage the space of health and care – both individual and collective – from positionalities grounded in experiences of oppression and stigmatisation, mental health issues, physical illness and mourning and grief. The artists' projects unhinge dominant conceptions of health and illness, making room for more expansive conceptions of what it means to be well. Reflecting on the rites and rights of mental and physical healthcare in the contemporary moment, The Sustenance Rite makes space for rituals that sustain us.

1   Audre Lorde, *A Burst of Light: Essays* (Ann Arbor: Firebrand Books, 1988).

2   This is a revised excerpt of the article 'Can The Work Heal Us', published in the Disability Justice issue of *The Peak Magazine* 56, no. 4 (2017).

3   I owe so much of my current knowledge of disability justice and healing justice to the wisdom and genius of Black, Indigenous, women, femmes and non-binary people of colour I've encountered URL and IRL, including but not limited to Spectra Speaks, Esther Armah, adrienne maree brown, Yashna Maya Padamsee, Mia Mingus, Ciel Sainte-Marie, melannie monoceros, Jassie Justice and Danielle Stevens. May our brilliance always light the way through the darkness.

4   Johanna Hedva, 'Sick Woman Theory', *Mask Magazine* (January 2016) (http://maskmagazine. com/not-again/struggle/sick-woman-theory).

5   *A Burst of Light*, op. cit.; Sarah Ahmed, 'Selfcare as Warfare', feministkilljoys (25 August 2014) (https://feministkilljoys.com/2014/08/25/selfcare-as-warfare).

Lauren Fournier, Lynx Sainte Marie and Sarah Sharma, 'Antinomies of Self-Care', *The Blackwood*, issue 1 – 'Take Care' (July 2017) 14–15.

Maria Puig de la Bellacasa
Thinking with Care//2017

> Reality is an active verb.
> – Donna Haraway, *The Companion Species Manifesto*

> Corrosive scepticism cannot be midwife to new stories.
> – Donna Haraway, 'In the Beginning Was the Word'

The epigraphs above disclose that this text unfolds as an intimate reading of Donna Haraway's relational ontology, where 'beings do not pre-exist their relatings', as a way of exploring how styles of thinking and writing technologies can contribute to relations of care in moving worlds. It is more particularly Haraway's take on the situatedness of knowledge[1] that I read speculatively as a way of thinking with care. That knowledge is situated means that knowing and thinking are inconceivable without the multitude of relations that make possible the worlds we think with. The premise from which I begin this chapter is thus quite simple: relations of thinking and knowing require care and affect how we care. In tune with a non-normative approach to care as a speculative ethics, the grounds of this premise are ontological rather than moral or epistemological: not only relations involve care, care is relational per se.

Caring and relating share ontological resonance. Again, Tronto's generic definition of care says this well: care includes *'everything that we do* to maintain, continue and repair "our world" [...] which we seek to *interweave in a complex, life sustaining web'.*[2] This vision of caring presupposes heterogeneity as the ontological ground on which everything humans relate with exists: myriad doings – everything we do – and of ontological entities that compose a world – selves, bodies, environment. It speaks of care as a manifold range of *doings* needed to create, hold together, and sustain life and continue its diverseness. This also means that an understanding of human agencies as immersed in worlds made of heterogeneous but interdependent forms and processes of life and matter, to or not to care about/for something/somebody, inevitably does and undoes relation. Its ontological import gives to care the peculiar significance of being a non-normative necessity. Feminist ethics of care argue that to value care is to recognise the inevitable interdependency essential to the existence of reliant and vulnerable beings.[3] Interdependency is not a contract, nor a moral ideal – it is a *condition*. Care is therefore concomitant to the continuation of life for many living beings in more than human entanglements – not forced upon them by a moral order, and not necessarily a rewarding obligation.

Of course, not all relations are caring, but very few could subsist without some care. Even when caring is not assured by the people/things that are perceptibly involved in a specific form of relating, in order for them to merely subsist somebody/something has (had) to be taking care somewhere or sometime. Even neglect, the biocidal absence of care, reveals it as inescapable: when care is removed, we can perceive the effects of carelessness. But if care is necessary, it is not given. Speaking of care as (non-moralistic) *obligation* denaturalises care – for life to even be, it needs to be fostered in some way. That it requires *doing* something indicates not only that it is in its very nature to be about labours of mundane maintenance and repair that require agency (though, as I will argue later in this book, not necessarily intention) but that a more than human world's degree of liveability – degree of 'as well as possible' living – might well depend on the caring it manages to realise. Standing by the vital necessity of care means standing for sustainable and flourishing relations, not merely survivalist or instrumental ones. Continuing to hold together a triptych vision of care doings-practice/affectivity/ethics- politics helps to resist to ground care as an ethico-affective everyday doing that is vital to engage with the inescapable troubles of interdependent existences.

Haraway's relational ontology has been an inspiration for this journey into care[4] before the theme of care appeared explicitly in her work. First, because for Haraway knowledge and science are relational practices with important material consequences in the shaping of possible worlds. My claim that care matters in knowledge politics – as contributing to the mattering of worlds – is sustained by Haraway's call to pay attention to the workings and consequences of our 'semiotic technologies' – that is, to practices and arts of fabricating meaning with signs, words, ideas, descriptions, theories.[5] Following Katie King in recognising the force of literary apparatuses, Haraway showed us how 'bodies' as objects of knowledge are also 'material-semiotic generative nodes'.[6] Another important source of inspiration are her situated politics of resistance to normativity, both moral and epistemological. These notions are particularly crucial for thinking that intervenes in the more than human worlds of technoscience and naturecultures, with their broken boundaries and imploded worlds where knowledge and ontology collapse. Reading Haraway speculatively is an inspiration for thinking with care in its transformative, non-innocent, disruptive ways. [...]

1   Donna J. Haraway, 'Situated Knowledges: The Science Question in Feminism and the Privilege of Partial Perspective', in *Simians, Cyborgs, and Women* (New York: Routledge, 1991) 183–201; Donna J.

Haraway, *Modest_Witness@Second_Millennium. FemaleMan©_Meets_Onco-MouseTM: Feminism and Technoscience* (New York: Routledge, 1997).

2   Joan C. Tronto, *Moral Boundaries: A Political Argument for an Ethic of Care* (New York: Routledge, 1993) 103 [emphasis added].

3   Eva Feder Kittay & Ellen K. Feder, *The Subject of Care: Feminist Perspectives on Dependency* (Lanham: Rowman & Littlefield, 2002); Daniel Engster, 'Rethinking Care Theory: The Practice of Caring and the Obligation to Care', *Hypatia: A Journal of Feminist Philosophy* 20, no. 3 (2005) 50–74.

4   Maria Puig de la Bellacasa, 'Think We Must: Feminist Politics and the Construction of Knowledge', PhD diss., Department of Philosophy, Université Libre de Bruxelles (2004); Maria Puig de la Bellacasa, *Les savoirs situés de Sandra Harding et Donna Haraway: Science et épistémologies féministes* (Paris: L'Harmattan, 2014).

5   'Situated Knowledges: The Science Question in Feminism and the Privilege of Partial Perspective', op. cit., 187.

6   Ibid., 200.

Maria Puig de la Bellacasa, extract from 'Thinking with Care', in *Matters of Care: Speculative Ethics in More than Human Worlds* (Minneapolis: University of Minnesota Press, 2017) 69–71.

DISABILITY
IS
STRUCTURALLY
REINFORCED
BY
ABLEISM

ON CRIPPING

Eli Clare
Stones in my Pockets, Stones in my Heart//2009

Gender reaches into disability; disability wraps around class; class strains against abuse; abuse snarls into sexuality; sexuality folds on top of race... everything finally piling into a single human body. To write about any aspect of identity, any aspect of the body, means writing about this entire maze. This I know, and yet the question remains: where to start? Maybe with my white skin, stubbly red hair, left ear pierced, shoulders set slightly off centre, left riding higher than right, hands tremoring, traced with veins, legs well-muscled. Or with me in the mirror, dressing to go out, knotting my tie, slipping into my blazer, curve of hip and breast vanishing beneath my clothes. Or possibly with the memory of how my body felt swimming in the river, chinook fingerlings nibbling at my toes. There are a million ways to start, but how do I reach beneath the skin? [...]

Our bodies are not merely blank slates upon which the powers that be write their lessons. We cannot ignore the body itself: the sensory, mostly non-verbal experience of our hearts and lungs, muscles and tendons, telling us and the world who we are. My childhood sense of being neither girl nor boy arose in part from the external lessons of abuse and neglect, from the confusing messages about masculinity and femininity that I could not comprehend; I would be a fool to claim otherwise. But just as certainly, there was a knowing that resided in my bones, in the stretch of my legs and arch of my back, in the stones lying against my skin, a knowing that whispered, 'not girl, not boy'. Butch, nellie, studly, femme, king, androgynous, queen: how have we negotiated the lies and thievery, the ways gender is influenced by divisions of labour, by images of masculinity and femininity, by racism, sexism, classism, ableism, by the notions of 'real' men and 'real' women? And how, at the same time, have we listened to our own bodies? For me the answer is not simple.

I think about my disabled body. For too long, I hated my trembling hands, my precarious balance, my spastic muscles so repeatedly overtaken by tension and tremor, tried to hide them at all costs. More than once I wished to amputate my right arm so it wouldn't shake. My shame was that bald. All the lies contained in the words *retard, monkey, defect*; in the gawking, the pats on my head, and the tears cried on my shoulder; in the moments where I became someone's supercrip or tragedy: all those lies became my second skin.

I think about my disabled body, how as a teenager I escaped the endless pressure to have a boyfriend, to shave my legs, to wear make-up. The same lies that cast me as genderless, asexual and undesirable also framed a space in which

I was left alone to be my quiet, bookish, tomboy self, neither girl nor boy. Even then, I was grateful. But listen, if I had wanted to date boys, wear lipstick and mascara, play with feminine clothes – the silk skirt and pumps, the low-cut blouse, the outrageous prom dress – I would have had to struggle much longer and harder than my non-disabled counterparts. The sheer physical acts of shaving my legs and putting on make-up would have been hard enough. Harder still would have been the relentless arguing with my parents, resisting their image of me as asexual or vulnerable to assault, persuading them that I could in truth take care of myself at the movies with Brent Miller or Dave Wilson.[1] But in truth I didn't want to date Brent or wear the low-cut blouse. I shuddered at the thought. How would I have reacted to the gendered pressures my younger, non-disabled sister faced? For her the path of least resistance pointed in the direction of femininity; for me it led toward not-girl-not-boy. But to cast my abiding sense of gendered self simply as a reaction to ableism is to ignore my body and what it had to tell me. When I look around me in disability community, I see an amazing range of gender expression, running the gamut from feminine to androgynous to masculine, mixed and swirled in many patterns. Clearly we respond in a myriad of ways to the ableist construction of gender.

How do we negotiate the lies and listen to our bodies? I think about my disabled body, my queer butch body read as a teenage boy. The markers of masculinity – my shaved head and broad stance, direct gaze and muscled arms – are unmistakable. And so are the markers of disability – my heavy-heeled gait; my halting, uneven speech; the tremors in my hands, arms, and shoulders. They all twine together to shape me in the ableist world as either genderless or a teenage boy. The first is all too familiar to disabled people. The second arises from the gender binary, where if I am not recognised as a woman, then I am presumed to be a man or more likely, given my lack of height and facial hair, a teenage boy. These external perceptions match in large part my internal sense of gender, my bodily comfort with gender ambiguity. But if the external and internal didn't match, what then?

Once I sat in a writing workshop with heterosexual, feminine, disabled women, and we talked for an entire afternoon about gender identity, precisely because of the damage inflicted when the external ableist perceptions don't match the internal sense of self. All too often, the thieves plant their lies, and our bodies absorb them as the only truth. Is it any surprise that sometimes my heart fills with small grey stones, which never warm to my body heat?

The work of thieves: certainly external perception, stereotypes, lies, false images, and oppression hold a tremendous amount of power. They define and create who we are, how we think of our bodies, our gendered selves. How do I write not about the stones, but the body that warms them, the heat itself? That question haunts me because I lived by splitting body from mind, body from consciousness, body from physical sensation, body from emotion as the bullies threw rocks and called *retard*, as my father and his buddies tied me down, pulled out their knives. My body became an empty house, one to which I seldom returned. I lived in exile; the stones rattling in my heart, resting in my pockets, were my one and only true body.

But just as the stolen body exists, so does the reclaimed body. I think of disabled people challenging the conception of a 'perfect' body/mind. Ed Roberts sits out front of his house talking about crip liberation. Ellen Stohl shapes herself into a sex symbol for the disability community. I think of queer people pushing upon the dominant culture's containment of gender, pleasure and sex. Drag queens and kings work the stage. Dykes take to the streets. Gay men defend public sex. Trans people of all varieties say, 'This is how we can be men, women, how we can inhabit all the spaces in between.' Radical faeries swirl in their pagan finery. Bisexual people resist a neat compartmentalising of sexuality. I think of people of colour, poor people, working class people all thumbing their noses at the notion of assimilation. Over and over again, we take the lies and crumble them into dust.

But how do I write about my body reclaimed, full of pride and pleasure? It is easy to say that abuse, ableism, transphobia and homophobia stole my body away, broke my desire, removed me from my pleasure in the stones warm against my skin, the damp sponginess of moss growing on a rotten log, the taste of spring water dripping out of rock. Harder to express how that break becomes healed, a bone once fractured, now whole, but different from the bone never broken. And harder still to follow the path between the two. How do I mark this place where my body is no longer an empty house, desire whistling lonely through the cracks, but not yet a house fully lived in? For me the path from stolen body to reclaimed body started with my coming out as a dyke. [...]

I want to take the stone between my tremoring hands – trembling with CP, with desire, with the last remnants of fear, trembling because this is how my body moves – and warm it gentle, but not, as I have always done before, ride roughshod over it. I want to enter as a not-girl-not-boy transgender butch – gendered differently than when I first came out, thinking simply, 'This is how I'll be a woman', never imagining there might be a day when the word *woman* was too small; differently from the tomboy who wanted to be a hermit; but still connected to both. Enter with my pockets and heart half-full of stone. Enter knowing that the muscled grip of desire is a wild, half-grown horse, ready to bolt but too curious to stay away.

In the end, I will sit on the wide, flat top of my wall, legs dangling over those big, uncrackable stones, weathered smooth and clean. Sit with butch women, femme dykes, nellie men, studly fags, radical faeries, drag queens and kings, transsexual people who want nothing more than to be women and men, intersex people, transgender people, pangendered, bigendered, polygendered, ungendered, androgynous people of many varieties and trade stories long into the night. Laugh and cry and tell stories. Sad stories about bodies stolen, bodies no longer here. Enraging stories about false images, devastating lies, untold violence. Bold, brash stories about reclaiming our bodies and changing the world. [...]

1   [Footnote 2 in source] I now recognise the disturbing irony of this, given the ways in which my father was sexually abusing me.

Eli Clare, extracts from 'Stones in My Pocket, Stones in My Heart', in *Exile and Pride: Disability, Queerness and Liberation* (Durham, NC and London: Duke University Press, 2009) 143, 150–53, 160.

Carolyn Lazard
Accessibility in the Arts: A Promise and a Practice//2019

PART I: WHY ACCESSIBILITY?

PART II: ACCOMODATIONS
American Sign Language Interpretation
Audio Description
Communication Access
Real-Time Translation (CART)
Chemical Sensitivity and Air Quality
Childcare
Closed Captioning
Communication
Consent
Content warnings
Food and Dietary Restrictions
Harm Reduction and Overdose Preparedness
Image Captions for Web Accessibility
Lighting and Flash Recording
Live Streaming Events
Mobility

Part 1: Why Accessibility?
Accessibility in the Arts: A Promise and a Practice is an accessibility guide geared toward small-scale arts non-profits and the potentially expansive publics these organisations serve. It details specific ways in which disabled people are excluded from cultural spaces and offers possible solutions to those barriers. Moving away from historical and juridical definitions of accessibility, this guide considers the unique capacity of small scale arts organisations to meet the needs of disabled communities. It engages principles of disability justice to think through what can urgently be done to create more equitable and accessible arts spaces.

Developed by queer and trans activists of colour in the Bay area, Disability Justice (DJ) is the second wave of the disability rights movement, transforming it from a single issue approach to an intersectional, multisystemic way of looking at the world. Within this framework, disability is defined as an economic, cultural, and/or social exclusion based on a physical, psychological, sensory or cognitive difference. Disability Justice movements understand disability to be unevenly distributed, primarily affecting black and indigenous communities, queer and trans communities, and low income communities. Disability is structurally reinforced by ableism, a system rooted in the supremacy of non-disabled people and the disenfranchisement of disabled people through the denial of access. Accessibility is the primary tool that organisations can engage to dismantle ableism and create a more inclusive space; it defines the degree to which all people can engage with certain resources and participate in cultural, social, political and economic spheres.

Arts institutions without considered accessibility measures are facing significantly diminished audience members and visitors. According to the US Census Bureau, one-fifth of the US population is disabled. Investing in accessibility is a sure-fire way for any small-scale arts organisation to expand its viewership. It can include a wide variety of actions and policies from making a physical space wheelchair accessible and ensuring ASL interpretation for public events, to all-gender restrooms and sliding-scale ticketing. Prioritising accessibility in arts spaces begins with asking oneself some basic questions: who comes to our events? Why do those people come to our events? Who doesn't come to our events? Why do those people not come to our events?

Conversations about access have traditionally been explored within a juridical framework. Our current understanding of accessibility is heavily reliant on the terms set by the Americans with Disabilities Act (ADA). This landmark piece of legislation, signed into effect in 1990, requires employers to support the needs of disabled workers and provide accommodations to make the workplace accessible. It also mandates certain accessibility measures for governmental organisations, non-profits, and businesses which service the public. ADA compliance is not a set of predetermined standards; the law exempts businesses and organisations with less than fifteen employees, meaning that many small-scale arts non-profits are not legally obligated to have accessible spaces. As a result, many organisations are motivated by the desire to protect themselves legally instead of viewing accessibility as indispensable.

And yet the very definition of 'small-scale' that allows organisations to evade ADA compliance can be seen as a strength, as small-scale arts organisations are perhaps more capable of meeting the needs of their audiences than larger institutions. Big museums, for example, might have access to more financial resources, but are often plagued by bureaucracy and inaccessible leadership. A smaller staff can lead to less bureaucracy and closer contact with an institution's public. The person introducing the event at a small-scale arts non-profit might also be the person who set out the seats earlier in the evening. These systems of organisation allow for more flexibility and change within an organisation. Programmes and exhibitions tend to bend to the frameworks presented by large arts institutions, whereas smaller arts institutions can be redefined with each project they engage.

ADA compliance is not the only way to create truly inclusive cultural spaces. It is critical to address not just the infrastructure but the very exhibitions and programmes that make an institution accessible. Do your exhibitions, screenings, performances and talks reflect the community that you want to bring into your space? Do they address the concerns, needs and discourses of said community? How can institutions think through their programming and exhibitions in holistic ways that fold into and expand out from various communities? Supporting the cultural labour of disabled artists and thinkers must happen in tandem with infrastructural changes. Additionally, arts organisations need disabled art workers in positions of leadership to create actual substantial shifts. There is often a striking discord between an institution's desire to represent marginalised communities and a total disinvestment from the actual survival of those communities. The ideal arts space is simple: it's one in which art and culture are not sequestered from the lived experience of artists and their communities.

The creation of accessible spaces cannot be done without dismantling the pernicious liberalism that pervades our lives and our relationships with each other, not just as artists and art workers, but as subjects of the state. To commit to disability justice is to redefine the terms of subjecthood. It's to undo the rampant individualism that is a fiction for both disabled and non-disabled people: everyone has needs. If followed, this guide will not produce an ADA-compliant institution, but it will hopefully provide some entry points into building a more inclusive foundation for the cultural work that an arts organisation does. Conversations about disability often rely on the idea of accessibility as a set of particular, preset interventions, but accessibility requires great flexibility. It demands a malleable infrastructure that shifts, in real time, with the needs of the community. We cannot account for every need that every person will ever have. To this end, this guide is in no way meant to be comprehensive, but will hopefully change the institutional landscape of the arts. Accessibility is a promise, not a guarantee. It's a speculative practice. [...]

Carolyn Lazard, extract from *Accessibility in the Arts: A Promise and a Practice* (Los Angeles: Common Field and New York: Recess, 2019) 4–10.

Canaries and Taraneh Fazeli
Canaries Manifesto//2017

WE ARE THE RELUCTANT VANGUARD
REGISTERING MODERN IMBALANCE AND TOXICITY;
THERMOMETERS AND FIRST RESPONDERS
GAUGING THE EARTH'S WELLBEING
THROUGH OUR OWN. WE ARE CANARIES
IN THE COAL MINE SEEKING NEW FORMS
OF ADDRESS THROUGH THE ASSERTION OF VULNERABILITY.

WE ARE ARTISTS.
WE ARE A SUPPORT GROUP.

OUR MALFUNCTIONING PARTS ARE SILENCED
OR REPLACED WITH APPROXIMATIONS,
OUR GROWTHS ARE REMOVED AND IRRADIATED
WHILE WE SHRINK IN A DISCOURSE
THAT DENIES OUR EXPERIENCE AND ITS CAUSES.
OFTEN OUR BODIES DEFY POSITIVIST LOGIC
AS WE FIND OUR OWN SOLUTIONS
TO 'INVISIBLE' PROBLEMS.

WE ARE SICK.
WE ARE GROWING IN NUMBER.

WE INJECT OURSELVES WITH MOUSE PROTEINS
AND EAT BUGS ENGINEERED TO REGULATE
ENDOCRINE AND GASTROINTESTINAL FUNCTIONS.
HOW CAN WE BE LEGIBLE WHEN DOMINANT LANGUAGE EXCLUDES US?
CAN THERE NOT BE, IN SOME WAY,
A NEW SCIENCE FOR EVERY PERSON?

Canaries and Taraneh Fazeli, 'Canaries Manifesto', in *Notes for the Waiting Room*, 2017. Available at https://static1.squarespace.com/static/57798de320099e9ea5949651/t/59cd301ccd39c3e808d1 edf3/1506619444570/NFTWR_LincoV5.pdf

Sara Jaspan
On Cripping//2018

Readers may be familiar with the term 'crip', but the friends, family and colleagues I mentioned it to ahead of attending 'On Cripping' at the Institute of Contemporary Arts – once I'd explained that the event wasn't about the Los Angeles street gang – reacted blankly. A reclaiming of the derogatory word 'cripple', the term has been around since the 1970s and refers to a distinct culture of identities forged in sickness and ill-health (encompassing physical disability, chronic illness, mental illness and more). Necessarily political in stance, the crip position regards disability as being caused by the way society is organised rather than by a person's impairment or difference and looks at ways of removing barriers that restrict life choices for crip people.

'On Cripping' took the form of a 90-minute series of presentations, readings and screenings by Leah Clements, Elena Colman, Alice Hattrick and Lizzy Rose – four members of a new Crip Theory Group founded by Clements (also including Rebecca Bligh and Uma Breakdown) – reflecting on their experiences as both crips and artists who identify as crips, as well as their collective aims for an upcoming residency at the Wysing Arts Centre in October. These revolved around community – forming a professional and peer-support network of fellow crip artists; advocacy – organising public talks and workshops on crip issues; and consultancy – helping art organisations to better understand and meet the needs of crip practitioners, from practical solutions like providing spaces for people with chronic fatigue or pain to lie down to introducing slower working models.

Concerning this last point, Clements states: 'The art world is predicated on over-work, especially for those who have to hold down other jobs to make a living. If you're sick/crip/disabled, over-work simply isn't possible, so how do we deal with that?' Failing to deal with it marginalises crip voices within mainstream art. Additionally, it perpetuates the wider capitalist labour model which has contributed to the rapid spread of autoimmune diseases in industrialised nations; many crip-theorists regard cripness as a form of unintended bodily resistance.

As Giulia Smith writes in 'Health v Wealth'[1], the art world is becoming more concerned with debates and practices that pivot on concepts such as health, healing and care. Indeed, the lead organiser of the event, curator Rosalie Doubal, explained that 'I wished to start an ongoing collaboration with Crip Theory Group so that we may think together how we can best reimagine the ICA from a crip position', and Clements reports feeling 'really encouraged' by interactions with the ICA and Wysing so far. There is, however, still a long way to go before we reach Clements' ambition for a consideration of 'cripness' (like gender, race or sexuality) to 'become more of a habit for anyone thinking practically and critically about art'.

Cripness is far from an issue confined to the art world, and the wider social invisibility and political silencing effect of chronic illness was discussed by all four speakers. 'Long-term sick people are not running television channels, newspapers or art galleries', Rose read from her grassroots zine, *chronicles*, 'mostly they are at home trying to keep themselves alive.' Likewise, plenty of references were made to Johanna Hedva's seminal 'Sick Woman Theory' from 2016 in which the artist writes of being bed-bound during the Black Lives Matter protests: 'So, as I lay there, unable to march, hold up a sign, shout a slogan that would be heard, or be visible in any traditional capacity as a political being, the central question of Sick Woman Theory formed: How do you throw a brick through the window of a bank if you can't get out of bed?'

The presentations also addressed the need to tackle the cultural shame and stigma attached to illness, the internalised guilt of not being a 'productive' member of society, the common struggle for diagnosis, distrust of the medical-industrial complex and common anxieties surrounding a perceived lack of legitimacy – connected with a historical and continuing pattern of women and other marginalised groups being judged unreliable narrators of their own experience (something Hattrick explores in her forthcoming book *Ill Feelings*).

Against these experiences, the internet inevitably emerged as a vital social space and democratic knowledge-sharing tool for all four speakers, which, in Rose's words, 'has greatly expanded the experience of chronic illness'. Rose has been following a Tumblr community since 2012 that posts under the hashtag #chronicillness, and described how many of the memes 'reveal a side of illness we don't often see…they spoke about illness in a way that could be difficult, funny, ungrateful, disgusting, callous, stupid or angry'. She has spent the past year in and out of hospital, documenting the experience on Instagram. Browsing her images, what's striking is how at odds they appear on a platform (and in a society at large) which generally privileges a filtered version of reality, where users generally only publicise the 'best versions' of themselves, and where good health and vitality rule supreme.

While Rose's posts are powerful in the way that they give voice to her experience of chronic illness, the event's overriding theme of 'voicelessness' was eventually challenged by an audience member who asked: 'How do you balance this with all your other identities?' Upon entering the ICA's Lower Gallery, the first thing that leapt out was how similar the speakers appeared: all white, female, young and not visibly disabled. To take issue with this last category seems misaligned with a non-hierarchical, all-embracing approach to illness and disability, yet for a movement that champions intersectionality, the apparent homogeneity felt odd.

The group acknowledged this as something they want to address but have found difficult to do so far. One potential explanation they gave was that cripness is not something people are often very open about, and those already experiencing other forms of marginalisation (e.g. transphobia or racism) may feel less willing or able to publicly identify as crips. The ICA event marked only the beginning of the group's work and Clements stressed that 'solidarity and intersectionality will definitely be at the front of our minds going into the Wysing residency'. She added: 'There are crips of colour like Carolyn Lazard and Hedva doing great things. Hopefully more will be given the platform going forwards, and we can be part of achieving that.'

Though crip networks are only nascent in the UK, 'it feels like this is a moment when people are more willing to listen, which I think owes much to the work done by queer people, people of colour and other marginalised groups', Clements states. Though she later qualified: 'while requirements that are more established in public consciousness like wheelchair access are still often not met, there are also other common needs that are kind of unheard of as something you could actually ask for'.

Interestingly, the movement is more developed in the US. Thinking back to Smith's article, maybe this is partly connected to the two countries' divergent – though increasingly similar – approaches to public healthcare. In a nation where a stint in hospital can leave citizens financially ruined, perhaps there is a more unavoidable urgency for a crip-rights movement. As the UK moves from a '"public-spirited holistic approach to health and community" in favour of a neoliberal model premised on the individual management of mental and physical fitness' (Smith quoting Maria Walsh's 'Art: A Suitable Case for Treatment?'[2]), the final audience question of the afternoon – 'Is what you're talking about not in fact more to do with belonging to a sick society?' – feels somewhat unsettling. Hopefully, the conversation will gain wider public attention. After all, a society with a 'healthier' approach to health (of all forms) would surely benefit everyone.

1   Giulia Smith, 'Heath v Wealth', *Art Monthly*, no. 418 (July–August 2018).

2   Maria Walsh, 'Art: A Suitable Case for Treatment?', *Art Monthly*, no. 145 (April 2018).

Sara Jaspan, 'On Cripping', *Art Monthly*, no. 420 (October 2018) 44.

Clare Barlow
Whose Body? Disability in the Museum//2020

This is a tale of three bodies. Firstly, the normative body, which none of us possess but which many, perhaps even most, of us measure ourselves against. Secondly, the individual body, which each of us have in all their glorious difference and diversity. And finally, the body as presented and affirmed in the museum: a fictive body, or bodies, created out of assumptions and expectations about who might be looking, what experiences and identities they might have and what might be familiar or unfamiliar to them. For many museums, despite valiant work by activists, protestors and visitors outside the museum and individual curators, learning and interpretative professionals within, this body remains stubbornly white, male, cis, heterosexual and non-disabled. This essay will focus on disability, but it is important to note that identities are intersectional and that many people experience exclusion from the assumed audience of museum displays in a variety of ways simultaneously. I will discuss one attempt to shift this fictive body, in the development of 'Being Human', a new permanent gallery at Wellcome Collection which opened in September 2019.[1] I was curator on this project, which aimed to create a space that would be more welcoming and affirmative of difference. Here, I will set out the context of the redevelopment, the process we adopted to achieve it, the conceptual framework for the changes we made in the form of the social model of disability (discussed below), and some of the insights we gained from this process.

'Being Human' replaced a gallery titled 'Medicine Now' and the aspiration was that the new gallery would similarly address themes of contemporary health and medicine. 'Medicine Now' had been in place for just over ten years, a period in which attitudes towards health and medicine had changed radically. Visitor research showed that audiences were struggling to connect with the gallery or articulate its themes and purpose. More damagingly, amongst other responses, the gallery's treatment of obesity was interpreted by some visitors as an example of fatphobia.[2] In its live programme, the museum had hosted a dance performance titled *But Is It Healthy?* by fat activist Dr. Charlotte Cooper that foregrounded these concerns, but there had been no changes to the permanent display.[3] The space was therefore ripe for reappraisal. Wellcome Collection had also undergone a shift in focus, culminating in a new vision: to challenge how people think and feel about health by connecting science, medicine, life and art.[4] This purpose put an explicit spotlight on the question of who would be challenged or affirmed by the new displays.

Inspiration and possible models for this project of renewing the display came from diverse sources. Museums have generally been more affirming of difference in temporary projects such as exhibitions or events programmes. Such programmes offer an opportunity to experiment with alternatives to the narratives in permanent galleries and can connect with audiences who are otherwise marginalised. Wellcome Collection had repeatedly engaged with diverse audiences through its temporary exhibition programme, through exhibitions such as 'The Institute of Sexology' or 'Bedlam: The Asylum and Beyond'.[5] There is, however, a danger in relying solely on temporary exhibitions to redress the balance. Firstly, once in the building, visitors don't stay put. If the exhibition embraces difference but the permanent hang reinforces prejudice, visitors may leave with no greater sense of being valued by the museum than when they arrived. More insidiously, the affirmation of diversity in temporary programme can reinforce ghettoisation. Difference can be acknowledged but not in the permanent spaces: the core of the museum remains untouched. Measures which reframe the permanent collection can be more effective: talks, tours, or labels that reveal the diversity of stories on display, such as the volunteer-led LGBTQ+ tours at the V&A Museum in London. Programmes like these do valuable work in revealing hidden connections for visitors and for museum staff (who may not realise the range of stories that the collection supports) but can still seem an ephemeral presence compared to permanent interpretation. A more comprehensive approach has been taken by specialist museums such as Bethlem Museum of the Mind, London, whose displays are a masterclass in how to embrace complexity and diversity of opinion. Institutions and projects such as these point to the enticing possibility of a wider re-orientation of the museum, shifting its fictive body towards a model that permanently embraces difference. It was this spirit that we wished to capture.

But how to create that shift? The assumptions we make about audiences are embedded in every aspect of an exhibition. In most conventional displays the list of artworks and content, the texts on the wall, the fonts, design, exhibition furniture and lighting are all formed through curatorial choices about who will see what and how that interaction is supported and framed. This brings us to another aspect of the question of 'whose body' – who gets to make those choices, and based on what information? Currently museum professionals are overwhelmingly white, middle class, university-educated and non-disabled. It is perhaps no surprise that those of us who fall into these categories so often frame the fictive audience in our own image, remaining tone deaf to the ways our choices are setting up barriers to inclusion. The only thing that will challenge and change our assumptions is having a more diverse set of voices round the table – something that, longer term, will only be achieved through a radically changed recruitment process and transformed career opportunities, particularly in the early stages of museum careers. Paid consultation, the process we adopted for 'Being Human', is helpful but it is important to recognise that it can only be a temporary stopgap for a genuinely transformative approach across the sector as a whole.

This consultation process for this project was organised in partnership with Professors Richard Sandell and Jocelyn Dodd from the University of Leicester Research Centre for Museums and Galleries. We worked with a small group of disabled experts convened by Leicester in a series of workshops throughout the gallery's development. Across the sessions, they set a conceptual framework for the redevelopment, examined challenges in the existing space, critiqued the proposed content, developed an interpretation strategy and refined design of the space. We met when plans in any particular area had taken shape enough to provoke discussion but when there was still scope for changes to be made in response to the group's recommendations. While some of this work focused on the 'Minds and Bodies' section, the section where themes of disability and difference were most prominent, we did not limit it to this area as we didn't want to pre-empt the group's responses. Looking at the whole space also allowed us to think about change in context.

The primary method that we used for consultation – pinning up texts, images of artworks, and design options on the walls and giving consultants post-it notes to add their comments and questions – allowed us to look at a lot of material in a short space of time. This approach was flexible enough to be used across the different workshops. At each session, we also reported back on what changes we had made in response to feedback the previous session. Reporting back in this way helped to keep us accountable, which was also aided by repetition of some of the activities. This consultation with the disabled experts ran alongside other important conversations and consultations: with other individuals, organisations and groups of potential users, including research scientists. At times, we had conflicting advice to reconcile. However, it was striking that the groups were in agreement more than they were in opposition. As the gallery took shape, it became clear that an inclusive approach was going to make the space more exciting for all users.

One of the earliest recommendations that we received from our disabled consultants was the need for a new conceptual model for the space: the social model of disability. This model originated out of the Union of the Physically Impaired Against Segregation (UPIAS) and was developed by scholars such as Profs. Vic Finkelstein and Mike Oliver. ShapeArts, which adheres to this model, describes it in the following terms:

'The Social Model holds that a person isn't 'disabled' because of their impairment, health condition, or the ways in which they may differ from what is commonly considered the medical 'norm'; rather it is the physical and attitudinal barriers in society – prejudice, lack of access adjustments and systemic exclusion – that disable people. To say that someone is 'just different' or 'differently-abled' ignores the fact that they face these disabling barriers created by society, and implies that they do not experience discrimination, and that society does not need to change to become more accessible and inclusive.'[6]

The social model is utopian, in that it imagines and encourages us to work towards a society in which barriers are removed so that all can freely participate. It is in opposition to the medical model of disability, which focuses on individual diagnosis. As our consultants advised us, one common way of distinguishing the two models is the medical model locates 'the problem' in the disabled person's own mind or body (which can be summarised as 'a broken person') while the social model identifies 'the problem' as lying in prejudice, poor design and inadequate provision (a broken society). The social model has sometimes been challenged as an all-encompassing model of disability but we found it helpful as a foundation for socially-engaged curatorship.[7] It drew our attention to the scale of the problem: the many barriers and ways in which museums are discriminating against or discounting the experiences of disabled artists, contributors and audiences by representing certain minds or bodies as normative or representative. It also encouraged us to consider how to make visible the underlying political, social and economic inequalities that disabled people face. This had a profound effect on the exhibition's content, leading us to seek out and include a greater range of work by artists who explicitly explore inequality and prejudice in their practice. While we had included Katherine Araniello's *Pity* (2013), with its sly deconstruction of the abject stereotype of the disabled person as object of charity, we now added *Meet the Superhuman* (2012), a performance critiquing the heroic stereotype of the Paralympian. We also included *Austerity Cuts* (2019), a powerful and thought-provoking performance which takes as its starting point the hidden emotional, psychological and societal impact of the current system of 'work capability' assessments.[8] Changes such as these increased the breadth of the gallery and ensured that it was not avoiding challenging works and subject matter.

The content list's development would, however, have counted for little if the interpretation continued to reinforce tired assumptions that *other* disabled people and experiences. We therefore asked the consultants for help in developing an interpretation strategy for the gallery based on the social model of disability: a set of principles that would shape the gallery's wall texts. First, however, we needed to work out what it would mean to write museum labels from a social model perspective. The workshop to address this was, for me, one of the most exciting in the project. It began with a presentation by Tony Heaton, reminding us of the distinctions between the medical model and social models of disability. He demonstrated this difference by reframing questions from a census, written from a medical perspective, into a social model perspective. Questions about 'your inability' were rewritten as questions about poor design and inadequate provision. We then split into groups, each consisting of a consultant and a group from Wellcome, and together tried to rewrite pre-existing labels for objects. This pair-writing exercise revealed the extent to which museum texts reinforce ableist assumptions. The original texts included labels for prosthetics and wheelchairs that focused on technological developments rather the user's perspective and stories of oppression and discrimination that had been tidied away behind that overused curatorial euphemism: 'problematic'. The process of re-writing was exhilarating, showing us not only that change was possible but also how we could achieve it. While none of the revised texts drafted in this session were intended for display, they became the foundation for the interpretation strategy, which was developed by Richard Sandell and Jocelyn Dodd in discussion with the consultants. This distilled the learning from the session into a set of clear principles and guidelines. We held a subsequent workshop in which we pinned up the first drafts of wall texts for the group to critique, to ensure that the spirit of the guidelines was manifested in the actual texts. This was an essential step, allowing us to ensure that we had understood the full implications of the social model of disability in shaping approach, word choice, and phrasing across the interpretation.

Refining the curatorial voice was not, however, enough by itself. One of the recommendations by the consultants was that we should seek ways of introducing diverse responses to medical intervention into the space and explicitly break down the dichotomy between the disabled subject and the museum, whose staff are usually assumed to be non-disabled. In discussion with the group, we approached these concerns through a display on prosthetics. We reached out to Wellcome Trust staff, and asked them if they, their families, friends or acquaintances might be prepared to lend us used prosthetics for the displays, together with a short paragraph about their associated experiences. We defined 'prosthetics' in this context as anything worn on, or in, the body that assisted with a particular function. We then selected an extract from each account that would be short enough for the gallery label and sent it to the lender for their approval. Some lenders suggested alternative wording or a different passage from their text and we followed their requests. Throughout this process, we were overwhelmed by the lenders' generosity. Objects ranged from a pair of glasses to a prosthetic knee, from a prosthetic breast to a hearing aid. The owners' responses were similarly varied, revealing a range of emotions towards the objects, from relief to hate. This variety emphasised each lenders' individuality. While curatorially, it can be tempting to present one object or experience as 'typical', this often leads to the dehumanisation of disabled people, who are represented as examples of a particular condition rather than as people, with complex lives and opinions. From the perspective of visitors, hearing people describe their responses in their own words made for an emotionally rich display that brought the objects to life.

In the gallery's design, we wanted to create a space that was seamlessly beautiful and accessible. Here, we had the benefit of previous evaluation work that Wellcome Collection had carried out on exhibitions, prototyping and testing displays with different groups. Findings from this process had been shared with Assemble, the architects for the space, who found creative and elegant responses to these recommendations and to the suggestions of the disabled consultants in the joint workshop that we held. We heard from several of the consultants how frustrated they felt to be constantly directed to a side entrance half-way through displays as it was the only door with a wheelchair ramp. It therefore became a key aim of the design to ensure that the lift entrance and stair entrances to the gallery had an equally strong sense of arrival. We also prototyped part of the design, to ensure that the plinths and captions worked for not only for standing visitors but also for visitors with different types of wheelchairs. The design process revealed the benefit of sustained consultation in supporting conversations outside the parameters of dedicated workshop sessions. Ideas such as off-setting the seating in front of the video works – one of the simplest design innovations in the space – came from a remark from one consultant that, as a wheelchair user, he was never able to see the screen full-on or have the best position for audio. Moving the bench in front of the work to create equal space for a wheelchair was an easy, free solution. If we had had less contact with the consultants, we might have missed out on these insights, which came from engaging with their everyday experience. Such moments highlighted not only the benefits of consultation but also its limitations: a more diverse workforce, with more disabled people in positions of authority, might have addressed such repeated mistakes earlier.

Curating from the social model of disability was at times challenging. It required us to open ourselves up to criticism, to recognise the mistakes we had made in the past and to be willing to work creatively to find design solutions, new objects and new ways of approaching the material. It also required significant commitment from all involved. The consultants were overwhelmingly generous in sharing their insight, knowledge, experiences and criticisms with us throughout the process. We benefitted greatly from being able to work in a sustained way with the same group of experts across this period of development. Achieving this level of deep engagement requires a dedicated budget, curatorial will and institutional support. There are no shortcuts to this process: no guidelines would have had the same impact as repeatedly presenting back on concrete changes and answering questions about what steps we had taken in response to advice. 'Being Human' is far from perfect: like all galleries, there will have been successes and failures which will reveal themselves across the years to come, as visitors explore the space. The fictive body of the museum with which I started this piece is stubborn and pervasive, reflecting prejudices and assumptions that are deeply engrained in society. Yet museums are utopian projects, showing us not only what has been but also encouraging us to reflect on what could be. Embracing the utopian ideals of the social model of disability is a step towards pluralising that fictive body and creating a space in which we all are affirmed.

1   'Being Human', curated by Clare Barlow, Creative Producer Fiona Romeo, designed by Assemble with Kellenberger-White, Wellcome Collection, London (September 2019–ongoing).

2   This display included diet books, medical apparatus associated with weight loss surgery and John Isaacs's sculpture, *I Can't Help the Way I Feel* (2002).

3   Cooper discussed this performance in a zine: http://charlottecooper.net/downloads/zines/ theblob_charlottecooper.pdf, and an article in *The Guardian* newspaper: www.theguardian.com/ commentisfree/2016/oct/26/rhetoric-obesity-toxic-new-language-fat-people

4   'Wellcome Collection Access Policy', https://wellcomecollection.org/pages/Wvmu3yAAAIUQ4C7F

5   Curated respectively by Honor Beddard and Kate Forde, and Mike Jay and Bárbara Rodríguez Muñoz.

6   www.shapearts.org.uk/news/social-model-of-disability?gclid=CjwKCAiA3uDwBRBFEiwA1Vsaj D35z4H4a_mZ5H3zSoGrDWGy5Yw5gubuFBRQJR_qErszpC4m50P9dBoCnpYQAvD_BwE

7   For a discussion of the strengths and weaknesses of the social model of disability, see: Tom Shakespeare, 'The Social Model of Disability', *The Disability Studies Reader*, ed. Lennard J. Davis (New York: Routledge, 2010) 266–73.

8   For an introduction to these assessments, see: Disability Rights UK, 'The Work Capability Assessment' (www.disabilityrightsuk.org/work-capability-assessment).

Clare Barlow, 'Whose Body? Disability in the Museum', a new text written for this book, 2020.

Emily Watlington
Critical Creative Corrective Cacophonous Comical:
Closed Captions//2019

This essay highlights works of video art that critically and creatively engage the closed caption. These works toy with the caption's limited capacity to translate, the importance of providing access, and present the caption as a generative site for poetic, humorous and critical perspectives. The author presents video art as an important site for experimenting with new forms of so-called 'audiovisual media' that do not presume sighted and hearing audiences and do not treat access as an afterthought that can be turned on and off.[1]

'THEN NO ONE GETS ANY', reads a voice in Carolyn Lazard's video *A Recipe for Disaster* (2018). 'IMAGE AND SOUND THAT CANNOT BE DISENTANGLED.' The voice is speaking over Julia Child's; she's teaching us how to cook an omelette on her 1960s television show *The French Chef*. 'A SUFFUSION. A CACOPHONY.' The text is printed in yellow, laid over footage of Child cooking in a bright kitchen. The text scrolls up slowly. 'NO LEGIBILITY FOR SOME. ILLEGIBILITY FOR ALL.' Pauses in Child's monologue are filled with another voice that describes what's on-screen: Child rotates the pan, adds a garnish. Sometimes the two voices overlap. 'A SENSORY FAILURE. A REDISTRIBUTION OF VIOLENCE.' 'WHAT IS PERFORMED IS WHAT IS DESCRIBED. WHAT IS SEEN IS WHAT IS HEARD. WHAT IS HAPPENING IS WHAT IS NARRATED… THIS IS A WHITE WOMAN WHO COOKS WHILE TALKING ABOUT HOW TO COOK. WHAT YOU HEAR, IS WHAT YOU GET. AND WHAT YOU GET, IS WHAT YOU HEAR. A REDUNDANCY FOR SOME. A CLARITY FOR OTHERS.' At the bottom of the screen, all dialogue and sounds are described: '[a pan scratching the stovetop].' These are closed captions (sort of). They're not subtitles; those transcribe dialogue only, not sounds like scratches. Closed captions are usually used to render audio content accessible to deaf/Deaf audiences.[2] Technically, Lazard's are open captions, because they cannot be turned off (closed captions can be). In *A Recipe for Disaster*, captions are not add-ons that render the video accessible after the fact. 'NO MORE INTERVENTIONS AS THE CONDITION OF ACCESS. A WORK MADE FROM THE CONDITIONS OF DEBILITY OR DIFFERENCE, NOT TRANSLATED FOR DEBILITY OR DIFFERENCE. SOMETHING MADE FROM SCRATCH.' Instead, captions and visual descriptions are the fabric of the work, a site for criticality and creativity, not only a corrective. But, of course, Lazard is actually retrofitting Julia Child's cooking show. Their remix shows both the importance and the limits of captioning sounds and describing images on media not made with deaf/Deaf and/or blind and low-vision audiences in mind from the start. Image descriptions are usually forced to fit in the seconds between spoken dialogue, for instance. Inevitably, either content is reduced, or voices overlap, producing a cacophony.

Lazard retrofitted Child's show, in particular, because this chef was already moving toward working accessibility into the fabric of her cooking show: she describes a lot of what she's doing, not necessarily in order to be considerate of blind and low-vision audiences necessarily, but under another rubric of access. Child was trying to bring French cooking to the masses; it's a didactic show. *The French Chef* (1962–73) was the first television show in the world to incorporate captions for deaf/Deaf audiences in 1972. Since 1993, the Americans with Disabilities Act has required built-in automatic closed-caption decoders on all televisions thirteen inches or larger in the US, where both Lazard and Child made their media. Since 2012, non-automated closed captions and visual descriptions have been regulated by the US Federal Communications Commission (FCC) for Netflix, television broadcasters, and movie theatres too. 'As accessible offerings increase,' writes Georgina Kleege in her book *More Than Meets the Eye: What Blindness Brings to Art*, 'it seems an apt moment to review the history of audio description and scrutinize current standards and practices.' *A Recipe for Disaster* and a number of other recent artist projects are doing precisely that.

Artists Christine Sun Kim and Joseph Grigely, for instance, have highlighted the countless errors, poetry, humour and subjectivity latent in automatically and human-generated closed captions. As Kim has put it, 'The multidimensionality of sound, or many layered sounds, are often reduced to brief captions.' She sampled some reductive captions, such as '(POEMING)' or '(VOICE BREAKING)' in her performance *Spoken on My Behalf* (2019). The work comprised a performance and three-channel video with white text on a black background, and it concerned Kim's experiences of having others speak for her. She performed live, signing and gesturing, while recordings of voices who've spoken for her regularly (her mother, her partner) played occasionally. One channel sampled closed captions from TV shows: Kim compared the ways in which having others speaking on her behalf in a language that's not her first can, like captions, be reductive. The sampled captions illustrate her point, reading reductive, hilarious, and perplexing things like '(BURNING QUESTION),' '(SOUND OF CONFUSED DEAF WOMAN),' '(INFLECTING BRIGHTLY),' '(OATMEAL MEOWS).'

For his in-progress series *Craptions* (ongoing), artist Joseph Grigely has been sampling a number of suspect captions as well. The series is made of printed screenshots also sampled from watching movies and television. Grigely's sarcastic title implies a sense of frustration with the limits of reductive captions and with the treatment of closed captions as mere afterthoughts. At the same time, its light-hearted and humorous tone posits the closed caption as a site for humour and for generative, new perspectives on a work of media.

In her piece *Close Readings* (2016), Kim pushed the humour, absurdity, and poetry that's often produced from this process of reduction even further. She sampled a range of movie clips concerned with the voice – literally and as a metaphor for agency, empowerment, and self-representation – from *The Little Mermaid* (1989), *2001: A Space Odyssey* (1968), and more. Then, she invited four deaf/Deaf friends to caption them according to what they felt important to describe. Some captioners and viewers might prefer to have every sound described, while others might privilege those overtly related to the narrative (though this, too, is subjective). The resulting four videos were presented side by side as a four-channel installation, inviting viewers to compare them and revealing the subjectivity inherent in the process. The captions made by and for deaf/Deaf people included more typical descriptions, as well as ones like '(the sound of a light that never flickers)' or '(sound of voice being extracted)': sounds I'm not sure I've ever heard and certainly can't conjure from their descriptions.

Kleege has critiqued the ways in which the subjectivity inherent in providing closed captions or visual descriptions can reflect biases. For instance, only recently did it become standard to visually describe the race of every character in a movie. Previously, it was up to the describer to determine whether or not a character's race explicitly bore on the plot. Non-white people were more likely to have their races identified, which reinforced whiteness as the default. Kleege also critiques requirements that visual descriptions always be 'objective', expressing frustration with a tendency to focus only on the plot and not on aesthetic experiences. She notes that visual descriptions often derive from 'problematic assumptions about what blind people can understand and should know about visual phenomena', and also notes that blind and low-vision people have a wide range of, for instance, education in art history, though they are usually assumed to have none at all. Kim's *Close Readings* demonstrates clearly that objective closed-captioning is not possible, and while basic standards can be fruitful, both she and Kleege seem to agree that objective or uniform descriptions are hardly desirable anyway. Kim figures describing and captioning as an art form itself: after all, we credit those who translate literary works from one language to another as interpreters. Why not do the same when translating from sound to text, or from image to words?

Artist Liza Sylvestre's *Captioned Series* (2017–18) considers what would happen if accuracy and objectivity were thrown out the window entirely. For *Captioned – Channel Surfing* (2017), she captioned her experience channel surfing without captions on, relying only on the visual information accessible to her: context clues, body language and lip reading (at least, when the actors' mouths face the camera). 'It is impossible to read cartoon lips', one caption reads. As a cartoon boy leads a princess down a path, Sylvestre sarcastically comments, 'He leads the way, of course.' Certainly, Sylvestre's interpretation is as (if not more) entertaining and enlightening as the original clips she samples; her interpretation is as valid as any 'objective' captioning. There's a sense that one would not be missing much if they couldn't experience yet another patriarchal hetero love story. Yet at the same time, Sylvestre also makes note of the ways in which movies and television often serve as crucial common cultural references: reflections of a zeitgeist or topics of dinner-party conversations. 'I'm left wondering how to make connections when I don't share the same content', reads one caption as the artist recounts her discomfort with making small talk. It's true that many people elect to opt out of mass media out of boredom, busyness, or a countercultural affinity, that not all of us have a desire to keep up with the Kardashians. Yet, of course, many people do, and forcing this exclusion is simply unfair. Sylvestre's video interventions thwart any notion that television and movies are so precious and wonderful they cannot be rethought in order to be more accommodating at the level of both form and narrative. 'NOT AN ACCOMMODATION, WHERE WE HAVE TO BE GRATEFUL FOR GETTING TO JOIN THE PARTY' – that's Lazard's video again. 'WELL YOUR PARTY SUCKS.'

Sylvestre, Grigely, Lazard, and Kim critique, with humour and sarcasm, the limits of the closed caption: it's reductive, an add-on, never objective, prone to errors, and it creates cacophonies when it means to render legible. But, of course, all of this is preferred to no closed captions at all. Still, we cannot conceive of them as a corrective, as having solved a problem: instead, closed captions are figured as sites for poetry and criticism. Lazard asks how access might be folded into the very fabric of audiovisual media, calling for 'A MEDIA OF MEDIAS. A NEW MATERIALISM. A WAY OF MAKING AND CONSUMING THAT REFUSES TRANSLATION, THAT WE DO NOT UNDERSTAND, THAT WE CANNOT IMAGINE, BECAUSE WE HAVE NOT CREATED THE CONDITIONS FOR ITS PRODUCTION. THE POSSIBILITY FOR AN INTEGRATED AUDIENCE.' A media that doesn't have to be mediated.

April 4, 1980 (2018) by Constantina Zavitsanos and Amalle Dublon pushes toward this new kind of media. It's actually Zavitsanos's voice reading the manifesto in Lazard's video, and they, with Dublon, offer a proposal for fulfilling its demands. The piece has no image (instead, a black rectangle): the artists describe the materials of the work as 'open captions, closed image, sound.' *April 4, 1980* privileges those accessing the work via closed captions rather than audio: for instance, the audio speed is slowed; caption reading is primary. There are no characters on-screen to match dialogue with, and no image that needs to be described. The resulting audio track sounds a bit broken, though this brokenness bears no obvious relation to the narrative. It also challenges what it means to work right or sound right: it gets the message across, after all. For once, hearing viewers are put into a rare experience of watching a piece not made to privilege them. 'A MEDIA SLOW ENOUGH FOR EVERYONE TO FOLLOW. A MEDIA QUICK ENOUGH FOR EVERYONE TO GET LOST… TOGETHER', reads Zavitsanos's voice in Lazard's video. The lack of image also addresses the problem of having to fit visual descriptions within pauses between dialogue, conforming to the speed of the original, which privileges sighted and hearing audiences.

Joseph Grigely actually made a work in the late 1990s in a similar vein: it's an episode of the TV series *Everybody Loves Raymond* (1996–2005) with the image and sound turned off, leaving audiences with only the captions. But he never showed it: critics and curators were not interested at the time. It was the days before YouTube and Vimeo, where many of the other videos mentioned in this essay live, and Grigely's piece still exists today only on Beta tape. Work by marginalised artists is often passively erased when it is not actively preserved, especially in the case of audiovisual works, which need to be constantly updated to new formats in order to remain playable. 'The visual description isn't creating access to something that separately exists,' wrote Dublon. 'Access is the material and form of the artwork.' She was referring to Park McArthur's *PARA-SITES* (2018), the audio guide that comprised the majority of McArthur's recent MoMA exhibition. The observation can be applied to all the videos in this essay.

In their book *The Biopolitics of Disability: Neoliberalism, Ablenationalism, and Peripheral Embodiments*, David Mitchell and Sharon Snyder note that 'disability subjectivities are not just characterised by socially imposed restrictions, but, in fact, productively create new forms of embodied knowledge and collective consciousness.' They note that much of disability studies has, until recently, focused so much on the removal of disabling barriers – by adding, for instance, closed captions or image descriptions – that 'the active transformation of life that the alternative corporealities of disability creatively entail' is often neglected. Like Lazard, they critique the ways in which neoliberal inclusionism is supposed to make disabled people feel grateful for getting to join the party, rather than challenging the notion of what counts as celebration and asking that we rethink the kind of party that had exclusion built into it from the start. The critical and experimental approach of artist projects offers a crucial way to imagine a future for audiovisual media – a term with hearing and seeing built into its name.

1   [Ed. note: This introduction was written and included in the original place of publication by *Mousse Magazine*.]

Emily Watlington, 'Critical Creative Corrective Cacophonous Comical: Closed Captions', *Mousse Magazine*, no. 68 (Summer 2019) [footnotes omitted]. Available at http://moussemagazine.it/critical-creative-corrective-cacophonous-comical-closed-captions-emily-watlington-2019/, updated by the author for this book, 2020.

Miguel A. López
Queer Corpses: Grupo Chaclacayo and the Image of Death//2013

To Helmut, to whose rage and love the ensuing lucubration is due.

The deeply transgressive sexual dissident work of Grupo Chaclacayo (1983–1994) has remained largely unknown until today. Narrated more like a myth or a rumour (almost no one has been able to see their actual works in almost thirty years), this collective endeavour was one of the most daring episodes of artistic experimentation and sexual-political performance to emerge in Peru during the 1980s. These experiments were carried out amidst a violent armed conflict between communist subversive groups and the Peruvian government. Grupo Chaclacayo consisted of three artists (the German Helmut Psotta and his Peruvian students Sergio Zevallos and Raul Avellaneda), who, from 1982 to early 1989, voluntarily sequestered themselves in a house on the outskirts of Lima. In 1989 they were forced to move to Germany by the lack of economic resources in Peru and by the social and political hostility resulting from a war that would leave a death toll of 70,000 people in nearly two decades (1980–2000)[1]. After arriving in Germany a few months before the fall of the Berlin Wall, Grupo Chaclacayo organised an exhibition summing up their work in Peru and including new installations and performances. The exhibition was entitled *Todesbilder. Peru oder Das Ende des europäischen Traums (Images of Death: Peru or the End of the European Dream)* and was shown in cities such as Stuttgart, Bochum, Karlsruhe and Berlin, among others. The group disbanded around 1995. The works and materials they produced never returned to Peru.

The group's extensive work is an explosive reworking of the surplus materials of urban modernity (such as city waste and detritus), merging representations of mystical pain and religious martyrdom with thousands of images of tortured and mangled bodies. The terror, incomprehension and fascination their experiments provoked was the result of the darkness of their work: cheap, anti-glamorous stagings that alluded to ideological dogmatism and sickness; homoerotic representations between abjection and necrophilia; transvestite recodings of mystical pain; the use of coffins and bodily remains, excretions and fluids; and references to foetuses, corpses and mutilated and crippled bodies. Far from being an orthodox claim to a homosexual sensibility, their work was an experiment in the production of abnormal and deviant subjectivities that undid gender and social identities, using a sadomasochistic and ritual vocabulary to exorcise the oppressive effects of ideology, religion and the legacy of colonialism.

It is no coincidence that the emergence of Grupo Chaclacayo paralleled the appearance of an unprecedented countercultural and alternative cultural scene in Lima between 1982 and the early 1990s, known as the '*subte*' [underground] movement. These disruptive practices took the form of collective experiences at the intersection of rock and punk, ephemeral and precarious self-constructed architecture, DIY fanzines, anarchist movements, junk aesthetics, scum poetry and shock theatre. A characteristic of these new radical groupings was the refusal to be silent in the face of the torture and disappearances that were part of the 'dirty war' that the Peruvian state conducted against many sectors of the civil population as a response to subversive activities and attacks by Shining Path.

Rock groups such as Leuzemia (a changed spelling of 'Leukemia'), Narcosis, Zcuela Cerrada (a changed spelling of 'Closed School'), Guerrilla Urbana (Urban Guerilla) and Autopsia (Autopsy), as well as album covers, agit-prop flyers, and collages produced by artists such as Herbert Rodríguez, Jaime Higa and Taller NN, testify to the willingness of anarcho-punk artists to confront the dire situation in Peru.[2]

This radical moment in music was similar to one that took place in architecture, with the anarchist, ephemeral public interventions by a collective called Los Bestias (1984–87), or in poetry, with the ephemeral 'commune' founded by Movimiento Kloaka (1982–84), which used literary production as a space of social struggle. The rebellious attitudes of these freaks, queers, misfits, drunks and malcontents caused some friction with Shining Path and orthodox communist discourses, but also with traditional socialist parties, including the spokespeople and critics of the new cultural Left, who saw in these scandalous activities the signs of social disintegration instead of the yearned for socialist unity. These new subcultural groupings demanded a distinct form of identification and collective communication through their socially marginalised bodies, which had no place in traditional society.[3] The reactions to Grupo Chaclacayo illustrated the hostility and revulsion that attended the rise of Lima's underground movement. [...]

Where to situate the overlooked practices of sexual disobedience, sadomasochistic actions and 'crip' representations of Grupo Chaclacayo?[4] How to intervene in the rhetorics employed by artistic discourses to differentiate the moralising and 'correct' aesthetic of the heterosexual body from others marked by disability, deviance and abjection? Is it possible to recover these episodes of subaltern visibility and sexual disobedience for art history without turning them into mere exotic figures or footnotes in dominant narratives? What political strategies do theatricality, ridicule and sickness offer for imagining micro-histories that shatter the privileged space of heterosexual subjectivity? [...]

The Soldier and the Priest, the Child and the Corpse
The actions and representations of Grupo Chaclacayo on the subject of queer religiosity can also be understood as an attempt to revive the stories of androgynous devotion and transvestite rituals that have been constantly suppressed throughout history. The use of Catholic imagery by the group exalts the cheap forms of visual representation of Andean Virgins and local saints, establishing operations of self-identification with popular and lumpen culture (everything considered poor and vulgar from the urban, upper-class perspective), which the group interspersed with images of prosthetic limbs, crosses, portraits of children, blood, mangled bodies, gunpowder and semen, proposing a renewed space of political antagonism. The images are a staging similar to what queer theorist [Paul] B. Preciado has described as the 'unspeakable attraction between the soldier and the queer, between the dyke and the queen, between the cop and the whore, between the artist and the illiterate, between the aesthetic of the martyrs and sadomasochistic sexual culture'.[5]

These queer forms of theatricalising power and of resignifying religious morality can be related to a wide repertoire of Latin American sexual disobediences and pagan feasts, which have rarely been shown and discussed. For instance, the drawings of phallus-altars for the Virgin of Guadalupe by the Mexican feminist Mónica Mayer in the late 1970s; the feminist religious posters and stickers printed with prayers for abortion rights and freely distributed by the Argentine collective Mujeres Públicas (Public Women); the liturgical experiences and subversive actions of the Chilean duo Yeguas de Apocalipsis (Mares of the Apocalypse) during Pinochet's dictatorship; the performances, graffiti, protests and street theatre by the Bolivian anti-capitalist anarcho-feminist collective Mujeres Creando (Women Creating) in open confrontation with hegemonic political and religious systems of power since the early 1990s; the recent street pilgrimages of Chile's first trans saint, Karol Romanoff, organised by the Coordinadora Universitaria de Disidencia Sexual [University

Coordinator of Sexual Dissidence] (CUDS); and the surreptitious public appearances of Peruvian drag queen Giuseppe Campuzano as an Andean Virgin. These deviant performances undo devout models of femininity (the mother, the Virgin, the wife, the blessed), but also undermine the strong component of morality that organises behaviour in public space. National ideologies, traditional family values and Catholic devotion are part of a strong conservative social matrix in South America. Abnormal sexual-political practices confront and subvert this matrix by intervening in the codes that divide the social body into normal subjects and sick subjects, into proper sexualities and wrong sexualities, into people who deserve to live and people who deserve to die.

It is the denunciation of heteronormative protocols and the pathologisation of queer and disabled bodies (subjects with either mental or physical impairments that make it difficult for them to meet the productive demands of capitalism) which have recently given rise to a collective platform for resistance and for enacting new political communities. The stance against concepts of normalcy (corporeal, sexual, social and mental) taken by both queer bodies and crip bodies does not advocate for inclusion into majority values, but rather for a radical transformation of certain systems of meaning and social structures that label non-normative bodies as 'disordered'. The political potential of crip as a means of fighting the hegemony of able-bodied, heterosexual standards lies in its ability to fracture the collective understandings of what is a desirable social body, thereby putting into question the reproductive/sexual and moral well-being of a nation.

In a recent, very moving silent performance entitled *Lifeline* (2013), Peruvian drag queen Giuseppe Campuzano (who was diagnosed with amyotrophic lateral sclerosis two years ago), in collaboration with Germain Machuca, asserts the experience of the queer and the disabled by showing his own vulnerable, almost motionless body in drag in a wheelchair. Campuzano is pushed along by his friend in a room filled with images and texts of deviant bodies from the pre-Columbian era to the present, which Campuzano collects as part of his project *Transvestite Museum of Peru*, a queer counter-reading of history. As the artist Renate Lorenz has written regarding the queer resignification of pain, the drag 'prevents the body perceived as sick from being completely integrated into the discourse on sickness and from eliciting pitying or sentimental reactions'.[6] Like the work of Grupo Chaclacayo, the action by Campuzano reclaims the devalued body and returns to the public eye that which had previously been expelled and labelled as abnormal or sick. These representations resignify queer and crip culture in a process through which bodies that had been denied their human status acquire, by other routes, the possibility of being subjects of enunciation, of being political agents of knowledge production.

The crip vocabulary mobilises the subversive possibilities of disability, pain and even death. In Grupo Chaclacayo's work, the presence of prosthetic bodies, skeletons, corpses and mummies, which are used to stage scenes of annihilation, suggests a different war beyond the Peruvian armed conflict, one both underground and unnoticed: the war declared against effeminate, weird, ugly, monstrous and sick people. The social pleasure that the death sentence of the homosexual produces, the yearning for the disappearance of gender non-conforming and disabled bodies, emerge in the group's performances as a way of twisting the prevailing hypotheses about the origins of political violence in Peru. Contrary to these prevailing hypotheses, Grupo Chaclacayo locates one of the origins of this political violence in ideas of able-bodied heteronormativity, which are integral to the maintenance of the nation's healthy borders and to the accepted war against any subject disobeying the hegemonic regimes of the 'normal'.

The reading of these bodies advanced by certain critics, who asserted that these bodies required psychiatric rehabilitation or even incarceration, continued to hound the group's homoerotic artistic grammar. In a 1989 article, the art critic Luis Lama (who had rebuked their work on moral grounds in 1984) dismissed the group's work, then exhibited at the Künstlerhaus Bethanien in Berlin, accusing it of being 'shrill and frivolous apologies' for Shining Path.[7] Beyond the threat that such accusation entailed for artists (at the time, it could mean persecution, kidnapping, torture or forced disappearance), it is revealing how these anarcho-queer outbreaks were associated with the terror produced by the Shining Path's armed raids in Peru.

Lama's denunciation represents a powerful example of how the group's inappropriate expressions of sexuality were interpreted as a threat to the national body. Equating 'terrorists' with 'queers', however subtly, was an example of how this hyper-sexualised theatricality and cripple-homosexual fiction that blended the soldier and the priest, the child and the corpse, could be a metaphor just as explosive and threatening to heteronormative discourses as the murderous Shining Path group.

1   [Footnote 2 in original] The armed conflict in Peru ended in 2000 with the fall of the right-wing dictator Alberto Fujimori and his criminal and corrupt government. The principal actors in the war were the Shining Path Maoist organisation (founded in a multiple split in the Communist Party of Peru), the 'Guevarist' guerrilla group Túpac Amaru Revolutionary Movement (or MRTA), and the government of Peru. All of the armed actors in the war committed systematic human rights violations and killed civilians, making the conflict bloodier than any other war in Peruvian history since the European colonisation of the country.

2   [5] For a short history of Lima's punk scene and 'subte' movement, see Shane 'Gang' Greene, 'Notes

on the Peruvian Underground: Part II', *Maximum Rocknroll*, no. 356 (January 2013). See also Carlos Torres Rotondo, *Se acabó el show. 1985. El estallido del rock subterráneo* (Lima: Editorial Mutante, 2012).

3 [6] For a longer reflection about the radical artistic interventions and the underground scene in Peru in the 1980s, see Miguel A. López, 'Discarded Knowledge: Peripheral Bodies and Clandestine Signals in the 1980s War in Peru', in *Removed from the Crowd: Unexpected Encounters*, eds. Ivana Bago, Antonia Majaca, and Vesna Vukovic (Zagreb: BLOK & DeLVe – Institute for Duration, Location and Variables, 2011) 102–41.

4 [8] 'Crip' is a play on the word 'cripple', and its use here refers to the political resignification of disability and the questioning of how and why disability is constructed and naturalised. The 'cripple' movement reclaims language and self-representation to direct them towards different modes of existence, confronting the dominant ideologies of 'normalcy' and its medical lexicon. The movement also aligns itself with other bodies that have been pathologised, such as the homosexual. Crip activism and theory mobilises the subversive potential of disabled bodies that refuse able-bodied norms, the productive demands of capitalism, and static identities. For the intersections of crip and queer, see Robert McRuer, *Crip Theory: Cultural Signs of Queerness and Disability* (New York: NYU Press, 2006).

5 [16] [Paul] B. Preciado, 'The Ocaña We Deserve: Campceptualism, Subordination and Performative Policies', in *Ocaña: 1973–1983: acciones, actuaciones, activismo* (Barcelona: Institut de Cultura de l'Ajuntament de Barcelona, 2011) 421.

6 [18] Renate Lorenz, *Queer Art: A Freak Theory* (Bielefeld: Transcript Verlag, 2012) 81.

7 [19] Luis Lama, 'Perversión y Complacencia', *Caretas* (20 November 1989) 74–6.

Miguel A López, extracts from 'Queer Corpses: Grupo Chaclacayo and the Image of Death', trans. Max Hernández Calvo, *e-flux Journal*, no. 44 (April 2013) (https://www.e-flux.com/journal/44/60146/queer-corpses-grupo-chaclacayo-and-the-image-of-death/) [some footnotes omitted].

Paul B. Preciado
Lorenza Böttner: Requiem for the Norm//2019

Overlooked by the dominant historiography of art until relatively recently, the work of Lorenza Böttner – an artist who painted with her mouth and feet, and who used photography, drawing, dance, installation and performance as means of aesthetic expression – emerges today as an indispensable contribution to the criticism of bodily and gender normalisation in the late twentieth century. Exercises of resistance to a medical and exoticising gaze that reduces the functionally diverse or trans body to the status of specimen or object, her works are characterised not only by the use of self-fiction, the dissident imitation of visual styles from the history of art and bodily experimentation, but also by criticism of the disciplinary divide between genders, between painting, dance, performance and photography, between masculine and feminine, between object and subject, between active and passive, and between valid and invalid. This exhibition, which brings together more than one hundred works, is the first international retrospective dedicated to the artist.

In what frame of representation can a body make itself visible as human? Who has the right to represent? Who is the represented? Can an image grant or deny a body political agency? How can a body construct an image to become a political subject? Is there any aesthetic difference between an image made with the hand and another made with the foot, or does this difference lie in a power relationship? These are some of the questions that Lorenza Böttner's visual and performative work poses.

The Art of Living

It is crucial to start with her biography, understood as a vitalist manifesto, because the most persistent practice in Lorenza's work is a blurring of the distinction between life and art. Lorenza Böttner was born on 6 March 1959 in Punta Arenas, Chile, into a family of German migrants. Assigned male at birth, she was recorded in the Chilean register as Ernst Lorenz Böttner Oeding. At the age of eight, Ernst Lorenz suffered a severe electric shock while climbing an electricity pylon in an attempt to get hold of a bird's nest. For several days after the accident, it was touch and go as to whether he would live or die. After the amputation of both his arms, Ernst underwent a long, painful process of hospitalisation, during which he unsuccessfully tried to commit suicide. That relationship between pain and death, which subsequently transmuted into hedonism and the exaltation of life, meant that her own body would become one of her main artworks: a vulnerable, neo-baroque monument to life.

In 1969, his mother took him to Germany so that he could have access to specialised therapies. An armless body, Ernst Lorenz was first institutionalised as a disabled person in the Heidelberg Rehabilitation Centre and then educated at the Lichtenau Orthopaedic Rehabilitation Clinic alongside the so-called 'thalidomide children'. Prescribed to pregnant women as a sedative between 1957 and 1963, the thalidomide-based drug (marketed under the trade name 'Contergan' in Germany) caused hundreds of thousands of babies to be born with modified limbs. The impact that this drug had in Germany led not only to the establishment of specialised learning centres, but also to the emergence of the 'Contergan child' as a pop image of the 1960s. 'The greatest contemporary composer is the Contergan child' declared Joseph Beuys in his 1966 performance entitled *Infiltration Homogen für Konzertflügel, der größte Komponist der Gegenwart ist das Contergankind* (*Infiltration Homogeneous for grand piano* [...]), which would later become a reference for Lorenza. The 'Contergan children' expression, by which the generation of children affected by the drug became known, indicated that the process of bodily modification caused by this drug meant that they were considered neither human nor children of their mothers. Spectacularised as invalids and deformed individuals, the 'thalidomide children' were the symbolic bodies of a pharmaco-pornographic capitalist transformation taking place in the West after the Second World War: illegitimate children of the pharmaceutical industry and the media, the 'thalidomide children' were the new lumpen of the consumer societies. It was there, in that damned, subaltern cradle, where Lorenza Böttner was born.

Lorenza emerged from resistance to the process of transformation from Ernst Lorenz into a 'thalidomide child': she rejected the prosthetic arms that would supposedly have rehabilitated her body into one deemed 'normal'; she rejected being educated as a disabled child and spent most of her time drawing, painting and dancing.

Lorenza's Birth

Going against the medical diagnosis and social expectations that promised her a future of 'social inclusion' as a disabled person, Ernst Lorenz was accepted into the Gesamthochschule Kassel (now a School of Art and Design) as a student from 1978 to 1984 under the supervision of teacher Harry Kramer. A sculptor of kinetic pieces as well as a dancer, choreographer and performer, Kramer had an undeniable influence on Lorenza's incorporation of dance and performance into the process of pictorial production.

While still an art student, it was in Kassel where Ernst Lorenz changed her name to Lorenza and assumed a publicly female identity. She then began a visual and performative exploration in which the self-portrait and dance served as techniques of experimental construction. Her degree project at the Kassel School of Art in 1984 involved the unprecedented use of the self-portrait as a dissident embodiment of the norm. It was a large oil on canvas mural painted using footprints like impressionist brushstrokes. The mural – shown for the first time in the school's exhibition room in the same year – returned to the city to take up one of the emblematic spaces at the exhibition in the great hall of the Neue Gallerie during documenta 14 in 2017.

For Lorenza, transvesting herself in images of the norm was a requiem for undoing the norm. The drawings, prints, paintings and performances she did over the intense 16-year period of her life as an artist (1978 to 1994) show her occupying a plurality of positions, not only of sex and gender, but also in history and time: an Elegant Victorian lady, a muscular young man with glass arms, a ballerina, a punk girl, a Greek statue, a flamenco dancer, Batman's bride, Miss World, a sex worker, a model, a traveller, a breast-feeding mother, a young BDSM enthusiast, an ephebe with the wings of Icarus, etc. Lorenza was interested in the simultaneity of embodiments and not identity as a static place. Her transvestism was not mimicry of femininity as an identity – it was usual to see her with a beard or naked – but rather an enlargement of the body's gestural repertoire, an expansion of the possibilities of action. In this sense, a photo that can be considered emblematic is the one of Lorenza with a beard and chest hair posing nude in front of a painted self-portrait, in which she had portrayed herself with smooth skin and female breasts. Both faces look straight at the viewer. Both assert: I am Lorenza. Because Lorenza was transition and not identity. Rather than transvestism, it would be more appropriate to speak of transition practices as counter-learning techniques through which the body and subjectivity deemed 'disabled' or 'sick' claim the right to represent and invent their own life practices. It would therefore not be accurate to say that Lorenza transvests her feet and mouth into hands, or that the artist transvests into a woman, but instead that she invents another body, another artistic practice and gender: neither disabled nor normal, neither male nor female, neither painting nor dance.

The Politicisation of Freaks: From Disability to Crip Pride

Besides the Impressionist-style self-portrait mural, Lorenza graduated from Kassel in 1984 with a dissertation entitled *Behindert?!* (*Disabled?!*), in which she examined the place that the non-conforming body had occupied in artistic representation. The dissertation, which included a first-person chronicle of her accident, and the processes of healing and learning to paint and dance, criticised the normative representation of the non-conforming body and advocated for an artistic practice capable of recognising an armless body as a social and artistic agent.

Until the Renaissance, the functionally diverse body, inscribed in a theological epistemology, was deemed to be an anti-natural monster that should be exterminated or could be the object of social ridicule. During the industrial revolution, a change in the politico-visual regime occurred: the functionally diverse body was considered an object of scientific research and institutional internment, a 'specimen' for which society demanded remedy and rehabilitation through plastic surgery and adaptive prostheses. The industrial revolution invented a new productive body, a new materiality in which the hand – and the male hand in particular – occupied a central place as an organ that enabled an articulation between body – as the productive force – and machine. It was within this context that the model of deficiency and disability emerged: a body whose hands had been mutilated was a body that heterosexual capitalism considered unproductive and asexual.

In resistance to this politico-sexual model, the dual process of artistic and gender vindication enabled Lorenza to construct a corporeality that was dissident and desirable at one and the same time: on the one hand, it was about resexualising a body that had been desexualised by medical and institutional discourse. It was the need to escape from the orthopaedy of the norm and to activate the political potential of the different gesture of a functionally diverse body that led Lorenza to transition from painting to dance, and even to the creation of her own dresses. On the other hand, Lorenza demanded political equality across all artistic practices, regardless of whether they were done with the hands or with any other living or technological organ.

The dissertation was accompanied by a performance project entitled *Lorenza, das Wunder ohne Arme. Freaks* (*Lorenza, the armless miracle. Freaks*). Lorenza researched the Freak Shows at the Leipzig Fair, the Tivoli in Copenhagen, the Prater in Vienna, the variety of Panoptikums (wax museums) in Germany and Austria, the Egyptian Hall in London's Piccadilly Circus, and the Théâtre des Variétés in Paris, among others.

The Freak Show was a crucial device in the modern invention of disability because it situated the non-conforming body on the boundaries of being human, while at the same time including it as part of a social spectacle. The Freak Show constituted a moment of transition between the theological regime in which the non-conforming body was seen as a monstrosity and its transformation into the object of scientific research and of the disability industries. It was within that narrow frame of visibility that Lorenza sought to act: between the regimes of popular spectacularisation of the body in Freak Shows and of medical devices rendering the body visible as sick. Lorenza obsessively returned to the images from the film *Freaks* (1932) by Tod Browning, collected Freak Show posters and included freak motifs in her performances.

During Ernst Lorenz's adolescence in the 1970s, bodily diversity was defined in the German Federal Republic's disability policies as an individual and functional deficit with regard to work and productivity. Integration demanded the reconstruction of the disabled body with the help of prostheses that should contribute to the visual normalisation of the body and its adaptation to the productive process.

Against this medical narrative, Lorenza sought to inscribe her body, her subjectivity and her artistic production in a political lineage of armless painters that went from Thomas Schweiker to Louis Steinkogler. But it was Aimée Rapin, whose work became an attraction at the 1889 Paris Universal Exposition, that she seemed to identify herself with the most. Rapin's eminently feminine themes, her floral compositions, the attention paid to the hair in her portraits, etc., were constant motifs in Lorenza's pictorial work. In the 1980s and 90s, during her trips to New York, Lorenza Böttner actively took part in the Disabled Artists Network with Sandra Aronson, but criticised the charitable and humanist models that framed disabled people as marginal artists. Unlike them, Lorenza understood the relationship between the hand and the foot, between the medico-pornographic and the artistic gaze, as a power struggle.

In the same way as feminist artists use works of art as a conceptual space in which to negotiate representations of the female body as an object of the heterosexual gaze, Lorenza's work questioned the technologies of normalisation, objectivisation and institutionalisation that had led to a functionally diverse body being constructed as disabled. In this sense, an extension of Lorenza's pioneering work can now be seen in the work of Jennifer Miller, Del LaGrace Volcano, Mat Fraser, Amanda Baggs and Park McArthur. [...]

Paul B. Preciado, extract from 'Lorenza Böttner: Requiem for the Norm', a text written for the exhibition 'Lorenza Böttner: Requiem for the Norm', Württembergischer Kunstverein Stuttgart, 23 February–28 March 2019 (www.wkv-stuttgart.de/uploads/media/Lorenza_Boettner_Booklet_final_kl_01.pdf).

TO INVOKE DECOLONIAL HEALING.

TO DEMAND DECOLONIAL HEALING. [...]

TO PRACTICE DECOLONIAL HEALING.

DECOLONIAL HEALING

Peter Pál Pelbart
Life and Death in the Context of Biopolitical Domination//2014

It would be necessary to start with the new relationship between *power* and *life*, as it manifests today. On the one hand, there is a tendency that could be formulated as follows: power 'took life by storm'. That is, power penetrated all spheres of existence, mobilised them totally, and put them to work: from the genes, the body, affectivity and psyche, to intelligence, imagination and creativity. If not directly expropriated by power, all these were violated, invaded, colonised, whether one evokes the sciences, capital, the state, or the media. The diverse mechanisms by which such powers are exercised are anonymous, widespread, flexible, rhizomatic. Power itself has become 'post-modern', wavy, decentred, reticular, molecular. It impacts therefore more directly on our ways of understanding, feeling, loving, thinking, even creating. If, in the past, we still imagined having spaces preserved from the direct interference of power (the body, the unconscious, subjectivity) and had the illusion of preserving some autonomy in relation to them, today our life seems instead totally subsumed by such mechanisms of modulation of existence; even sex, language, communication, oneiric life, even faith; none of them still preserve any exteriority in relation to the mechanisms of control and monitorisation. To put it in one sentence: power is no longer exercised from the outside, nor from above, but as if from the interior, controlling our social vitality from top to bottom. We are no longer dealing with a transcendent, or even repressive, power; it is rather an immanent, productive, power. Such *biopower* does not intend to block life, but to take care of it. It intends to intensify, to optimise life. Hence our extreme difficulty to resist, as we barely know where power is and where we are in relation to it, what is dictated by it and what we want from it. We oversee the management of our control, and such anonymous dynamics fully captures our desire. Never has power gone so far and so deep into the core of subjectivity and life itself.

Where the second axis intervenes, it is necessary to specifically refer to some Italian autonomists. We can summarise this axis as follows: when it appears that 'everything is dominated', as a Brazilian rap song says, a turning point is indicated at the end of the line: that which seemed submitted, controlled, dominated, that is, 'life', reveals, in the very process of expropriation, its indomitable capacity. Let us take just one example. Today capital does not need more muscles and discipline, but inventiveness, imagination, creativity, invention-force. Nonetheless this invention-force, which capitalism appropriates, making it work for its own benefit, does not emanate from the capitalist mode of production. At the limit, it could even do without it. This is what we confirm here and there: today, the true source of wealth is the intelligence of the people, their creativity, their affectivity. All of this clearly belongs to each and everyone. Three teenagers and a PC, and the conditions for the invention of a software programme that will earn them billions are already met. They do not need a capitalist that brings together the means of production and labour power. More profoundly, it means the following: disseminated everywhere, such intelligence, such life capacity, forces us to rethink the very terms of resistance. We could sum up such movement as follows: life's capacity responds to the power over life, bio-capacity (*biopuissance*) responds to biopower (*biopouvoir*).[1] But this 'response' does not mean reaction, for it is acknowledged that such capacity was already there from the beginning. Social vitality, when enlightened by the powers that aim to vampirise it, suddenly appears in its ontological primacy. What once seemed entirely submitted to capital, or reduced to mere passivity, 'life', now appears as an inexhaustible reservoir of sense, a source of forms of existence, a germ of directions that extrapolate the structures of command and the calculations made by constituted powers.

We would need to go through these two major paths as in a Möbius strip; biopower (*biopouvoir*), biocapacity (*biopuissance*), the power over life, the capacities of life. But we could do it here under a particular screen: the body. For, today more than ever, both biopower and biocapacity necessarily pass through the body. Traversing this Möbius strip, I propose therefore to work here with three modalities of 'life', that is, three concepts of life, followed by their corresponding bodily dimension. This way I might be able to make more tangible and more concrete that which challenges us today. […]

The Body

Let us take as an example the overinvestment in the body that characterises our present day. For some decades, the subject's focus has moved from psychic intimacy to the body itself. Today, the self is the body. Subjectivity has been reduced to the body, its appearance, image, performance, health, longevity. The predominance of the corporeal dimension in the constitution of identity makes the allusion to bioidentity possible. Indeed, we are not facing, as one hundred years ago, a body tamed by disciplinarian institutions, the body striated by the panoptic machine, the body of the factory, the body of the army, the body of the school. Nowadays, in gyms or surgery clinics, everyone voluntarily submits to an ascesis according to scientific and aesthetic instructions. This is a topic that our friend Denise Sant'Anna has been working on for years. Likewise, it is what Francisco Ortega, following Foucault, calls *bioascesis*. On the one hand, the issue is about adapting the body to the scientific norms of health, longevity, equilibrium; on the other, it is about adapting the body to the norms of the culture of spectacle, according to the celebrity model. Taking into consideration the endless possibilities of transformation proclaimed by genetic, chemical, electronic or mechanical protheses, the obsession with physical perfection, and the compulsion of the self to cause the desire of the other for itself through the idealisation of the body image – even at the expense of one's own well-being, despite the mutilations that compromise it – finally replace the promise of erotic satisfaction with self-imposed mortification. The fact is that we voluntarily embrace the tyranny of the perfect body in the name of a sensory pleasure whose immediacy makes the suffering it entails even more surprising. Bioascesis is a care of the self, but in contrast with ancient people, whose self-care aimed at achieving the good life, that Foucault called an aesthetics of existence, our care aims at the body itself, its longevity, health, beauty, fitness, scientific and aesthetic happiness, or what Deleuze would call 'a dominant and bloated health'.[2] Even under the modulating conditions of contemporary coercion, we do not hesitate in naming it a fascist body since, facing this unreachable model, a large part of the population is thrown into a condition of sub-human inferiority. Furthermore, the body has become also an information package, a genetic pool, a statistical dividual, with which we are thrown into the domain of biosociability ('I am part of the hypertensive group, of the seropositive group', etc…). This only reinforces the risks of eugenics. Any weekly magazine with its maxims on health, beauty, sexuality, food, which we happily adopt as scientific rules, hence as imperatives, is a fit illustration of this context. In any case, we are struggling with the register of biologised life… . We are reduced to a mere body: from the stimulated to the manipulatable body, from the body of spectacle to the self-modulating body. This is the domain of bare life. We are still in the domain of survival, of the mass production of 'survivors' in the broad sense of the word.

The Body that Cannot Take Anymore

What could yet shake us from such state of lethargy, lassitude, exhaustion? There is a fine Beckettian definition of the body, given by David Lapoujade: 'the body is that which cannot take anymore'. But the author asks, what is it that the body cannot take anymore? The body cannot take anymore of all that coerces it, from the inside and the outside. Firstly, the civilising training that, for millennia, has befallen the body, as Nietzsche showed exemplarily in *On the Genealogy of Morals* or, more recently, Norbert Elias, when he describes how what we call civilisation is the result of a progressive silencing of the body, its noises, impulses, movements… . Secondly, what the body cannot take anymore is the docilisation imposed upon it by the disciplines, by the panoptic machine; the army, factories, schools, prisons, hospitals… . In view of what we said before, we should finally add: what the body cannot take anymore is biopolitical mutilation, biotechnological intervention, aesthetic modulation, bioinformatic digitisation, the sensory numbness inflicted by this anaesthetising context… . Briefly, and in a very broad sense, what the body cannot take anymore is survivalist mortification, be it in the state of exception or in everyday banality. No matter how extreme their differences appear, the 'Cyberzombie', the 'Body-spectacle', 'dominant and bloated health', '*Bloom*', resonate with the anaesthetic and narcotic effect, configuring in nihilistic terminal conditions the impermeability of an 'armoured body'.[3] Facing this context, it would be necessary to recapture what is more proper to the body, the pain it faces in the encounter with the exterior, its condition as a body affected by the forces of the world, capable of being affected by them: its affectability. As Barbara Stiegler observes, for Nietzsche all living subjects are primarily affected subjects. They are bodies that, from the alterity that strikes them, suffer from their affections, their encounters, the multitude of stimuli and excitations that they have to select, avoid, choose, welcome… .

Along this line, Deleuze also insists: a body does not cease to be subjected to encounters with light, oxygen, food, sounds and incisive words – a body is primarily an encounter with other bodies, the power of being affected. But it is not the power of being affected by everything or in any way, as someone who gulps and vomits everything, with its phenomenal stomach, in the pure indifference of the unwavering; like the consumers of culture, or rubbish or luxury goods… . How to preserve, then, the ability of being affected? Would it not be necessary to cultivate a certain porosity, even fragility, a sensibility which would give us back the power of being affected? But how can the body have the strength to live up to its weakness, instead of remaining in the weakness of just cultivating its strength? Gombrowicz referred to an unfinishedness proper to life, *where it is in its most germinal state*, not yet completely 'caught' by form; the irresistible attraction that this state of Immaturity exerts is where the freedom of 'yet to be born' is preserved… . This could be particularly relevant in the domain of education. If we could see these 'beings not yet born' in the groping that they must experience, in the experimentation that should be their right, the pledge for their indeterminacy, without restrain or domestication, without desensitising them to all that that does not serve our targets of power, urgency, productivity, institutionalisation (with their armouring, formatting and ready solutions). More generally, perhaps that is why so many literary characters, from Bartleby to the Hunger Artist, need their immobility, emptying, pallor. They are at the limit of the dead body, in a kind of work-to-rule action. Maybe they need that gesture to enable the passage of different forces that an excessively 'armoured' or 'performative' body would not allow. As Deleuze says, we should not move too much, so as not to frighten the becomings.

In any case, it is a matter of establishing another relation with life, precisely with this life 'before' it is formed, or with life freed from its form, or, lastly, with a dimension of life behind and beyond the form which it tends to acquire. In the last text written by Deleuze, entitled *Immanence: a Life*, there is a telling example, Dickens. [...]

It is as if Deleuze probed below the empirical body and individuated life. As if he searched, not just in Kafka, Lawrence, Artaud and Nietzsche, but also throughout his own work, and also, we could argue, through the effects that this body of work produced in different fields; as if he searched that threshold between life and death, man and animal, madness and sanity, where being born and perishing resonate in each other, calling into question so many divisions and dichotomies bequeathed to us by tradition.

With regards to our concrete context, the questions remains: considering that we still do not know what can a body do, how can we distinguish Spinoza's splendid perplexity (and open an unprecedented experiment), from the voracity with which power, capital and technoscience research and experiment precisely what is possible to do with the body and with life within the production of survival? How to move away from the obsession of researching 'what is possible to do with the body and with life' (the biopolitical question: which interventions, manipulations, improvements, eugenics?), and retake the vitalist and Spinozian question, 'what can the body and life do' in this context? How to insist on that minor, trivial postulate that says that living is not surviving? On the one hand, we have life capacities that need to get rid of their crystalised forms in order to experiment; on the other, we have the power over life that needs a post-organic body or a post-organic life to attach to the axiomatics of capitalism.

Perhaps for one side to appear the other side needs to be fought, or at least displaced. For instance, it is necessary to divest life of everything intended to represent or contain it, so that what Deleuze called *a life* can emerge in its immanence and affirmative capacity. The whole conceptualisation of the body-without-organs is, par excellence, a variation around this biopolitical theme. It is life getting rid of what imprisons it: the organism, the organs, the inscription of several powers upon the body; life getting rid of its reduction to bare life, death-life, mummified life, shelled life. But if life must dispose of all these social, historical and political ties, is it not to regain something of its naked, dispossessed animality? Is life stripped from these bonds in danger of amounting to the bare life that Agamben refers to? Perhaps we should return to Artaud, via the fine comment of his Japanese translator and interpreter, Kuniichi Uno: 'But he [Artaud], never lost the intense sense of life and the body as genesis, or auto-genesis, as an intensive, impervious force; a mobile force, without limits, which would not let itself be determined, even by the terms *bios* or *zoē* (the two names given by the Greeks to life. One refers to the form of life; the other, to the mere fact of life). For Artaud, life is indeterminable, in all senses, while society is made up of infamy, trafficking, commerce, which continues to besiege life and, above all, the body.'[4] It would be sufficient to meditate on Artaud's enigmatic phrase: 'I am innately genital, and if we examine closely what it means, it means that I never made the most of myself/ There are some fools who think of themselves as beings, as innately beings/I am he, who in order to be, must whip its innateness'. Uno remarks that someone innately genital is someone who tries to be born through herself, originating a second birth beyond given biological nature. With Artaud we could therefore say that, in the strong sense of the term, we are innate, not yet born. Let us consider Beckett hearing Jung's comments about a patient: the fact is that she was never born. Carrying this phrase to the context of his work, Beckett builds an 'I' that is not born. This 'I' that was never born writes about the other 'I' who has already been born. The refusal of biological birth is not a rejection coming from a being who does not want to live; instead, it is the refusal of the one who demands to be born again, always, all the time. The innately genital carries the history of a body that questions the body already born, with all its functions and organs, representative of orders and institutions and the visible and invisible technologies aiming to manage the body. This is a body that has the courage to challenge the socio-political complex that Artaud called the Judgement of God, and we name biopower. It is a power that is falling upon our own body... . Uno claims that the refusal of birth, in favour of self-birth, does not amount to the desire to dominate one's own commencement; it is rather the desire to recreate a body with the power to commence. Uno insists that life is this body, as long as the latter finds the vigour of genesis and frees itself from the weight of determination – a war on biopolitics... . Perhaps this is one of the few points where we agree with Badiou, as he claims that, for Deleuze, life is the name of being. Life not grasped as a gift or treasure, or survival, but as a neuter that rejects all categories. As Badiou claims:

> All life is denudation, divestment, the dissolution of all organs and codes. Not in order to move towards some sort of nihilistic black hole, but rather to maintain oneself at that point where actualisation and virtualisation are exchanged into one another; to be a creator... .

But is Badiou right in designating this life as bare? In any case, as Uno had already noted, the denuded life Badiou refers to cannot be simple *zoè*, the name given by the Greeks to designate the fact of life, a mere biological or animal fact, or life reduced to the biological bareness affixed to juridical order by the state of exception. It cannot be life destined to technoscientific manipulation enacted by the nihilistic movement of capital. As Deleuze conceived it, *a life* is virtuality, difference, invention of forms, impersonal capacity, beatitude. As Agamben conceptualised it, *bare life is,* on the contrary, life reduced to its state of mere actuality, indifference, deformity, incapacity, biological banality. Furthermore, *beastly life* is the entropic exacerbation and dissemination of bare life at its nihilistic limit. If these lives are so counterposed – but, at the same time, so superimposed – it is because in the biopolitical context life itself is at stake, as it becomes the field of battle. However, as Foucault puts it, at the juncture where power pushes with its utmost strength, life initiates an anchorage to resistance, as if changing signals... . In other words, sometimes it is at the extreme of *bare life* that *a life* is discovered; it is at the extreme of manipulation and decomposition that the body can discover itself as virtuality, immanence, pure capacity, beatitude.

If those who better diagnosed beastly life, from Nietzsche and Artaud to the young experimenters and researchers of today, have the conditions to regain the body as affectability, flow, vibration, intensity, even as a power to begin, is it not because for them beastly life has become intolerable? Are we not all at that point of suffocation that pushes us precisely towards another direction? Maybe for life to emerge differently there is something in the extortion of life that must come to an end... . Something must exhaust itself, as Deleuze suggested in his essay 'The Exhausted' (1992), so that another game can be thinkable. [...]

Conclusion

I will try to wrap it up from the first stance, when I mentioned the Moebius strip to characterise our current situation. On the one hand, we can see everywhere power creeping into all spheres of life, engulfing it altogether, in its most infinitesimal dimensions. On the other hand, we detect everywhere, even in tiny gestures, minor desertions, collective affections and assemblages, the unsubordinated vitality that our mediated perception and dampened sensibility hardly grasp. But this antagonism – 'on the one hand/on the other' – does not indicate two opposite fields separated by a clear border; they are instead like the two sides of the same coin, or rather, the two coextensive and inseparable sides of the same twisted strip, the two dimensions that traverse and constitute us. As we imperceptibly pass from one to the other. We are both of them at the same time. And the war between these two sides happens inside us and tear us from the inside, forcing us not so much to take a stand, but to reinvent the tactics for life. For this reason, the geometry of conflict has changed completely.

Every struggle is also a struggle against ourselves, against certain powers that traverse and constitute us. Through our passivity, our support and adherence to these powers, we become their product. No one can imagine living on the right side, the independent margin, the place of the Great Refusal, for no one can consider themselves protected from what constitutes us, inside and outside. For those who yearn for easy dichotomies, visible enemies, definite resolutions – the final assault on the Winter Palace – this context might seem claustrophobic, giving the feeling that there is no way out. But the actual context, that some call the Empire, is more subtle and complex, more mobile and molecular. Despite the unimaginable ability to expand, capture, and impoverish life, this context is nonetheless closer to the explanation that Kafka gave to Janouch: 'we live not in a ruined but bewildered world. Everything creaks and rattles like the rigging of an unseaworthy sail ship'. Maybe the current challenge is to intensify this rattling and creaking from that which irrupts everywhere: the modes of cooperation that emerge here and there; non-organic life; the buzzing collective intelligence; the counter-subjectifications that ask for a way through and redesign our collective landscape.

As Negri, inspired by Spinoza, claims, power is superstition, the organisation of fear: 'Alongside power, there is always capacity. Alongside domination, there is always insubordination. It is about digging, to carry on digging, from the lowest point: that point is not prison as such; it is quite simply the place where people suffer, where they are at the most impoverished and exploited; where language and the senses are most removed from any power of action. And yet this is where such power exists; because this is all about life, not death'.

1   [Trans. note: *capacity-potência*. In line with Negri's Spinozism, the author draws a clear opposition between *potência* (potentia) and *poder* (potestas). In order to underline this distinction, I have translated throughout the essay *poder* as power and *potência* as capacity.]

2   [Ed. Note: Gilles Deleuze, *Essays Critical and Clinical*, trans. Daniel W. Smith & Michael A. Greco (Minneapolis: University of Minnesota Press, 1997) 3. [Translation modified by the author, 2020].]

3   [Ed. note: 'Bloom' is a reference to the fictional protaganist of James Joyce's *Ulysses* (1922)].

4   [Trans. note: I have translated the quote from PPP's text, and not from the original French. In source, footnote says 'unpublished', but I found the text in Kuniichi Uno, 'As pantufas de Artaud segundo Hijikata', in *Leituras da morte*, eds. Christine Greiner and Claudia Amorim (São Paulo: Annablume, 2007) 40. Here, the translation from the French to Portuguese is slightly different].

Peter Pál Pelbart, extracts from 'Vida e Morte em Contexto de Dominação Biopolítica', *Territórios de filosofia* (28 August 2014) https://territoriosdefilosofia.wordpress.com/2014/08/28/vida-e-morte-em-contexto-de-dominacao-biopolitica-peter-pelbart/2013) [footnotes omitted]. Translated by Nuno Rodrigues.

Tamar Guimarães
A Man Called Love: Reading Xavier//2010

These three sections are part of a longer text by Tamar Guimarães that extends the research which lead her to the slide projection A Man Called Love *(2008). Xavier was a Brazilian civil servant who became famous as a psychic medium and scribe to the spirits and has been described as 'the biggest and most prolific psychographer worldwide at all times' having channelled over 400 books. In his channelled writings about a city where the dead receive medical care, learn and work, Xavier questions earthly medical knowledge with regards to the illnesses of the soul, qualifying positivism as soul murdering.* Reading Xavier *attempts to discuss the medium's devotional practice in ways other than neurotic symptoms. Yet along the way it grapples with the complex and unresolved internalised racism at the core of Brazilian twentieth-century discourse.*

Reading Xavier

To begin with there was this queer figure whose camouflage included amusing wigs and dark glasses, and who became a national celebrity at the age of 60, having spent his life notating the words spoken to him by disembodied spirits.

Francisco Candido Xavier was a Brazilian psychic medium and psychographer – a 'channeller' of spirits in order to write. The dead spoke and he wrote it down, as a kind of secretary – a task similar to the civil servant job he held until retirement. He has been described as 'the biggest and most prolific psychographer worldwide of all times', having written over 400 books. In the 60s and 70s he was a celebrity in Brazil, drawing large crowds whenever he appeared in public.

I have scrutinised Xavier for some time as the case of a predicament – that of a man entangled in the lace of racism in disguise, the cordial racism prevalent in Brazil – a country that has not come to terms with the gap between its reality of white supremacy and its myth of racial democracy. So perhaps this is about Brazil – its race relations, its social malaise – with the scrivener to the spirits himself a channel for Brazil's turbulent history and social political anxieties – anxieties which seem to coalesce, crystallise and find new 'incarnations' in his work.

Xavier's literary work speaks of an 'other-world' remarkably similar to the one in which he lived. My endeavour is to conjure up some of the historical developments restaged, or shall I say reincarnated, in his work. I will diverge from Xavier to some of the figures and events implicitly and explicitly alluded to in his writing as well as digress to other texts which have come to shape my reading of him. Even, or especially, if this is to concede that the meaning of one text does not reside within it, but within the world of other texts.

One of the questions raised here, and one for which I have no answers, is: what produces consent? Why does one say 'yes' to the law? How does one come to love the law with abandon? And, with this, another question – how autonomous can one ever be?

Reading Xavier's public life and work without doing violence to him constitutes a substantial difficulty. How to avoid reducing him, his context and his work to a set of sociopolitical and psychoanalytic signs? How to discuss his devotional practice in ways other than neurotic symptoms and/or anthropological data? Xavier's 'love' is also a form of radical non-violence.[1] A solution for this problem would be deferring too quick a reading of Xavier in order to understand his works differently – that is, delaying this violence in order to produce different readings.[2] But on this occasion 'devotion' will remain a leftover, a residue, untouched by whatever seemed necessary to address first, in order to clear the way for its postponed approach. For now, the social-political events recounted in *Our Home*, the 'neighbouring' city on the astral plane described in one of Xavier's most famous books, will be seen in the light of symptomatic restagings of social structures in disarray. [...]

The Doctor, His Right of Intervention and a Poisonous Black Substance

Throughout *Our Home* the notion of investiture is touched upon, particularly with reference to the narrator's rights (or sufficient knowledge) to be a doctor. The narrator realises that as an earthly doctor his 'right of intervention' was based on the references to academic sources ('known books') and on the titles he acquired, but in *Our Home* he is demoted since he does not yet understand bodies.

The minister tells the narrator:

How could I appoint you to treat spirit patients, when on Earth you insisted on limiting your professional observations to the physical body? I do not deny your capacity as an excellent physiologist, but the field of life is much wider. What would you think of a botanist who based his definitions on the mere examination of the dry bark of a few trees? A great number of earthly physicians prefer mathematical conclusions in their anatomical work. Now, I quite agree that Mathematics is a most respectable science, but it is not the only one in the Universe. As you are already aware, a doctor cannot draw the line at diagnoses and terminologies – he must go deeper, and scrutinise the innermost recesses of the soul.[3]

The narrator then rejects the sceptical positivism (or the 'soul murdering') of his generation and gains spiritual consolation ('mystical consolation'). Now he is a doctor who knows that the soul is not dead, but he still works as an assistant at the correction chambers of the Ministry of Regeneration, which appears to be a mental hospital. The narrator speaks of 'vast inter-communicating wards crowded with carcass-like human forms' where a 'strange clamouring filled the air – groans, sobs and plaintive phrases uttered at random. Ghastly faces, bony hands and monstrous faces bore witness to their terrible spiritual misery'. He walks 'between numerous rows of well-kept beds' and notes 'unpleasant smells which filled the place, caused […] by the mental emanations of those […] dominated by the low vibrations of inferior thoughts'.[4] Some of the patients lay in continuous deep sleep for years, plagued by 'sinister nightmares', and when treated with 'passes'[5] they vomit a fetid and poisonous 'black substance, a dark and viscous matter with cadaverous emanations'.

The narrator's first service at *Our Home* is the outcome of his voluntary assistance in cleaning these poisonous and fetid substances. He speaks of how he intuitively picked up the 'hygiene tools'.

All these monstrous bodies and physical and psychic impurities, fetid smells, dirt and materialised nightmares urge that something be hygienically cast away before progress can follow. But what?

For Xavier, the extent to which the body is a mere vessel for a spiritual soul that transcends human differences would seem to specifically negate race. Not wash away, as something dirty, but render it unimportant. Unlike Schreber's Germany, obsessed with the purity of the body-politic, Xavier's Brazil is precisely obsessed with the mixing of the body politic which is supposedly, if not actually, transcended, once by the state and then again by the spirit (or perhaps, in *Our Home*, they are the same thing).

But more to the point, the impure matter one must get rid of is neither the body nor race; one must get rid of 'impure thoughts'. The proof that 'thinking is doing' is to be found on the 'fetid matter' produced by mental habits. One must get rid of 'nasty' ideology and its poisonous fumes, one must overcome the pull of the drives. What this utopian city-state of work and learning provides is an environment conducive to cleansing one's mind from self-harm and from injustice to others – an infinitely benevolent view of state ideology and its hygiene. The factories where workers toil away to the sound of music are only a few hundred metres away from the Regeneration chambers.

Gobineau's Carnival, Sheila the Healer, Meimei and Civilisation

Lighter than his mother's black skin, Xavier's skin was eventually understood as white, due to an accumulation of fashion, discourse and demeanour. Colour lines in Brazil are blurred, and perhaps this has to do with the way the Portuguese went about their lives in the colonies. Instead of segregation as a principle, it seems that the Portuguese formula for spreading the empire was to be carried out in bed.

During the slave trade – a trade which the Portuguese had the dubious honour of inventing – the mixed race children born out of the liaisons between the Portuguese and local women in West Africa served as the go-between from the white fathers in the coastal towns to the inland communities of their mothers. Mixed blood children were of vital importance in bringing slaves from inland to the coast. No, it was not segregation as in the British colonies. The Portuguese were keen on bodily contact with their colonial subjects.

Feeling somehow implicated in the chain of power implies one is less likely to have a clearly antagonistic relationship to the ones in power. Nepotism being a veiled norm, the possibility of eventually gaining power due to blood relations, even remote ones, makes the issue of who feels white and who feels black obscure and hard to ascertain. Internalised racism is a force we will have to contend with for a long time to come.

Eugenics gained force among the Brazilian elite in the 1870s. Its theories were elaborated upon by, among others, the French aristocrat Comte de Gobineau[6], who after publishing four volumes titled 'An Essay on the Inequality of the Human Races', landed in Brazil during Carnival in 1869 to fulfil his diplomatic function as French ambassador. During his fifteen-month stay in Brazil he amassed enough 'evidence' to support his claim that Brazil was undergoing a process of degeneration due to racial mixing.[7]

When eugenics gained currency in Brazil, psychometric tests were applied to measure the aptitudes of different segments of the population, especially black and mixed ancestry groups. Religious practices of African influence were one of the main targets for psychiatrists and doctors with eugenic sympathies. As well as a sign of inferiority, their practices seemed not only to represent a threat to Catholic morality, but were also viewed by the medical profession as posing a 'sanitary hazard' to the mental health of subjects already deemed to be predisposed to insanity. 'Primitive' manifestations were not welcome in a country aiming at fast development. The question implied wasn't whether Brazilians were 'civilised', but whether they were 'civilisable', that is, taking as a premise that it was a 'mixed blood country', could it ever catch up with 'advanced civilisations'.[8]

The practice of magic and religions other than Catholicism was not only condemned but actually persecuted in Brazil since its inception as a colony. But even if the Portuguese Inquisition visited at least three and possibly four times between 1591 and 1650[9], Brazil became known as a laboratory of religious syncretism.

Yet despite syncretism and religious tolerances, Spiritism wanted no connection with *Candomble* (an Afro-Brazilian practice). Besides differing religious beliefs this differentiation also marks divisions of race and social class.

Xavier's books and TV appearances in the late 1960s and 70s helped to establish a pietistic form of Kardecist Spiritism as one of the main religions among the middle class in the Brazilian South East, establishing not only Spiritism but also Xavier as a respectable figure.

Was the docile pietism and saintly humbleness associated with Xavier the only approach he could have followed to be both socially visible and acceptable in Brazil? He might have 'become' white but he lived in near deprivation having donated the large profits from his book sales to charity.

Looking through the portraits and the names of the spirit messengers who spoke through Xavier, one is surprised, or perhaps not, to find they were all white and in large part European, or else had been doctors, lawyers, judges and nurses. Sheila, the healer whose presence was preceded by a strong smell of roses, had been a German nurse who died during WWI.

At first I thought of the kind of self-hatred this must have implied. Then I thought of blonde Sheila as a kind of aspirational vector, pointing to an idea of 'becoming'. Like becoming 'Meimei', a woman who'd died of tuberculosis in her youth. Perhaps this 'becoming' is to be thought of as an alchemic process – a self, in transit, from lead to gold. [...]

1   The love in question is perhaps best described as *agape* and *caritas*. Xavier was well known for his charitable work, his kindness and for a life of material deprivation. His biographers write that all of the profits of the estimated 25 million copies sold of his books, were 'channelled into charitable organisations' (Jussara Korngold & Marie Levinson, *Endearing Gems from Francisco Xavier* (New York: Spiritist Alliance for Books, 2004). In the introduction to one of his books, Xavier writes on behalf of his guiding spirit: 'I speak to you as an anonymous friend, in this anonymity which stems from brotherly love.' (Francisco Candido Xavier/dictated by the spirit Andre Luiz, *Nosso Lar (Our Home)* (Brasilia: Federaçao Espírita Brasileira, 2006) 56–9. I am using the 56th edition of the book.

2   That is Reading as *differance* in Derrida's sense. The French word *différer* means both different and differed, or defer and differ.

3   [Footnote 60 in source] *Our Home*, 94–5.

4   [61] Ibid., 173.

5   [62] A magnetic pass is a healing procedure where the healer does not touch the patient but 'sweeps' the contours of the body at a distance, to redirect its energy flows.

6   [63] Gobineau was an essayist, novelist and a man of strange passions who elaborated on racial purity regardless of the fact that both his grandmother and the mother of his children were of Creole origins.

7   [64] André Luis Masiero, 'Psicologia das raças e religiosidade no Brasil: uma intersecção histórica', *Psicologia: ciencia e profissão*, vol.22, no.1 (March 2002) 66–79 (http://pepsic.bvs-psi.org.br/scielo. php?script=sci_arttext&pid=S1414-98932002000100008-&lng=pt&nrm=iso).

8   [65] Ibid.

9   [66] Carole A. Myscofski, 'The Magic of Brazil: Practice and Prohibition in the Early Colonial Period, 1590–1620', *History of Religions*, vol. 40, no. 2 (November 2000) 55.

Tamar Guimarães, extracts from *A Man Called Love: Reading Xavier* (São Paulo: Capacete Produções and Copenhagen: Forlaget * [asterisk‾, 2010) n.p.

Margarida Mendes
Molecular Colonialism//2017

Consumption and Growth Under Climate Austerity

The recent acquisition of Monsanto agrochemical and agricultural biotechnology corporation by Bayer chemical and pharmaceutical company is symbolic of a crucial moment in the course of planetary politics. The growing demand for food has allowed intensive agriculture to be promoted globally. These modes of food production take up methods of monocultural production that began in colonial regimes, and saw their growth intensified with the industrial revolution, in what was a planetary agro-economical turn with a major impact.

Targeting key ingredients such as corn or soya that have a wide application in many derivative products used in the food industry, a handful of multinationals such as Monsanto jumped into the chain of the food industry and patented seeds, chemical herbicides, GMOs, and pesticides. These products intervene directly in cultivation methods to enhance crop production rates but signs of a cartel-type domination of the market have also begun to appear.[1] And as a result of this widespread genetic modification of key elements in the food chain these corporations are intervening directly in the natural cycles of life and ecosystems, thus implicating their genetically-modified seeds in the natural world and the causal interrelations of the food cycle.

The modes of intensive monoculture promoted by these corporations, such as the absence of crop rotation, cause an increase in the risk of pests and require aggressive pesticides (also produced by them) that in their turn exhaust the land and make soil infertile and profoundly destabilise agricultural rhythms.[2] Pesticides rich in nitrogen and phosphorus have accelerated the acidification of soil and the oceans,[3] and have led to a loss of biodiversity over the past decades, while the use of neonicotinoid insecticides in corn plantations has also been associated with the decrease of the bee population.

Moreover, the implication of this agricultural regime has also created a debt economy for farmers related to the increase in GMO seed prices, despite the market domination by these corporations. In the case of countries such as India where most crops are still produced by small farmers and a big portion of the population is vegetarian, this was a tragic move, as it created major debt loops that deregulated the market and caused a regime of dependency that resulted in a major suicidal tendency among small farmers, as has been cautiously pointed out by environmental activist Vandana Shiva.[4]

The merge between the two giants, Monsanto and Bayer, makes explicit the relations between healthcare research, genetic patenting, and food consumption. With it, a top-down pyramid of biosovereignty is taking shape that stretches beyond the nation state and governs a macro-economical panorama. In particular, it discloses an interrelated ecosystem of products that both create and offer remedies for contamination under the arch of the same company: quality control and environmental fitness assessment of food production, prevention, and healing of diseases, and research into future therapeutics.

Furthermore, multinationals like Bayer and Monsanto have over the last two decades become further empowered by international trade and investment agreements such as the NAFtA (North American Free Trade Agreement) signed in 1994 by the US, Canada and Mexico; and more recently the TPPA (Trans Pacific Partnership Agreement) signed in 2016 by twelve of the Pacific Rim countries, the CETA (Comprehensive Economic and Trade Agreement) signed in 2016 by Canada and the twenty-eight EU states, or the TTIP (Transatlantic Trade and Investment Partnership), which is currently under discussion between the EU and USA. The TTIP envisions the reduction of regulations for trade and big business in an unprecedented move that will allow corporations to sue governments over contract infringement and challenge national environmental policies, by putting forward market measures that go against the goals signed at the COP21 where nation states committed to a reduction of greenhouse gas emissions by 80% by 2050.[5]

In allowing the intensification of rapacious power structures between corporations and their host countries, the neocolonial intentions of such agreements become evident. Before, colonial regimes in the Western world were implicated in the notion of race and territoriality by their exchange of people as currency, and use of military control and cartographic knowledge of colonial territories to maintain their sovereign control on foreign land. Nowadays, the emerging power structures that take shape move beyond the horizon of the individual and the geographic into the infinitesimal domain of the gene and the molecule.

Body as Corporate Territory

At the present moment, bodies can no longer be understood as finite unities, but instead as distributed networks of corporate agency. The colonial influence of big business over populations extends its outreach beyond the limits of visibility, invading the chains of biological evolution with its vampiric quality. Navigating through the breaches of law, capitalism transgresses the ethical limits of earth democracy while operating through a surveillance mode of action that ruthlessly infiltrates populations through policy-making lobbying. As patented GMO genes are absorbed into our bodies in a proprietary relationship of biological subjugation, the body itself becomes an expanded, multiple infrastructure, where intervention can happen at many different scales. Moving bodies become fluid cartographies that cross different juridical regimes.

The mechanisms of an administration of life have their roots in a history of implementation of pervasive measures, such as the regime of hygienisation imposed over the colonies, demographic management such as birth control and one-child policies due to overpopulation fears, or the Global Vaccine Action Plan pushed forward by the World Health Organisation (WHO).[6] In his detailed writings on the topic, Eugene Thacker recalls, after Foucault, that colonialism began the 'biologisation of the state' we currently live under,[7] a moment when statistical forms of knowledge are applied in monitoring the population, used in management and the prediction of evolutionary conditions, a period defined by 'a significant move away from earlier notions of the state grounded in territory'.[8] Bodies become expanded territories for sovereign intervention, where the managerial hand of the state has a say about the liability of one's biorhythms. If in Mark Fisher's *Capitalist Realism* population monitorisation is associated with the regulation of affects and expectations, contributing to the suppression of difference and revolt under widespread neoliberal imposition,[9] Thacker's work on the politics of biometrics points to the fact that this monitorisation itself incites new forms of governance both at the molecular level, and through channels as vast as those of big data circulation. This wide scope then informs areas as different as jurisdiction or scientific predictions regarding the genetic evolution of life.

To this effect, the modes of collection, analysis, and distribution of information become just as relevant as the programming languages of the data megastructures that circumscribe the world, that should be also subjected to legal scrutiny. Along with the positivist predominance of statistical forms of knowledge, data provides the groundwork for a mode of governance that directly intervenes on the relation between information and matter. As Thacker argues, this happens precisely at a time when the field of ethics is extended to computer code, just as the public disclosure of DNA becomes the main basis for intervention into physical reality.

On Unprecedented Ground: The Financialisation of the Molecule

The heyday of DNA study we currently live in allows not only for a wider medical understanding of disease helping explain morphogenetic reactions, but has unveiled an unprecedented ground for intervention into and transformations on the level of genetic encoding. Coincidently, the cracking and public dissemination of the genetic codes of humans, plants and animals gave way to an exponential rise of biological patents, as currently 'nearly 20% of the human genome is now privately owned',[10] and an investment in a managerial viewpoint of bodily politics as a form of endocolonialisation.[11]

At the same time, the methodologies of administration operation of finance have broadly invaded the spectre of the bios, with their modes of analytical and statistical treatment of reality, that deploy methods of computation as modes of assessment of performance, capability and evolution of life.

The proprietary status of these patents originated from a supremacist framing of terrestrial ontologies, where the assumption of human speciesism is pivotal. Moreover, it is responding to a market logic that addresses life as a commodity to be manipulated and replicated under the volatility of market consumption.

The last century helped produce eighty thousand new molecules that were subsequently released into the ecosystem and whose behaviour we can not fully predict. Scientists such as Giuseppe Longo are concerned with both the creation of anthromes, new molecules produced by man, and the circulation of GMOs and their effects; especially given that the endocrinal crisis that our systems are living with has increased rates of infertility and cancer development. The interaction between hybrid agents such as anthromes and natural organisms was chain motivated in an unprecedented manner, leading to the unexpected behaviour and evolution of the various components and an unpredictable turn out of its mutations.

A new arena of capitalisable potential is thus unravelled, bringing along with it a strategic cartography of intervention in forms of life. As large sums of transnational capital are allocated in the administration of planetary health, enzymatic reactions have become financialised spaces. But how can one address the intricacy of this managerial relation we have developed with matter without bringing to the foreground the very aims beneath the tools that we operate with? This neoliberal approach to the natural realm as a potential platform for profit leads irrevocably to ethical controversy, in which life is handled as information: a language that can be coded and decrypted. [...]

1   Ken Roseboro, 'The GMO Seed Cartel', *The Organic and Non-GMO Report* (1 February 2013) (www.non-gmoreport.com/articles/february2013/the-gmo-seed-cartel.php).

2   Union of Concerned Scientists, 'Expanding Monoculture, 8 Ways Monsanto Fails at Sustainable Agriculture: #4' (9 January 2012) (www.ucsusa.org/food_and_agriculture/our-failing-food-system/

genetic-engineering/expanding-monoculture.html#.WC-7NGXPzrc).

3   Will Steffen et al., 'The Anthropocene: conceptual and historical perspectives' (31 January 2011) (http://www.rsta.royalsocietypublishing .org/content/369/1938/842).

4   'Instead of controlling pests, Bt. Cotton has led to the emergence of new pests and a thirteen-fold increase in pesticide use. The farmers suffer twice over. Costly seeds and costly chemicals push them into debt trap, and debt pushes them to suicide. 200,000 farmers have committed suicide in India since 1997. Most of these suicides are concentrated in the cotton belt, and 95% of cotton is now Monsanto's Bt. Cotton.' Vandana Shiva, 'Making Peace with the Earth', Sydney Peace Foundation (3 November 2010) (http://sydneypeacefoundation.org.au/wp-content/uploads/2012/02/2010-SPP_Vandana-Shiva1.pdf).

5   Arthur Nelsen, 'Leaked TTIP energy proposal could "sabotage" EU climate policy', *The Guardian* (11 July 2016) (www.theguardian.com/environment/2016/jul/11/leaked-ttip-energy-proposal-could-sabotage-eu-climate-policy).

6   World Health Organisation, 'Global Vaccine Action Plan 2011–2020' (www.who.int/immunization /global_vaccine_action_plan/en/).

7   Eugene Thacker, *The Global Genome: Biotechnology, Politics, and Culture* (Cambridge, MA: MIT Press, 2005) 151.

8   Ibid.

9   'In his book *The Selfish Capitalist*, Oliver James has convincingly posited a correlation between rising rates of mental distress and the neoliberal mode of capitalism practiced in countries like Britain, the USA and Australia. In line with James's claims, I want to argue that it is necessary to reframe the growing problem of stress (and distress) in capitalist societies. Instead of treating it as incumbent on individuals to resolve their own psychological distress, instead, that is, of accepting the vast privatisation of stress that has taken place over the last thirty years, we need to ask: how has it become acceptable that so many people, and especially so many young people, are ill? The "mental health plague" in capitalist societies would suggest that, instead of being the only social system that works, capitalism is inherently dysfunctional, and that the cost of it appearing to work is very high.' Mark Fisher, *Capitalist Realism* (Winchester: Zero Books, 2009) 19.

10   'Over the past thirty years, more than 3,000 gene patents have been granted. Nearly 20% of the human genome is now privately owned. The US Patent and Trademark Office has issued nearly 50,000 patents involving human genetic material. Patents have been granted for microorganisms, genetically modified plants and animals, stem cells, tissue and many other living things.' David Bollier, 'The Chakrabarty Case and the Ownership of Lifeforms' (5 October 2012) (www.bollier.org/blog/chakrabarty-case-and-ownership-lifeforms).

11   'Biocolonialism is also a phenomenon within First World countries, where the pharmaceutical industry stands to gain the most returns. This "endocolonisation" – not only of the body but of medical practice itself – focuses on the ways in which the biological body can be turned into a value generator, either in drug development or through novel medical techniques such as gene therapy.' Thacker, op. cit., 157.

Margarida Mendes, extract from 'Molecular Colonialism', in *Matter Fictions* (Berlin and New York: Stenberg Press, 2017) 127–33 [some footnotes omitted].

Catalina Lozano
Crossroads//2018

> If it is necessary to resort to the spirits in order to unchain a system, then the spirits exist, at least as invisible souls of that apparatus.
> – Tobie Nathan[1]

In 1946, American filmmaker Maya Deren received a Guggenheim Fellowship to go to Haiti. She was influenced by the research of anthropologists Gregory Bateson and Margaret Mead, especially by a film they made of a ritual dance in Bali. Deren, who had already made four short experimental films, wanted to make one about Haitian dance in Vodou ceremonies, but she failed in her objective. While footage she gathered over a period of seven years was released posthumously as an attempt to collate her writing and moving images into a finished film,[2] Deren however had recognised that the reality she found had far exceeded her capacity to create a form out of it:

> I had begun as an artist, as one who would manipulate the elements of a reality into a work of art in the image of my creative integrity; I end by recording, as humbly and accurately as I can, the logics of a reality which had forced me to recognise its integrity, and to abandon my manipulations.[3]

In Vodou, the figure at the crossroads bears powerful qualities. It is at the crossroads, its Petro master being Kafou (of Kalfu), where the divine and the human, and the spirits of the dead and living, meet. In her book, *Divine Horsemen: The Living Gods of Haiti*, Deren explains these relationships and how the godly derives from the living: it transcends in death and reincarnates during Vodou ceremonies where a process of collective healing is carried out. A ceremony is 'a grand *travay* (from the French 'travail', meaning 'work')' that opens the door between the worlds of the visible and the invisible.[4]

> The complete process can be understood as [a] closed chain circling life and death. The power of the *loa* to become manifest in living matter marks their final mastery of matter.[5]

French ethno-psychiatrist Tobie Nathan has strongly criticised Western psychotherapy for strengthening rather than weakening the patient's association with their symptom and isolating them both from society. He writes, 'our divisions between a medicine of the body and a medicine of the soul have no other interest than to contribute to the construction of a discipline. I prefer by far the notion of "disorder".'[6] Nathan states that, in several African cultures, curing means the disassociation of the patient and their symptom through their kinship to others within their community. For Nathan, there is no such thing as an isolated disease; actually, a disease is really a disorder and this disorder is not individual, but it is a reflection of a wider social construct that needs healing. In Vodou, ceremonies have a collective character, they serve a community and the community serves its divinities, invisible ancestors take possession of a body while their 'soul' (*grosbonange* in Creole) temporarily leaves. Hence, the patient 'cannot, as a person, himself benefit from that possession. The function and purpose of such divine manifestation is the reassurance and the instruction of the community.'[7]

Nathan calls non-Western doctors 'masters of hidden knowledge' who interrogate the invisible. Divination talks to the unseen, the collective and the repairable. Instead, modernity's diagnosis establishes rulings in a univocal universe where the invisible does not operate, privileging a retinal approach to truth. The eye is the foremost tool to confirm it. Deren, as an artist, used film as a transformative medium. Her works are not representational; they were engendered in multiplicity and the idea of travelling through different dimensions and states of materiality. In *Ritual in Transfigured Time* (1948), a mortal body momentarily acquires the inertia of a stone set upon a plinth; in *Meshes of the Afternoon* (1943), a mirror announces the intuition of a reality that is accessible only through art, or through that coherent reality that Vodou later came to represent for her. Vodou engenders art, not as representation, but as tool. For instance, in Vodou, a '*Pwen*' refers to the precise point of contact between divine force and the earthly plane. The point is usually an 'art object' created by those who believe.'[8]

I stress that Haitian Vodou, as a religion born in the crosswinds of the Atlantic trade, not exactly rooted in Africa but 'engendered in the cross-currents of the Atlantic World,'[9] has an important political and historical dimension. The beginning of the Haitian slave revolt that unchained independence and the abolition of slavery was a Petro Vodou ceremony in August 1791. In Vodou, there are two sets of ceremonies – Rada and Petro. The first is identified more directly with African divinities that came from and were embedded in a stable system of government, but the latter,

> was born out of this rage. It is not evil; it is rage against the evil fate which the African suffered, the brutality of his displacement and his enslavement. It is the violence that rose out of that rage, to protest it. It is the crack of the slavewhip sounding constantly, a never-to-be-forgotten ghost, in the Petro rites. It is the raging revolt of the slaves against the Napoleonic forces. And

it is the delirium of their triumph. For it was the Petro cult, born in the hills, nurtured in secret, which gave both the moral force and the actual organisation to the escaped slaves who plotted and trained, swooped down upon the plantations and led the rest of the slaves in the revolt that, by 1804, had made of Haiti the second free colony in the Western hemisphere, following the United States.[10]

Vodou is ever-changing in the sense that the cycle between life, death and divinity requires constant work. A ceremony is a transformative process. Collective healing and historical process are intertwined it seems: 'The dispossession accomplished by slavery became the model for possession in Vodou, for making a man not into a thing but into a spirit.'[11]

1   [Footnote 41 in source] Tobie Nathan, 'Les bienfaits des thérapies sauvages' in Tobie Nathan & Isabelle Stengers, *Médecins et Sorciers* (Paris: La Découverte, 2012) 24.

2   [42] Maya Deren, *Divine Horsemen: The Living Gods of Haiti* (London: Thames & Hudson, 1953) 6.

3   [43] Ibid.

4   [44] Beatriz Santiago Muñoz, *A Universe of Fragile Mirrors* (Miami: Pérez Art Museum, 2016) 30.

5   [45] Deren, op. cit., 30. Deren further explains that a *loa*, or *lwa* in Haitian creole is ' a divinity… the archetypal representative of some natural or moral principle'. The *lwa* were later assimilated as Christian saints and the symbol of the cross represents not only the body of Christ, but also the crossroads and the intersections of the two planes where vodou operates. According to Deren, Haitian vodou also incorporated indigenous Taíno practices and beliefs.

6   [46] Stengers, op. cit., 61.

7   [47] Ibid.

8   [48] Vladimir Lucien, 'André Pierre (1915–2005)' (http://www.documenta14.de/en/notes-and-works/22037/andre-pierre-1915-2005).

9   [49] Alex Farquharson, 'Kafou – At the Crossroads', in *Kafou: Haiti Art and Vodou*, eds. Alex Farquharson & Leah Gordon (Nottingham: Nottingham Contemporary, 2012) 8.

10   [50] Deren, op. cit.

11   [51] Colin Dayan, 'The Call of the Gods, The Making of History', in *Kafou: Haiti Art and Vodou*, op. cit., 29.

Catalina Lozano, extract from 'Crossroads', in *The Cure* (Askeaton: A.C.A. PUBLIC, 2018) 62–70.

Rizvana Bradley
Incalculable Lives: Oreet Ashery's *Revisiting Genesis*//2019

The twelfth episode of Oreet Ashery's web-based digital video series, *Revisiting Genesis*, extends a larger aesthetic-philosophical intervention into reconceiving the lived and imagined horizons for life and death. The previous eleven episodes of Ashery's web series offer a complex mosaic of stories and conversations between people who relay their experiences of surviving life-limiting illnesses. The intricate seriality and multifaceted complexity of this work unfolds around the central figure of the series, Genesis, whose very name provokes questions about origin and birth, and subsequently, derivations and beginnings. The stories threaded through the fragmented episodes that comprise *Revisiting Genesis* thwart any desire for narrative closure, as well as assumptions about the lived finality of the event of death.

The work aims its critique at the death industry and its violently extractive biomedical economy. The virtual and actual characters who inhabit the digital environments in *Revisiting Genesis* hijack the digital means of production, so to speak, intervening in the systems of control that propel the online exploitation of those living with chronic illness. We see and hear these characters interrogate the future projection of their death as they play with slideshows meant to photographically reproduce, capture and archive their living as well as the intimate process of their decline. In this way, the work taps into the precise nexus where neoliberal management and preservation economies meet the biopolitical practice and necropolitical desire to make live and let die. Nursing, more precisely, relational networks of material and affective labour, are urgently at the quintessential centre of this biopolitical contouring of durational living, as caring for others and for other bodies continues, within the increasing neoliberal precaritisation of work, to mark and target life, desire, and death through regulated economies of care. As a character in one episode approaches the subject of work, care, and burnout: 'burnt out emotionally because you're having to grieve and you're having somewhat to confront your own self and your mortality'. *Revisiting Genesis* highlights the harnessing of digital technologies for necropolitical ends. Gravestones are scanned with iPads or accessed online through posthumously constructed websites[1] - surely the humour here, however cruel, encompasses, or at the very least touches upon, 'the slow wearing down of populations',[2] which involves the production of a certain distinction and the expression of a certain tension between 'targeting the disabled and targeting to debilitate'.[3]

Revisiting Genesis revalues both the subject and the practice of dying. The centring of care collectives in this performative digital environment reimagines the possibilities for collective care against the grain of the economic drive toward the medical marketisation and commodification of ill, disabled, debilitated bodies. Collective resistance to the corporate medical establishment is here given in and through performative gathering, as study and counterstudy, as modalities of re-engaging and redeploying the body in the midst of the 'capitalist colonisation of death'.[4]

Following eleven episodes that feature actual subjects as well as fictional characters like Bambi and Genesis, whose identities serve as both living and virtual avatars for real or historical figures triggering various personas – the Russian sculptor Dora Gordine, the nostalgic drag of Amy Winehouse, and the fictional Nurse Jackie from the American television show, for example, are all inventively interwoven here – the arrival of the anonymous aerialist seems unprompted, and curiously out of sync within the arc of the project. But the non-specificity of the aerialist, the episode's vital central spectre, brings together notions of bodily finitude and questions about life and death, about the imagination of the afterlife, and about the universalisation of death constructed and lived in consort with an image of universal humanity.

The last episode of *Revisiting Genesis* provokes a substantial shift in the critical and imaginary horizon of the work in relation to the preceding episodes. This culminating moment of Ashery's precisely woven yet improvisational biomedical fiction produces an episodic break from the discursive environments and the encounters between the characters. The episode, 'Aerialist, Prayer', is a scored performance by Johnny Parry. The score, which itself is based on a Jewish prayer for the dead, the Kaddish, lends its sonic contour to the smooth footage of an aerialist. Most striking is the crystalline whiteness of the image. Episode 12 presents the angular perfection of a body, masked and sheathed in a white suit, in flawless, circuitous rotation. This body, which transcends the imperfections, deficiencies, and deformities of this material world, achieves an optimum visual harmony with a milky-white background that seems to suffuse, saturate and pervade that body's form. The aerialist's translucent straps are the sole tether to any mortal platform.

This figure's disappearance, reappearance, and wraithlike presence ushers in the shadow of violent biopoliticality, while simultaneously gesturing toward the existence of 'alternative modes of life alongside the violence, subjection, exploitation, and racialization that define the modern human'.[5] Here is where *Revisiting Genesis* expands the scope of its own necropolitical critique. The work gets at the heart of the division between universal man, normative humanity, and its conventional life vectors. Deviation from the norms of living delineates not merely the inhuman but the abnormally subhuman – coded precisely as *sick*. This subhuman declension is the moment Eli Clare describes, where *retard* passes into *monkey*,[6] where the fold of the subhuman, the nonhuman, and the sick actively tropes what Denise Ferreira da Silva refers to as *the racial*.[7]

The dehumanisation and reduction of the sick and debilitated crudely to serial numbers and mere data relegate the visceral and non-cognitive affectivity of bodies, emotions and passions to the 'irrationalities' of illness. We might consider 'death in advanced capitalism', as art historian T.J. Demos has worded it, precisely as a totalising system of calculation and control, but not one without precedent.[8] The field of Black Studies continues to theorise the massive implications of the political violence of racial slavery as a fully instantiated instance of biopolitical control over life, in particular, the necropolitical scene in which 'death lives a human life', according to Achille Mbembe.[9] Here, also we might consider Hortense Spillers' historical genealogy of racial slavery and its direct bearing on medical biopolitics, and the ongoing regulation and administration of death: 'We could argue that the culture of slavery… its modalities of work and celebration, its civic functions and legal codes, its elaborate orders of brutality and mutilation – presents the spectacle of a *culture* in the service of death.'[10]

The aerialist's prayer gives motional form to grieving. The performance is a lament for the biopolitical regulation of bodily vulnerability and intimacy. Important in this instance is what the whiteness of this body betrays, as it renders the impassable form of the disembodied fantasy that subtends mainstream humanity's violent commodifiability. The whiteness of the figure stands in sharp contrast to the appearance of Akiya Henry, who plays Nurse Jackie in the web series. A close-up of Henry's face, done up in a silvery-bluish purple lip, matching eye shadow and gold brow highlighter, suggests a vital portrait of brilliantly enfleshed life – of incalculable existence that, as Alexander Weheliye has put it, 'excavates the social (after) life' of 'bare life and civil death'.[11]

1   T. J. Demos, 'The Death of Death: Oreet Ashery's Revisiting Genesis', *Afterall* (10 March 2016); later online (3 October 2016) (https //www.afterall.org/online/the-death-of-death-oreet-ashery-s-revisiting-genesis#.XaSrcy3MwXp).

2   Patrick Wolfe, quoted in Liat Ben-Moshe, 'Weaponizing Disability', *Social Text Online* (25 October 2018) (https://socialtextjournal.org/periscope_article/weaponizing-disability/#marker-11561-1).

3   Furthermore, the distinction between disability and debility is parsed by Jasbir Puar, who asserts that 'debilitation and the production of disability are in fact biopolitical ends unto themselves' that move neither toward life nor toward death but whose aim is 'the right to maim'. The scope of this brief essay prevents me from discussing the bearing of Puar's argument on the current work. See Jasbir Puar, *The Right to Maim* (Durham, NC: Duke University Press, 2017) xviii.

4   Demos, op. cit.

5   Alexander Weheliye, *Habeas Viscus: Racializing Assemblages, Biopolitics, and Black Feminist Theories of the Human* (Durham, NC: Duke University Press, 2014) 2.

6   Eli Clare, *Brilliant Imperfection: Grappling with Cure* (Durham, NC: Duke University Press, 2017) 181.

7   See Denise Ferreira da Silva, *Toward a Global Idea of Race* (Minneapolis: University of Minnesota Press, 2007) xix. Here she writes of the racial as an ontological context that 'fuses bodily traits, social configurations, and global regions, in which human difference is reproduced as irreducible and unsublatable.'

8   Demos, op. cit.

9   Achille Mbembe, 'Necropolitics', *Public Culture*, vol. 15, no. 1 (Winter 2003) 15.

10   Hortense Spillers, *Black, White, and in Color: Essays on American Literature and Culture* (Chicago: University of Chicago Press, 2003) 103.

11   *Habeas Viscus*, op. cit., 2.

Rizvana Bradley, 'Incalculable Lives: Oreet Ashery's *Revisiting Genesis*', in *How we live is how we die only more so*, eds. Oreet Ashery & George Vasey (Milan: Mousse Publishing, 2019) 87–92.

Portia Malatjie
Ritual, Song and Spirituality as Radical Healing Praxes in the Work of Dineo Seshee Bopape//2020

During a research trip to Sharjah in preparation for the 2017 Sharjah Biennale, Dineo Seshee Bopape paid a visit to a number of gardens. The purpose of these visits was to ascertain names of indigenous plants that were historically used in the area for different purposes, including for their healing properties and everyday use. The research revealed the use of the following plants: Yaas for healing diarrhoea, diabetes, bleeding, tumours, inflamed pimples and sores; Qaysoum whose oil was used for urinary tract infections, eye infections and as a muscle relaxant; Al Ja'ada (Nepata), which was used as an insect repellent and for the management of cholesterol and blood pressure; Arabic Gum to reduce pain, for the promotion of oral health and to soothe coughs and sore throats; Hermal for the treatment of asthma, period pains or regulating one's period, and for insomnia; as well as Khitme to reduce skin inflammation, and whose dried bark can be used to clean one's teeth.

Some of the herbs and plants were acquired and later included in the installation *+/-1791 (monument to the Haitian revolution)* (2017). The herbs, along with others such as sage that are not specific to the area, were intuitively and carefully placed in and around the installation. Bopape added crystals such as jade – known for its protective property – and amethyst – famous for its ability to activate spiritual awareness and as a calming device – to the installation. The installation bears traces of other material, such as rose water – believed to aid in headaches and heart diseases – and water contained in plastic bottles from the nearby sea. A number of African cultures believe in the healing property of sea water, and swimming in the sea can be a self-actualised cleansing ritual. The *+/-1791* installation, with its rich constellation of materials, is dedicated to the Haitian revolution of 1791, which is said to be have been inspired by a spiritual ceremony.[1] In the installation, a curious and alternative form of healing material is presented.

Bopape included petrol in plastic bottles, covered with either red or white cloths for caps. The different coloured cloths carry different meanings in traditional healing and spiritual practices and have a close affiliation with communications with one's ancestors. The importance of ancestral practice in the lived experiences of blackness is thus brought to the fore; Bopape compels us to think about ancestrally-based healing practices that are often at the core of black culture. The marrying of the plastic bottles, petrol and cloths are reminiscent of petrol bombs used by the black population against the apartheid government in South Africa.[2] Conversely, they are reminiscent of the brutality done towards black bodies that have been incinerated in their neighbourhoods as a result of the political tensions during the apartheid regime. While this brutality and scarring is alluded to by Bopape, she mentions that in the right context, the consequences of lighting and throwing a petrol bomb can have a therapeutic outcome – the resultant fire has the capacity to cleanse through destruction and regrowth, to rid the land of the ills that have been done onto it, and to potentiate a new beginning.[3]

Bopape's use of herbs and other healing materials intersects with her continued interest in history, memory, colonialism and a politics of blackness. Throughout her practice, Bopape signals to enactments of ritual, and makes use of song, herbs and cosmology as modes of potential healing. The healing that Bopape helps us think about is not only located in the body, but extends to the land, to history and to the spirit. Healing in the context of South Africa can be thought through the spiritual healing work performed and carried out by traditional healers. Robert Thornton states that, 'indeed, the term "traditional healers" is a misnomer if by "tradition" we mean an unchanging conservation of past beliefs and practices, and by "healer" someone who practices some version of physiological therapy aimed at organic disease'.[4] If we are to imagine the limiting and limited definition of healing that Thornton argues against, we would limit potentialities of different forms of healing practices. It is with this in mind that I want to think through Bopape's healing practices as radical forms of refusal and resistance. These practices that Bopape employs are related to memory and futurity, and are intended to heal the distress of past traumatic events that are rooted in and mobilised through anti-blackness. By working through these events and moments with reference to healing practices, what is aspired towards is a different kind of black futurity, one that would be freed from the abrasions and hauntings of wounded pasts.

Bopape's practice exists alongside a number of other African art practices that are continuing the longstanding tradition of engaging spirituality as a mode of reflection, contemplation and healing. Bopape makes use of song and sound, and African spiritual practices to think through ways of healing the brutality done unto blackness. She often makes use of impepho, a plant and incense used in South Africa in traditional medicine and ceremonies.[5] Impepho – an indigenous African plant that, like amethyst, is said to have calming properties – is often burnt by traditional healers to communicate with ancestors, or to cleanse an area of evil spirits.[6] Bopape's use of impepho evidences a commitment and recourse to spirituality as vehicles with which we can begin to imagine and heal differently and otherwise. It also evidences a move towards an embracing of African knowledge systems that have been erased or undermined for centuries. Traditional healing in Africa has often been tied to primitivism, and presented as an other and lesser alternative to Christianity. As such, a claim for the use of mechanisms of traditional healing is a form of both refusal and resistance. By boldly making use of this property, there is an overt performing of decoloniality by Bopape. This enactment of decoloniality is mobilised as a healing strategy, one that puts previously undercut knowledge systems to the fore as valid forms of being in the world. It is also a means with which we can begin to heal the 'spirit' of those who have had to endure the ills of colonialism.

Bopape's practices of healing are generated through different forms of ritualistic practice. In the video *is i am sky* (2013), the artist performs a kind of ritual of singing a South African struggle song, *Hamba Kahle Mkhonto (Go Well Spear of the Nation)*, to a landscape in San Francisco. The song that she is singing is often sung as a community activity, with a group of people, and as a response to a traumatic event. It is often sung at the funerals of fallen struggle heroes. In the video, Bopape contemplates the dispossession of South Africa black people from their lands during settler colonialism, and the fact that black people are forced to occupy a state of nothingness by being landless.[7] Through this engagement with blackness and nothingness, Bopape feels compelled to remedy the ontological disjunction that black people are forced into. Bopape's singing to the landscape in *is i am sky* generates contemplation about continued structures and implementations of anti-blackness that are intended to continuously pick at the scab left by colonialism and the apartheid regime. By singing to the land, she thinks with and through the song and the land, while simultaneously offering potential healing modalities. The inaudible singing of such a politically and spiritually loaded song washes over the land, is carried through it by the wind that is heard rustling through the trees, and cleanses the lacerations of a traumatic history of blackness. That a kind of healing takes place is alluded to by the smile that Bopape wears on her face, which alerts us to the potential for recovery. Bopape's use of song extends to her reflections on choral music, seen in works such as *Sa koša ke lerole* (2017) which acts as a travelling museum for the Polokwane Choral Society. Choral music, along with other modes of song such as struggle songs, has a rich history in South Africa. It has been used as a recording device for events and history, and is later disseminated to different people across the country through competitions.[8] The installation comprises a number of collages, some video and sound recordings, and charts the political history of South Africa that can be traced through the choral genre. This history is one that needs rewriting, and the record of these practices act as an alternative form of preserving and disseminating histories. By being immersed in the installation and being immersed in the music and sound, a kind of healing of the manner in which history is typically told takes place. The importance of choral music also lies in its call and response mechanism, and the community aspect of collectively thinking and being together.[9] It is indicative of the right to congregate, and the right to exercise freedom of artistic expression.

What Bopape's practice helps us understand is the multifariousness of healing practices, and the fact that they are not only rooted in the body or in ubiquitous modalities. Through her practice, we begin to imagine song as a healing strategy, to imagine violent symbols such as petrol bombs as potential medicine, and to accept strategies of refusal and resistance as radical healing praxes. As indicated in *+/- 1791* Bopape places importance in Afro-diasporic spiritual practices, from the premonition of a Haitian priestess as a propellant for a possible healing revolution, to the traditional healers who use impepho in their practice. This signalling to different forms of knowledge systems is itself a kind of remedy, a healing of past colonial impositions and the ills they inflicted on the black body, on black land and on the black spirit. Through an engagement and introduction of radical healing practices, Bopape contributes to new modalities of being and of healing.

1   Kameelah Martin, *Envisioning Black Feminist Voodoo Aesthetics: African Spirituality in African American Cinema* (Lanham: Lexington Books, 2019).

2   Petrol bombs have a long history of resistance against oppressive regimes in other areas of the world.

3   Dineo Seshee Bopape, personal communication, 2019.

4   Robert Thornton, 'The Transmission of Knowledge in South African Traditional Healing', *Africa*, vol. 79, no. 1 (2009) 17.

5   Jean-Francois Sobiecki, 'The Intersection of Culture and Science in South African Traditional Medicine', *Indo-Pacific Journal of Phenomenology*, vol. 14, no. 1 (2014) 6.

6   Ntshangase, 'Some Gendered African Ritual Practices: The Case of Impepho (An Indigenous African Plant)' (MA thesis), University of Kwazulu Natal (2012) 1.

7   For more on *is i am sky* see Malatjie, 'Nang'umfazomnyama: Race and Technology in Dineo Seshee Bopape's *is i am sky*', *Afterall*, no. 48 (2019) 5–9.

8   Mugovhani, 'Muzika Wa Dzikhwairi: An Essay on the History of Venda Choral Music', *Muziki*, vol. 10, no. 2 (2013).

9   Ibid., 75.

Portia Malatjie, 'Ritual, Song and Spirituality as Radical Healing Praxes in the work of Dineo Seshee Bopape', a new text written for this book, 2020.

Patricia Domínguez
Technologies of Enchantment//2019

The original text was presented as a broadsheet paper and included a variety of images and patterns in the background based on striped business shirts and Diaguita ceramics.[1] It was designed in collaboration with Futuro Studio Madrid.

I met Señora Rosa while I was shooting my video, *Eyes of Plants*. Rosa told me she had a son who bio-transformed into a white man. She is the direct descendent of a Mapuche chief, her grandfather. She married 'a dark-skinned man, though *mino* (handsome)', who was a Special Investigations police officer. When she bore her fourth son, he left her (although he always regretted it, according to her).

Rosa's parents often talked about whether the *wawas* (babies) were white, or nearly white, or dark-skinned. Though her husband was dark, her three first sons were white like her. But the fourth turned out to be dark. One day he caught hepatitis and became white. 'Well, not white-white', said Rosa, 'he was rather yellow'. Her son wanted so hard to belong that his body underwent a process of bio-whitening. Not unlike Jacko, the King of Pop.

> *Rosa, your story is a real bio-drama.*
> *Rosa, your son's bio-depigmentation*
> *is a myth.*
> *Rosa, I will make a bio-video for you about*
> *the myth of bio-tears.* […]

Shapeshifting lines
Once I finished shooting the video, I put the *jarro pato*[2] back in its cabinet. That very night, I dreamed about the vase. In my dreams, I visited a museum built underground. It was cold and dark inside. The museum walls were all metallic grey and I could only distinguish rows and rows of display cabinets dimly lit by LED lights. The cabinets contained white corporate shirts with thin blue stripes. The shirts had been meticulously folded in such way that they formed abstract and geometric designs so wonderful that they resembled origami. They had been starched and were stiff enough to hold all the pre-Columbian objects from my grandfather's collection.

I looked closer into one of the cabinets. Resting on the upper folds of a business shirt, I could see a black obsidian knife crowning a pyramid made of dozens of blue-striped corporate shirts.

The duck-shaped vase was in another cabinet. But it rested on someone's torso, a nondescript someone who was wearing a pink-and-white striped shirt. On a second glance, I noticed that this person was rubbing the vase against his or her back. The vase had healing properties and eased their pain. I then noticed other office workers and businessmen who were also rubbing pre-Columbian pottery over their exhausted bodies, looking for some relief, brushing the passing of time from their weary bones.

My eyes squinted as I tried to focus simultaneously on the geometric designs of the pre-Columbian pottery and the regular stripes in the business shirts.

As they combined into a single stereoscopic image, new patterns emerged. I understood that the abstract patterns from those ceramics had mutated into the stripes in the shirts. I recognised new cosmologies and hybrid patterns taking shape in this geometry.

For the Diaguita people, the lines painted in zig-zag, ripples and chain-like patterns that decorate their pottery were like visual litanies or mantras. These geometric designs provided an order to their world. Likewise, the thin stripes in today's corporate shirts are not just ornamental. They convey a way of ordering the world. Namely, the neoliberal world order. These stripes outline the arms of employees while they are signing invoices or investment contracts. Like the lines in a legal contract, the stripes in business shirts are no less straight, regular, orderly. […]

It takes minutes for a contract signed in Europe to set into motion natural resources in Chile. Forests disappear, cities flourish in the desert, the courses of rivers are altered, ancestral cemeteries are replaced by garbage dumps, new industrial suns light up the sky 24 hours a day without interruption.

However, restless productivity does not come free. Back pain is pretty much inevitable for those who sit all day in front of a computer. Blue light emitted by screens is harmful for your eyes. Typing produces joint pains. Bones ache. While financial markets run at full speed, our bodies are left behind.

The last time I was in London, I explored the financial centre of Canary Wharf, a privately-owned commercial state in the Isle of Dogs. British writer Iain Sinclair has described the Isle of Dogs as 'a Hong Kong principality with its own private security. Lands disappear and you get this financial centre that's just been parachuted in from somewhere else and it isn't where it is. It sort of is there, but it isn't'. I found several healing centres, wellness facilities and prayer rooms hidden in the basements of the office buildings in Canary Wharf. They were concealed beneath the earth, guarded by her. The names of these places are telling: *Healing Earth Centre, Nomad Travel Clinic, Island Health Clinic, Freedom Clinic, Mobile Male Massage…*. Above ground, in the streets and in the office blocks, appearances were kept up 24/7. Beneath the Earth's surface, office workers consumed by deadlines waited for their wounds to mend.

OH earth! good earth.
unproductive, silent earth.
there are no treasures beneath the
ground, but only consumed bodies
waiting to be healed.
earth is entrusted
with healing our sorrows.

Earth's transformative potential is not just spiritual, but physical too. Think for example of mud poultices and how they have been used for thousands of years. These poultices appeal to the intelligence of earth. They can absorb toxins from the body, reduce inflammations and trigger processes of healing. When placed on a painful area, cold mud tempers any excessive heat from the body as it gets warmer and eventually dries. After each use, it can be sanitised just by exposing the mud to sunlight, since the sun's radiations have well-known antibacterial properties. The body knows about its balance and mud is an ally to restore it. Years ago, I accompanied my ex-partner in his process of healing from a colon cancer. In case every other treatment failed (of the Western and non-Western types), it was suggested that he meet with a traditional healer in South Korea, who, as a last resort, would bury him for days until the earth brought his body back into balance.

Restore his order.
His order.
Bring him back into balance.
Earth is a body hosting
other bodies.

I have carried out research on some of the most comprehensive collections of pre-Columbian artefacts in Chile, Bolivia, Peru, Colombia, Mexico, United States, Britain, Netherlands and Spain. Most precolonial objects found on earth belong to these museums. They offer their geometric patterns as a gift to anyone who looks at them.

My soul is traversed by these patterns when I look at them.

Like fractals, pre-Columbian ceramics often look alike but they are never the same. Having spent so much time in archaeological museums, I have begun to recognise the hands of the artists that modelled them. Some are pretty easy to identify, for example the artist who made the sculptures of Xipe Tótec. They have the same look, the same faces, the same expression. One of them is on display at the Chilean Museum of Pre-Columbian Art, and another one belongs to the National Museum of Anthropology, in Mexico City.

The abstract patterns in this art are not just ornamental, but a synthesis of indigenous worlds. Each of these objects contains a microcosm within itself. The fear of emptiness (*horror vacui*) that led these artists to fill the entire surface of their ceramics with such intricate detail is a reminder of human search for meaning. According to archaeologist Paola González, the geometric patterns in Diaguita pottery were a visual technology of shamanic healing and hypnotic attraction.

The pre-Incan visual art of the Diaguita, explains Paola, does not pursue a semantic end. Rather, we are dealing with *technologies of enchantment*, involving the use of optical illusions, such as non-mimetic animation, as a way to captivate viewers. Today, decorative patterns with similar characteristics still play a crucial role in shamanic healing for some indigenous communities in the Amazon [...]. It's almost as if the eye comprehended senses of which the mind knew nothing.[3]

As the duck-shaped vase keeps spinning on its axis, the enchanting technology of its geometric patterns brings us to another dimension. We forget about deadlines. We escape from cyclical time. Black lines come forward, white lines recede and a new dimension unfolds before our eyes. Time and space open up in the ceramic vase, while its abstract patterns and geometric lines unfold throughout the body.

Let me quote from Paola's essay again; '*as if the eye comprehended senses of which the mind knows nothing*'. After comparing the Diaguita and Shipibo designs, Paola concludes that abstract and symmetrical patterns have in both cases not only aesthetic, but also therapeutic purposes:

The *kené* (sacred design) doesn't merely fulfil an aesthetic function, but it's also an active agent in the maintenance of the Shipibo's physical and spiritual health. Belaunde points out that both in the materialisation of abstract designs on their bodies, and in the immaterial vision of the same designs during a shamanic session, the purpose is the embellishment of people and things by covering them with graphisms of plants. This ritual embellishment allows the Shipibo to heal from physical, psychological, social and spiritual forms of distress.[4]

Just like every plant and every person, each object has its own code. Depending on their specific energy, there are objects that soothe us, objects that induce delirium, objects that trigger action. Objects are portals and vortices. They transfer their energy to us as we look at them. Their geometry imprints a new order on your hologram.

> *Graphisms of plants*
> *Wrap around me! […]*

1   The Diaguita people are a group of South American indigenous people native to the Chilean Norte Chico and the Argentine Northwest.

2   Duck-shaped ceramic belonging to the Diaguita Culture. Some are depicted weeping, three tears falling down from each of their eyes.

3   [Footnote 2 in source] See Paola González, 'Shipibo-Conibo Shamanic art of the Peruvian Amazon and its Relation to the Diaguita Culture of Chile', *Boletín del Museo Chileno de Arte Precolombino*, no. 21 (2016).

4   [3] Ibid.

Patricia Domínguez, extracts from 'Technologies of Enchantment: When a Ceramic Vase and a Drone Cry Together' (London: Gasworks, 2019) 2, 5, 6–7. Available at www.gasworks.org.uk/2019/07/02/Artist_publication_Technologies_of_Enchantment.pdf

Tabita Rezaire
Decolonial Healing: In Defence of Spiritual Technologies//2019

Invocation

I call upon the remaining wisdoms of those who have walked the path we are walking to inform and guide us. May the forces of creation reveal themselves to us, through us, as us. So be it. So it is.

To invoke decolonial healing. To demand decolonial healing. To imagine decolonial healing. To manifest decolonial healing. To honour decolonial healing. To practice decolonial healing. To sing decolonial healing.[1]

We breathe. We give. We struggle. We dream. We love. We fall. We resist. We dance. We care. We remember. We survive. We deserve. We trust.

I sing in remembrance of a time-space where data flows from the 'cosmos database' to our inner information portals.[2] I sing in defiance to restore our lineage of scientific knowledge. As considerable and crucial as all the applications of decolonial healing are; it is to harvest our potential for connection that these words are written. What is our collective state of connectivity? How do we connect? What do we connect to? From where? How does it feel? As electronic networks swiftly replace intuition-based technologies, what effects do computing technologies have on our heart-mind-womb-lands? How can we retrieve ancestral knowledge as a weapon against modern/colonial imperialism?

By engaging with African and indigenous ancestral technologies of information and communication, we dare to reconcile the worlds of organic matter, energy and electronics to nurture a mystic-techno-consciousness. So we sing to decolonise and heal our technologies.

To grasp the immensity and the responsibility decolonial healing demands, we must first apprehend the necessity and urgency of both decoloniality and healing in their singularity and multitude.

May this incantation soothe our burning tongues so that our words dance in ecstasy.[3]

On Decoloniality

Decoloniality is the theory and practice of delinking from Western hegemony and Euro-US-centric systems of governance. Decoloniality is defiance against the West's political, economical, cultural and epistemic (relating to knowledge and its validation) domination.

The term emerged from South America in the 1990s, yet decoloniality is as old as colonisation, as people have been resisting the hostage of their lands-bodies-minds-dreams ever since. From the time sovereignty was first impeded, salvation ordained, then genocide inflicted, and indigenous knowledge condemned, there have been guardians of the ancient ways of living and being. From the seeds that were kept, from the seeds that were planted in insubordination, we sprout to continue the missions of protection, emancipation and retrieval. Thus decoloniality is not a mere thinking but a radical doing; it is a call answered to 'delink from that overall structure of knowledge in order to engage in an epistemic reconstitution', and recover from the violence of Western ideology.[4]

It is not to be confounded with postcolonialism as some of us are still waiting for the postcolony. Not merely waiting but fighting, imagining and creating the path toward political, economical, cultural, epistemic and aesthetic liberation. Indeed, although colonialism per se has legally ended, its living legacy is ubiquitous in contemporary societies. This is coloniality. Coloniality is the colonial matrix of power that has been integrated and assimilated into the postcolonial social order.

Coloniality in pair with modernity is the foundation of Western ideology, which has been used to legitimise its hegemonic domination.

The coloniality of power[5] manifests as a set of hierarchies that define and organise social relationships between people, territories and knowledge; with everything non-Western deemed irrelevant, illegitimate or inferior. Inherited from the colonial enterprise, those hierarchies still rule our collective cognitive understanding today. Namely the institutionalised hierarchies between people according to race, ethnicity, social class, gender, sexual preference, religious belief, body and neurological abilities…with the urban, white, able-bodied, financially comfortable, heterosexual cis-man at the top of this hierarchy, making all alternatives to that fictional-historically fabricated 'norm' somehow deviant and consequently inferior; 2018, this is the world we live in, where being Black, Indigenous, trans, homeless, Muslim, refugee, a sex worker and/or disabled under coloniality means your life is less valued. To the point where your existence becomes a threat and thus undeserving of the same rights and access, let alone of the same respect or compassion.

When our bodies are disposable, only valuable to be used or abused and our existences dehumanised, demonised, not meant to be lived. Yet we dare to thrive.

As the underlying logic of all Western modern/colonial imperialisms, coloniality also maintains a hierarchy of cultures, with European-North American cultures appearing to be the pinnacle of modern civilisation – thus, justifying the hierarchy between systems of knowledge, with the West's Christian, then secular and now scientific paradigms as the sole source of legitimate knowledge.[6]

Granting itself the monopoly on truth and objectivity, the Western world designed its supremacy by rendering all other knowledge systems illegitimate, vehemently showing contempt for African and indigenous knowledge. Disdainfully labelled as 'archaic', 'primitive', 'naïve', 'underdeveloped', at best exotic or good enough to entertain, non-Western knowledge systems still suffer from this stigma as this demeaning rhetoric keeps being disseminated through formal education and mass media. We live under the tyranny of logic, rationality and dogmatic science.

Our histories, sciences, contributions erased, delegitimised, exploited or appropriated. Yet in our flesh and breath remains the wisdoms of our elders.

The Wound
Here is the land of the wound.

We hurt.
We hurt.

We hurt.
We hurt.
We hurt.
We hurt.
We hurt.
We hurt.
We hurt.
We hurt.
We hurt.

Repeat until it doesn't mean anything anymore.
Repeat until we can't feel it anywhere anymore.
Repeat until we stop spreading our hurts everywhere.

Coloniality affects us in all aspects of our lives, conditioning the way we think, feel, move, speak, dream, listen, desire, share and learn. The way we love, who and what we love and under which conditions. We are under siege, trapped in the colonial matrix of power. All wounded. All of us. All wounding. All of us.

Shame. Anger. Pain. Humiliation. Low self esteem. Anxiety. Fatigue. Restlessness. Addiction. Stress. Depression. Precarity. Loneliness. Disconnection… So do the symptoms of coloniality make themselves at home in our beings, in our siblings.

'When the world around is still sweating from yesterdays fever', said a friend to me.

Despite the waves of decolonisation of the Americas, Africa and Asia; coloniality survived, and we are sweating streams. This is why decoloniality is as necessary today as it was then, if we are to thrive – all thrive.

Decoloniality is fighting the struggle against the West's control of our options of emancipation. This disobedient living scheme is devising tools to confront and dismantle the institutionalised oppressive system we live in and suffer from: white supremacist-capitalist-imperialist-cis-heteronormative-patriarchy.

Decoloniality is a path for the retrieval of justice, a radical emancipation of the mind, body and soul from the subordination to coloniality.

Decoloniality is a path toward healing.

On Healing

The wound is the land of healing.

To overcome the disconnection to ourselves, to each other, to the earth and the universe mandated by coloniality, the healing we require is not solely physical nor mental but emotional, political, historical, technological and spiritual.

Healing as Transforming

Healing is transformation, it's becoming, it's blooming, it's being home and whole within oneself in order to be home and whole within our worlds.

Healing is necessary to transform, grow and realise one's full potential. To exist beyond pain, beyond trauma, beyond historical and political narratives, to become the spirits that we are.[7]

Healing as Unlearning

How can you be at peace with what and who you are when the world tells you that you are not worthy? To overcome that inner-voice which says I'm not enough, is a struggle of resilience.[8] This is our work against coloniality.

We have internalised so many toxic and harmful mechanisms of being and living, so to not reproduce how these mechanisms have wounded us, we need to unlearn them and let them go. Often the way we are, the way we behave, the way we talk to each other and ourselves is dreadful – that's because we have been taught to be as such, and because it's frightening for many of us to change and to break those automatic patterns by which we are wired. And possibly because we have come to define ourselves by our suffering, healing can also be terrifying. The unlearning we need is beyond historical narratives, but also on an emotional level – how do we deal with our emotions, how do we react when we are emotionally triggered, how do we communicate our pains? We must let go of what no longer serves us to make space within ourselves, our communities, our world for different patterns, perspectives, understandings, information. We need the courage and grace to walk the journey of self-respect, self-love and self-compassion. When you operate at the vibrational frequency of love, then hurtful patterns, negative thoughts, doubts and fear-based behaviours won't reach you; they'll just slide off you because you're up there. That's unlearning, and that's healing.[9]

Healing as Aligning

Healing means aligning. It means aligning with source, with your own rhythm, with your destiny and your vision. Often we are afraid. We're full of fears, full of doubts, full of insecurities, and we're unable to manifest our vision because we are broken inside. When you're broken you give birth to broken dreams. So healing is to allow a flow of infinite creative energy to move through you, with you and for it to work as you. How can you be yourself, a body in service of the infinite? By aligning with soul. That's what healing is for me, right now.[10]

Healing as Listening

I believe sound birthed the universe. Literally. That sound is the creative force behind our manifested reality. Thus from the cosmic primal sound, all material form – as in matter – was birthed and still keeps birthing. Everything has a vibratory frequency, even if inaudible, and this is the result of the primal sound, which set creation into motion. We are 'only' sonic residues from our cosmic sonic beginnings. The human pursuit is then to find that sound and resound in that sound, so as to vibrate in unison with the vibratory frequency of infinity. This is the ultimate healing.

Healing is overcoming transgenerational trauma, is reprogramming DNA memory, is raising vibrational frequency, is shifting consciousness, is living from heart, is dancing until exhaustion, is disciplining the mind, is taking responsibility, is trusting intuition, is honouring our ancestors and descendants, is companionate loving, is listening to soul, while holding each other's hands on the journey.

So that we may be whole, home, safe, enough, cared for, full and loved as intended.

I am loved
I am loving
I am love
I am loved
I am loving
I am love
I am loved
I am loving
I am love
I am loved
I am loving
I am love

Repeat until you smile inside.
Repeat until you believe it deep down.
Repeat again.
If decoloniality sets the relationship between the self and the world, healing reveals the inner relationship between one's finite and infinite self.

Decolonial healing is a praxis of love in service of collective consciousness and liberation. It is a remembrance and honouring of the land, the heart, each other and the wisdoms of those who listened to the unheard song. [...]

1   [Footnote 2 in source] Today I sing from Cayenne in French Guyana, one of my ancestral lands. A land in the Amazon that is legally (still) a part of France. To this day French Guyana is the only territory on the South American continent not to be independent. So we keep singing.

2   Tabita Rezaire, quoted in E. Ford, 'Artist profile: Tabita Rezaire', *Rhizome* (2018) (http://rhizome. org/editorial/2018/feb/ 01/artist-profile-tabita-rezaire/).

3   [3] Responsibility as response-ability. What is our ability to respond to any given circumstances?

4   Walter Mignolo, 'Interview with Walter Mignolo: Activism, trajectory, and key concepts' (2017) (http://criticallegalthinking.com/2017/01/23/interview-waltermignolo-activism-trajectory-key-concepts/).

5   [4] The term 'coloniality of power' was, for example, conceptualised by Aníbal Quijano, *Coloniality of Power, Eurocentrism and Latin America* (Durham, NC: Duke University Press, 2000) and later developed by Walter Mignolo, *Local Histories/Global Designs: Coloniality, Subaltern Knowledges and Border Thinking* (New Jersey: Princeton University Press, 2000), *The Darker Side of Western Modernity: Global Futures, Decolonial Options* (Durham, NC: Duke University Press, 2011).

6   'Interview with Walter Mignolo', op. cit.

7   Rezaire, quoted in H. Nestor, 'Tabita Rezaire: "Reclamation allowed me to glow into my blackness, womanhood and queerness"', *Studio International* (2018) (https://www.studiointernational.com/index.php/tabita-rezaire-interview).

8   Rezaire, quoted in 'Feel like a cyber slave? Meet Tabita Rezaire, Healer of souls' (2018) (https://www.huckmag.com/art-and-culture/decolonising-the-internet-artist-tabita-rezaire/).

9   Rezaire, quoted in J. Radley, 'We Carry a Lot in Our Wombs: An Interview with Tabita Rezaire' (2018) (http://www.berlinartlink.com/2018/01/13/truth-we-carry-a-lot-in-our-wombsan-interview-with-tabita-rezaire/).

10   Rezaire quoted in B. Stosuy, 'On the Infinite Flow of Creative Energy: An interview with artist Tabita Rezaire', *The Creative Independent* (2018) (https://thecreativeindependent.com/people/visualartist-and-healer-tabita-rezaire-on-the-infinite-flow-of-creative-energy/).

Tabita Rezaire, extracts from 'Decolonial Healing: In Defence of Spiritual Technologies', in *The SAGE Handbook of Media and Migration*, eds. Kevin Smets, Koen Leurs, Myria Georgiou, Saskia Witteborn and Radhika Gajjala (London: Sage Publications, 2019) xxix–xxxiii.

Aimar Arriola is a curator, editor and researcher based between London, Barcelona and the Basque Country, and a member of Eqipo re collective (with Nancy Garín and Linda Valdés).

Clare Barlow is a curator and has worked for museums such as Tate Britain and the Wellcome Collection, London.

Khairani Barokka is an Indonesian-born writer, poet and artist based in London.

Dodie Bellamy is an American author, journalist and editor based in San Francisco.

Anne Boyer is an American poet and essayist, and Associate Professor at the Kansas City Art Institute.

Rizvana Bradley is Assistant Professor of History of Art and African American Studies at Yale University.

Canaries is an international network of cis women, trans and non-binary people living with autoimmune and other chronic illnesses.

Eli Clare is an American poet, essayist and activist based in Vermont.

Patricia Domínguez is a Chilean artist based in Las Condes.

Taraneh Fazeli is a curator and educator, and Curatorial Fellow at Red Bull Arts Detroit.

John Foot is Professor of Modern Italian History at the University of Bristol.

Lauren Fournier is a writer, curator and artist, and SSHRC Postdoctoral Fellow in Visual Studies, University of Toronto.

Dora García is a Spanish artist and teacher based in Barcelona.

Nancy Garín is a journalist, art researcher and curator, a member of Eqipo re collective (with Aimar Arriola and Linda Valdés), and also part of Specters of the Urban research project.

Tamar Guimarães is a Brazilian artist based in Copenhagen.

Sunil Gupta is an Indian-born Canadian artist and teacher based in London.

Alice Hattrick is a British writer and producer.

Johanna Hedva is a Korean-American writer, artist, musician and astrologer based in LA and Berlin.

Martin Herbert is a writer based in Berlin.

bell hooks is an American author, feminist and social activist.

Sara Jaspan is a writer and editor based in Manchester, UK.

Alexandra Juhasz is an activist filmmaker, Distinguished Professor of Film at Brooklyn College, CUNY, and a founding member of What Would an HIV Doula Do?

Theodore (ted) Kerr is a Canadian-born writer and organiser based in Brooklyn, and a founding member of What Would an HIV Doula Do?

Mahmoud Khaled is an Egyptian artist based in Oslo and Cairo.

Eve Kosofsky Sedgwick (1950–2009) was a scholar in the fields of gender studies and queer theory.

R.D. Laing (1927–89) was a Scottish psychiatrist and writer, known for his work on mental illness and psychosis.

Carolyn Lazard is an American artist based in Philadelphia, and co-founder of Canaries.

Simone Leigh is an American artist based in New York.

Miguel A. López is Peruvian-born writer and curator based in San Jose, Costa Rica, and co-director of TEOR/éTica art + thinking.

Catherine Lord is an American writer, artist and curator, and Professor Emerita in the Department of Women's Studies and Department of Visual Culture, Claire Trevor School of the Arts, University of California, Irvine.

Audre Lorde (1934–92) was an American writer, feminist and civil rights activist.

Catalina Lozano is a curator and researcher based in Mexico City.

Portia Malatjie is a curator and lecturer in Art History and Discourse of Art at Michaelis School of Fine Art, Cape Town.

Park McArthur is an American artist based in New York.

Margarida Mendes is a writer, curator and educator based in Lisbon.

Pedro Neves Marques is a writer, artist and filmmaker.

Mujeres Creando is a Bolivian anarcha-feminist collective founded in 1992.

Naomi Pearce is a British writer and researcher.

Peter Pál Pelbart is a Hungarian philosopher, writer, teacher and translator based in São Paulo.

Paul B. Preciado is a Spanish theorist, curator and writer.

Maria Puig de la Bellacasa is Associate Professor at the Centre for Interdisciplinary Methodologies at the University of Warwick.

Filipa Ramos is a writer and lecturer based in London.

Pedro Reyes is a Mexican artist based in Mexico City.

Tabita Rezaire is a French artist based in Cayenne, French Guyana.

Anne Charlotte Robertson (1949–2012) was an American filmmaker whose work documented her battles with depression, paranoia and borderline schizophrenia.

Sur Rodney (Sur) is an American artist, writer and activist based in New York.

Lynx Sainte-Marie is an artist, activist and educator based in the Greater Toronto Area.

Sarah Sharma is Associate Professor and Director of the McLuhan Centre for Culture and Technology at the University of Toronto.

Susan Sontag (1933–2004) was an American cultural and literary critic, writer and filmmaker.

Jo Spence (1934–1992) was a British photographer and writer.

Patrick Staff is a British artist based in LA and London.

Mary Walling Blackburn is an American artist and writer based in New York and Dallas.

Emily Watlington is a writer and critic based in New York.

Simon Watney is a writer, art historian and activist based in London.

Bibliography

Acker, Kathy, 'The Gift of Disease', *The Guardian* (January 1997)

Ahmed, Sarah, 'Selfcare as Warfare', Feminist Killjoys (August 2014) (https://feministkilljoys. com/2014/08/25/selfcare-as-warfare/)

Basaglia, Franco, ed., *L'istituzione negata* (Turin: Einaudi, 1968)

Biss, Eula, *On Immunity: An Inoculation* (London: Fitzcarraldo Editions, 2015)

Bitelli, Jos and Nicola Guy, eds., *Patricide: The End of a 60-Year-Old-Mistake*, no. 1 (2018)

Bordowitz, Gregg, *General Idea: Imagevirus* (London: Afterall Books, 2010)

Bolaki, Stella, *Illness as Many Narratives* (Edinburgh: Edinburgh University Press, 2016)

Boyer, Anne, *The Undying: a Meditation on Modern Illness* (London: Allen Lane, 2019)

Boyer, Anne 'The Kind of Pictures She Would Have Taken: Jo Spence', *Afterall*, issue. 42 (Autumn/ Winter 2016) 4–11. Available at www.afterall.org/journal/issue.42/the-kind-of-pictures-she- would-havetaken-jo-spence

Butler, Judith, 'Capitalism Has its Limits' (March 2020) (www.versobooks.com/blogs/4603- capitalism-has-its-limits)

Cabañas, Karia M., *Learning from Madness: Brazilian Modernism and Global Contemporary Art* (Chicago: University of Chicago Press, 2018)

Chave, Anna C., 'Normal Ills: On Embodiment, Victimization, and the Origins of Feminist Art', in *Trauma and Visuality in Modernity*, eds. Liza Saltzman & Eric Rosenberg (Hanover: Dartmouth College Press, 2006)

Cohen, Michael, *Gran Fury: Read My Lips* (New York: 80WSE Press, 2015)

Costinas, Cosmin, Inti Guerrero and Lesley Ma, eds., *A Journal of the Plague Year* (Berlin and New York: Sternberg Press, 2015)

Crimp, Douglas, ed., *October*, no. 43 – 'Cultural Analysis Cultural Activism' (Winter 1987)

Didi-Huberman, Georges, *The Invention of Hysteria* (Cambridge, MA and London: The MIT Press, 1982)

Fazeli, Taraneh, 'Notes for "Sick Time, Sleepy Time, Crip Time: Against Capitalism's Temporal Bullying", in conversation with the Canaries' (2016) (http://temporaryartreview.com/notes-for-sick-time-sleepy- time-crip-time-against-capitalisms-temporal-bullying-in-conversation-with-the-canaries/)

Feder Kittay, Eva & Ellen K. Feder, *The Subject of Care: Feminist Perspectives on Dependency* (Lanham, MD: Rowman & Littlefield, 2002)

Fernández-Savater, Amador, 'Habitar la excepción: pensamientos sin cuarentena I' (March 2020) (www.filosofiapirata.net/habitar-la-excepcion-pensamientos-sin-cuarentena-i/)

Firestone, Shulamith, *Airless Spaces* (New York: Semiotext(e), 1998)

Fitzpatrick, Corrine, 'Illness as a Festival', *Triple Canopy* (February 2018) (www.canopycanopycanopy. com/contents/illness-as-festival)

Foucault, Michel, 'Therapeutic process and moral treatment', in *Psychiatric Power: Lectures at the Collège de France* (New York: Palgrave MacMillan, 1973–4)

Frank, Arthur W. 'The Restitution Narrative', in *The Wounded Storyteller: Body, Illness, and Ethics* (Chicago: University of Chicago Press, 1997)

Gabert-Doyon, Josh, 'Paranoia and the Coronavirus: How Eve Sedgwick's Affect Theory Persists Through Quarantine and Self-isolation' (March 2020) (www.versobooks.com/blogs/4597-paranoia-and-the-coronavirus-how-eve-sedgwick-s-affect-theory-persists-through-quarantine-and-self-isolation)

Gómez Peña, Guillermo and Elaine Katzenberger, 'On Illness, the Human Body, Performance, and Quantum Physics: a Psychomagic Script for a Hard Recovery', *TDR: The Drama Review*, vol. 58, no. 2 (Summer 2014)

Haraway, Donna J., 'Situated Knowledges: The Science Question in Feminism and the Privilege of Partial Perspective', in *Simians, Cyborgs, and Women* (New York: Routledge, 1991)

Hengehold, Laura, *The Body Problematic: Political Imagination in Kant and Foucault* (Pennsylvania: Penn State University Press, 2007)

Huska, Kat, ed., *Art, AIDS, America* (Tacoma and Washington: Tacoma Art Museum and University of Washington Press, 2016)

Juhasz, Alexandra, 'A History of the Alternative AIDS Media', in *AIDS TV: Identity, Community and Alternative Video* (Durham, NC: Duke University Press, 1995)

Kapil, Bhanu, *Schizophrene* (Callicoon: Nightboat Books, 2016)

Kerr, Theodore (ted), 'AIDS 1969: HIV, History, and Race', *Drain Magazine*, vol. 13, no. 2 – 'AIDS and Memory' (2016)

Laing, R.D., *The Divided Self* (London: Penguin Classics, 2010)

Lakshmi Piepzna-Samarasinha, Leah, 'Fragrance Free Femme of Colour Genius (2018) (http://brownstargirl.org/fragrance-free-femme-of-colour-genius/)

Lazard, Carolyn, 'How to be a Person in the Age of Autoimmunity' (2017) (https://static1.squarespace.com/static/55c40d69e4b0a45eb985d566/t/58cebc9dc534a59fbdbf98c2/1489943709737/HowtobeaPersonintheAgeofAutoimmunity+%281%29.pdf)

Lennard, J. Davis, 'The Social Model of Disability', in *The Disability Studies Reader* (New York: Routledge, 2010)

Letters & Handshakes, 'Take Care: Project Statement' (Mississauga: University of Toronto and The Blackwood Gallery, 2017). Available at https://lettersandhandshakes.files.wordpress.com/2017/06/takecarepreliminaryprojectstatement.pdf

Lord, Catherine, *The Summer of Her Baldness: a Cancer Improvisation* (Austin: University of Texas Press, 2004)

Lotringer, Sylvère and David Morris, eds., *Schizo-Culture* (Los Angeles: Semiotext (e), 2013)

McRuer, Robert, 'Coming out Crip', in *Crip Theory, Cultural Signs of Queerness and Disability* (New York: New York University Press, 2006)

Mignolo, Walter, *Local Histories/Global Designs: Coloniality, Subaltern Knowledges and Border Thinking* (Princeton: Princeton University Press, 2000)

Mingus, Mia, 'Access Intimacy: The Missing Link', Leaving Evidence (May 2011) (https://leavingevidence.wordpress.com/2011/05/05/access-intimacy-the-missing-link/)

Mitchell, David and Sharon Snyder, *The Biopolitics of Disability: Neoliberalism, Ablenationalism, and Peripheral Embodiments* (Ann Arbor: University of Michigan Press, 2015)

Nelson, Maggie, *The Argonauts* (Minneapolis: Graywolf Press, 2015)

Perkins Gilman, Charlotte, *The Yellow Wallpaper* (1892) (London: Virago, 1981)

Preciado, Paul B., *Testo Junkie: Sex, Drugs, and Biopolitics in the Pharmacopornographic Era* (New York: The Feminist Press, 2013)

Proctor, Hannah, 'Sedgwick, Laing and the Politics of Mental Illness', *Radical Philosophy*, no. 197 (May/June 2016)

Puar, Jasbir, 'Prognosis Time: Towards a Geopolitics of Affect, Debility, and Capacity', *Women and Performance: a journal of feminist theory*, vol. 19, no. 2 (2009)

Sagar, Ilona, 'Coda Cycle', in *Self-Service* (Glasgow: Glasgow International, 2018)

Scourti, Erica, 'Rituals, Self-care and Collectivity' (June 2017) (https://wrongdreams.com/2017/06/19/rituals-self-care-and-collectivity/)

Smith, Giulia, 'Carolyn Lazard', *Art Monthly*, no. 429 (September 2019)

Smith, Giulia, 'Health v. Wealth', *Art Monthly*, no. 418 (July 2018)

Sontag, Susan, *Illness as Metaphor* (New York: Farrar, Straus and Giroux, 1978; reissued London: Penguin Classics, 2009)

Spence, Jo, *Putting Myself in the Picture: a Political, Personal and Photographic Autobiography* (London: Camden Press, 1988)

Stengers, Isabelle, *The Invention of Modern Science* (Minneapolis: University of Minnesota Press, 2007)

Stengers, Isabelle, 'The Doctor and the Charlatan', *Cultural Studies Review*, vol. 9, no. 2 (2013)

Szasz, Thomas, *Anti-psychiatry: Quackery Squared* (New York: Syracuse University Press, 2009)

Thacker, Eugene, *The Global Genome: Biotechnology, Politics, and Culture* (Cambridge, MA: The MIT Press, 2005)

Thornton, Robert, 'The Transmission of Knowledge in South African Traditional Healing', *Africa*, vol. 79, no. 1 (2009)

Trawalter, Sophie, Kelly M. Hoffman and Adam Waytz, 'Racial Bias in Perceptions of Others' Pain', *PLOS.One* (November 2012) (http://journals.plos.org/plosone/article?id=10.1371/journal.pone.0048546)

Treichler, Paula, 'AIDS, homophobia and biomedical discourse: An epidemic of signification', *October*, no. 43 (Winter 1987)

Weeks, Jeffrey, *Sexuality and Its Discontents* (London: Routledge & Kegan Paul, 1985)

Woolf, Virginia, *On Being Ill* (London: Hogarth Press, 1930; reissued Ashfield, MA: Paris Press, 2002)

Wu, Danielle, 'The Medicalization of Blackness: Rashid Johnson and the Diseased Connotations of Race,' *Inquiries Journal*, vol. 7, no. 4 (2015). Available at www.inquiriesjournal.com/articles/1025/the-medicalization-of-blackness-rashid-johnson-and-the-diseased-connotations-of-race

Yanagihara, Hanya, 'The Burning House', in *Wojnarowicz: History Keeps Me Awake at Night*, eds. David Breslin & David Kiehl (New York: Whitney Museum of American Art, 2018)

ACKNOWLEDGEMENTS

Editor's acknowledgements
The assembly of this anthology has been shaped by conversations over the last few years with different friends and colleagues and through the projects I've developed at Wellcome Collection. Among them are Aimar Arriola, Oreet Ashery, Ana Botella, Johanna Hedva, Ruth Horry, Sita Reddy, Laura Vallés and George Vasey. Special thanks to Chris Fite-Wassilak, Filipa Ramos and Teresa Cisneros for their thorough feedback. Heartfelt thanks to Emily Sargent for our ongoing conversation.

I am grateful to Wellcome Collection for granting me research time, Wellcome Library for taking care of and expanding such an important resource on health. Thanks above all to the artists and writers who have granted the reprinting of their texts here, in particular to Patrick Staff, Clare Barlow, Portia Malatjie and Mahmoud Khaled for their newly commissioned contributions.

This book was conceived just after the birth of my child and finalised during the COVID-19 lockdowns, two moments of high upheaval and vulnerability. I am ever so grateful to my parents Raúl and Encarna, my sister Paloma and my partner Tom for creating the space I needed to remain focused.

Publisher's acknowledgements
Whitechapel Gallery is grateful to all those who gave their generous permission to reproduce the listed material. Every effort has been made to secure all permissions and we apologise for any inadvertent errors or omissions. If notified, we will endeavour to correct these at the earliest opportunity. We would like to express our thanks to all who contributed to the making of this volume, especially: Aimar Arriola, Clare Barlow, Khairani Barokka, Dodie Bellamy, Anne Boyer, Rizvana Bradley, T.J. Demos, Patricia Domínguez, John Foot, Lauren Fournier, Luke Fowler, Nancy Garín, Dora García, Tamar Guimarães, Sunil Gupta, Alice Hattrick, Johanna Hedva, Martin Herbert, Sara Jaspan, Alex Juhasz, Ted Kerr, Mahmoud Khaled, Carolyn Lazard, Portia Malatjie, Chus Martinez, Margarida Mendes, Miguel A López, Park McArthur, Mujeres Creando, Pedro Neves Marques, Peter Pál Pelbart, Naomi Pearce, Filipa Ramos, Helena Reckitt, Tabita Rezaire, Pedro Reyes, Nuno Rodrigues, Sarah Sharma, Patrick Staff, Mary Walling Blackburn, Emily Watlington.

We also gratefully acknowledge the cooperation of: Abner Stein, Christine Shaw at Blackwood Gallery, Casanovas & Lynch, Commonwealth and Council, Essex Street, Clare Mao at Europa Content, The MIT Press, Richard Saltoun, Semiotext(e).

Whitechapel Gallery

whitechapelgallery.org

Whitechapel Gallery is supported by

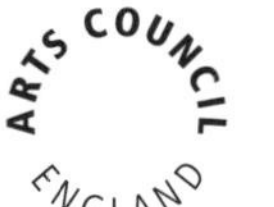

Supported using public funding by

**ARTS COUNCIL
ENGLAND**